Way Over in Beulah Lan'

Way Over in Beulah Lan'

Understanding and Performing the Negro Spiritual

André J. Thomas

With a Foreword by Anton E. Armstrong

HERITAGE MUSIC PRESS

A DIVISION OF THE LORENZ CORPORATION
Box 802 / Dayton, OH 45401-0802
www.lorenz.com

Editor: Kris Kropff
HMP Choral Editor: Mary Lynn Lightfoot
Book Design: Digital Dynamite, Inc.
Cover Design: Jeff Richards
Music Engraving: Linda Taylor and Jeanette Dotson

Heritage Music Press
A division of The Lorenz Corporation
P.O. Box 802
Dayton, OH 45401-0802
www.lorenz.com

Printed in the United States of America

ISBN: 978-0-89328-723-8

Little of beauty has America given to the world save the rude grandeur God himself stamped on her bosom; the human spirit in this new world has expressed itself in vigor and ingenuity rather than in beauty. And so by fateful chance the Negro folk-song—the rhythmic cry of the slave—stands today not simply as the sole American music, but as the most beautiful expression of human experience born this side of the seas. It has been neglected, it has been, and is, half despised, and above all it has been persistently mistaken and misunderstood; but notwithstanding, it still remains as the singular spiritual heritage of the nation and the greatest gift of the Negro people.

—W.E.B. DU BOIS, *The Souls of Black People*

CONTENTS

List of Music Examples ix
Foreword xi
Preface xiii
Acknowledgments xvi

Part I. Understanding the Spiritual 1

1. Singing in a Strange Land: The Origin and Development
   of the Spiritual 3

2. From the Oral Tradition to the Printed Page:
   Selected Collectors of the Spiritual 12
   Slave Songs of the United States (1867) 13
   Fisk Jubilee Singers (1878) 15
   Cabin and Plantation Songs (1874) 17
   Befo' De War Spirituals (1933) 18

3. Beyond the Printed Page to Shaping an Art:
   Selected Arrangers of the Spiritual 20
   Early Nationalistic Arrangers (1866–1896) 20
       Harry T. Burleigh 21
       John Rosamond Johnson 23
       R. Nathaniel Dett 24
       Hall Johnson 30
       Eva Jessye 32
       William Grant Still 33
   Middle Period Arrangers (1897–1927) 35
       Edward H. Boatner 35
       William L. Dawson 37
       John Wesley Work III 40
       Jester Hairston 42
       Undine Smith Moore 43
       William Henry Smith 46
       Roy Ringwald 48
       Leonard de Paur 50
       Mitchell Southall 52
       Alice Parker 54
       Albert J. McNeil 56
   Modern Arrangers (1928–1958) 58
       Betty Jackson King 58
       Lena Johnson McLin 59

Brazeal Wayne Dennard.. 61
Wendell Phillips Whalum 63
Eugene Thamon Simpson 64
Robert Harris 66
Robert Morris 66
Roland Carter... 67
Larry Farrow 68
Marvin Curtis 69
André J. Thomas 70
Moses Hogan 72

Contemporary Arrangers (1959–present) 73
David Morrow... 73
Stacey V. Gibbs 74
Rosephanye Powell... 74
Rollo Dilworth 75
Mark Butler.. 78
Jeffery L. Ames... 79
Damon Dandridge 80
Victor C. Johnson 80

Additional Arrangers 83

Part II. Performing the Spiritual 85

4. From the Printed Page to the Concert Stage:
Interpreting the Spiritual 87

5. Reflections on Six Spirituals 98
Soon Ah Will Be Done, arranged by William L. Dawson 98
Swing Down, Chariot, arranged by André J. Thomas.......... 111
Way Over in Beulah Lan', arranged by Stacey V. Gibbs 125
Beautiful City, arranged by André J. Thomas 136
Ride On, King Jesus, arranged by Moses Hogan 150
I'm Gonna Sing, arranged by André J. Thomas................. 164

6. Other Perspectives: Interviews with Dr. Anton Armstrong
and Prof. Judith Willoughby... 177

Index of Concert Spirituals by Arranger 198
Index of Concert Spirituals by Title 234
Notes 262
Bibliography 265
Selected Audio and Video Recordings 268
About the Author 271

MUSIC EXAMPLES

1.1 "Musieu Bainjo," from *Slave Songs of the United States*

1.2 Moses Hogan, "Mister Banjo" (m. 9–12)
© 1996 Hal Leonard Corporation

2.1 "Roll, Jordan, Roll" from *Slave Songs of the United States*

2.2 "Swing Low, Sweet Chariot" from *Fisk Jubilee Singers*

2.3 "Some o'dese Mornin's" from *Cabin and Plantation Songs, 1st Edition*

2.4 "Come An' Go Wit' Me" from *Befo' De War Spirituals*

3.1 Nathaniel Dett, "Were You There When They Crucified My Lord?" (m. 1–17),
from *Religious folk-songs of the Negro as sung at Hampton Institute*
© 1927 AMS Press

3.2 Nathaniel Dett, "Listen to the Lambs" (m. 62–74)
© 1914 G. Schirmer

3.3 Nathaniel Dett, "I'll Never Turn Back No More"
© 1918 J. Fischer & Bros.

3.4 Hall Johnson, "His Name So Sweet"
© 1925 Carl Fischer, Inc. (m. 11–14)

3.5 William Grant Still, "The Blind Man" (m. 13–21)
© 1974 Gemini Press

3.6 Edward Boatner, "Who Is That Yonder?"
© 1954 G. Ricordi

3.7 William Dawson, "I Wan' to be Ready"
© 1967 Neil A. Kjos Music Company

3.8 John Wesley Work III, "My Soul's Been Anchored in the Lord,"
from *American Negro Songs and Spirituals* (m. 1–7)
1998, Dover Publications. Replication of the edition published by Crown Publishers, Inc. in 1940.

3.9 John Wesley Work III, "Rock, Mount Sinai"
© 1962 Galaxy Music

3.10 Undine Smith Moore, "Daniel, Daniel, Servant of the Lord" (m. 59–end)
© 1953 Warner Bros. Music

3.11 William Henry Smith, "Ride the Chariot" (m. 1–4)
© 1939 Neil A. Kjos Music Company

3.12 Roy Ringwald, "IV. The Judgment Day" from *God's Trombones*
© 1955 Shawnee Press, Inc.

3.13 Leonard de Paur, "Jesus Hung and Died" (m. 1–3)
© 1960 Lawson-Gould Music

3.14 Mitchell Southall, "There's No Hiding Place Down There"
© 1959 Ralph Jusko Publications, Inc.

3.15 Alice Parker, "John Saw duh Number" (m. 1–16)
© 1963 Lawson-Gould Music

3.16 Alice Parker, "By an' By" (m. 25–30)
© 1988 Jensen Music

3.17 Betty Jackson King, "Sinner, Please Don't Let This Harvest Pass"
© 1978 Pro Art Publications, Inc.

3.18 Lena McLin, "Glory, Glory, Hallelujah" (m. 1–13)
© 1966 Neil A. Kjos Music Company

3.19 Brazeal Wayne Dennard, "Lord, I Want to Be a Christian" (m. 4–10)
© 1994 Alliance Music

3.20 Eugene Thamon Simpson, "Sister Mary Had-a But One Child" (m. 1–8)
© 1981 Bourne Music

3.21 Larry Farrow, "Ev'ry Time I Feel the Spirit"
© 1982 Gentry Publications

3.22 Rollo Dilworth, "Walk in Jerusalem" (m. 30–33)
© 1994 Hal Leonard Corporation

3.23 Victor C. Johnson, "Song of Freedom" (m. 63–70)
© 2007 Heritage Music Press, a division of The Lorenz Corporation

The following spiritual arrangements are included in their entirety in Chapter 5. Our thanks to their publishers, who generously granted permission to include them.

William L. Dawson, "Soon Ah Will Be Done"
© 1934 Neil A. Kjos Music Company (T102A)

André J. Thomas, "Swing Down, Chariot"
© 2003 Heritage Music Press, a division of The Lorenz Corporation (15/1778H)

Stacey Gibbs, "Way Over in Beulah Lan'"
© 2007 Gentry Publications (JG2370)

André J. Thomas, "Beautiful City"
© 2006 Heritage Music Press, a division of The Lorenz Corporation (15/2124H)

Moses Hogan, "Ride On, King Jesus"
© 1999 Hal Leonard Corporation (08703210)

André J. Thomas, "I'm Gonna Sing"
© 2005 Heritage Music Press, a division of The Lorenz Corporation (15/2023H)

FOREWORD

Way Over in Beluh Lan' by André J. Thomas is a long-awaited resource that combines practical scholarly analysis and insightful recommendations on the performance of the Negro spiritual. As both conductor and arranger, Dr. Thomas has been one of the most influential interpreters of the Negro spiritual in his work throughout the United States as well as on the global stage. His study commences with an overview as the African was seized into slavery and accounts of the turbulent passage to the New World, including the music that was part of this traumatic experience. Dr. Thomas examines the early influences which gave rise to the creation of the Negro spiritual as it permeated the lives of the slave and shaped the culture in which they existed. This early section also traces the development of the spiritual into a genre of art music.

This book brings together in one source several valuable historical collections of tunes and writings on the Negro spiritual, which will provide a unique view of these profound songs. Many of these historical sets will provide enlightening revelations for choral conductors and singers in their interpretations of this genre. These collections offer a wonderful opportunity to compare how these slave songs were transcribed from the oral folk song to a notated version, and the transformation of the tunes that occurred in that process. Additionally they provide examples of the important role of dialect and tempo in the interpretation of the Negro spiritual.

Significant in the monograph is Dr. Thomas's chronicle of arrangers who have been vital in the perpetuation of the Negro spiritual through their artistic choral/vocal settings. These arrangements serve as core repertory for the concert stage, music classroom, and worship settings throughout this country and abroad. Classified in a chronological sequence, this may be the most comprehensive compilation and examination of the musical styles of these arrangers, whose work has preserved this distinctive body of American song.

The concluding body of this book explores pedagogical issues related to the performance of the Negro spiritual. Topics including text, diction, rhythm, and tempo are addressed by not only the author, but also, when possible, Dr. Thomas weaves the arranger's intent into his analysis. He provides a unique, in-depth, personal discussion as to his teaching strategies of six selected settings. Dr. Thomas has included comments by two recognized African American conductors (including this writer) in regards to their process of selection and performance of the Negro spiritual. A valuable appendix of printed spiritual settings as well as an extensive bibliography and a discography/videography complete this much-needed resource.

André Thomas has furnished choral/vocal musicians throughout the world with a practical but well-researched study that can enable the reader to recreate these songs with greater integrity and artistry. The Negro spiritual has long been recognized as one of the most distinctive and rich musical contributions of the United States. These songs, beloved throughout the world, were borne from the trials and tribulations of the Africans ripped from their native soil, then forced into slavery to serve as the cheap labor force to build an important economic fabric of the budding American society. The wide variety of Negro spirituals serves not only as testimony to the lives of a noble people who persevered through the storms of life, but also a rich chronicle of the history and communal life of the African American people. In the twenty-first century, these slaves' songs transcend any one race of people and have become a universal musical expression of people seeking release from whatever personal or societal oppression enslaves us. They provide us with an inspiring treasury of song filled with the human exploration of pain, pathos, hope, courage, faith, and freedom. *Ain't a that good news!*

—ANTON E. ARMSTRONG, DMA
Harry R. and Thora H. Tosdal Professor of Music
St. Olaf College
Conductor, The St. Olaf Choir

PREFACE

The year is 1964 and schools in Wichita, Kansas, are basically segregated and busing had not been instituted. Black music in my world fell into two categories. There was the secular music I heard on the radio, if we could adjust our radio to get WOKJ in Jackson, Mississippi. At that time there were no Black or Soul stations in Wichita, Kansas. Of course, there were the forty-five recordings of R&B that my sister owned. The other music was the "church music" that I heard at the Baptist church I attended. We were a progressive church, so there were the four anthems that made the circuit throughout most black communities; these, of course, not being from the black tradition. There were the hymns, the deacons lining out the chants or, as they would sometimes call them, the "Dr. Watts." There were the songs found in the *Gospel Pearl*, and there were the latest gospel songs, performed by groups including the Caravans, Mighty Clouds of Joy, Roberta Martin, Clara Ward, James Cleveland, and, of course, Mahalia Jackson. I remember hearing Mahalia Jackson singing her gospel interpretation of the spiritual, "Soon Ah Will Be Done" in that wonderful movie *Imitation of Life*. But I did not associate that with that genera of music that W.E.B. Du Bois described; it was just church music.

Because education was indeed so very important in my household, my mother sent me to a junior high school that my sister could drive me to on her way to her teaching position at the high school. My world changed immediately. It went from one that was predominately black to a large junior high school of approximately 2,000 students that I would integrate. Initially it was not easy to feel at all welcomed or comfortable, but I soon found the music room. It was there that an introduction to the world of choral settings of spirituals was experienced. I must admit, I was not fond of these settings, even through high school. As a young black man, I really didn't identify. This was not the black music that I knew and it certainly wasn't the music that I experienced at my church! The text utilized dialect and it made me feel as if performing this music gave white people a chance to make fun of black people. I never really heard the message in the text; I only heard the way it sounded. We certainly weren't allowed to speak like that in my home and it denoted ignorance in my mind. For me it was not far from *Amos 'N Andy*. Being the racial minority—2,000 white students to one, until my friend could join me at that school—there was no place to hide. I took a great deal of pride in being able to play the latest

James Cleveland song and I had already won competitions playing Brahms, but oh, this music from the slaves! These feelings about this music continued during my brief two-year stay in high school. Every time one of these songs was brought out, the insides shrunk a bit of embarrassment.

College brought about a change. When I was a young sophomore student, my university brought in several guests to our campus. One of those guests was the incredible arranger, musician, and actor Jester Hairston. Although the racial balance was significantly better than in my junior high school, there were still only three of us in a choir of roughly 75 students. My lack of enthusiasm for this music became pretty obvious. Mr. Hairston said to me, "you don't like this much." I told him that this music felt like a caricature of black people. He began to explain to me things about dialect, particularly the "th" sound that is written as a "d" in dialect. He told me that the "th" sound is not present in any of the African dialects. This meant that the slave simply accommodated with the "d." He then began to explain to me about the strength of my ancestors, what they had endured, and how this slave song functioned in their lives. My embarrassment was quickly replaced with pride and admiration, and I was set on a path to learn more about this music. Later, I even began to arrange these songs myself. I am sure that Mr. Hairston affected many lives during that visit; he certainly affected mine! I then only hoped that I would someday be able to give to others the gift he had given me.

That opportunity came in a very special way years later in Austin, Texas. I was a Professor of Music at UT, Austin, and had been asked to be a clinician/adjudicator. The group that I was working with had chosen to sing one of my arrangements as their final number. In the clinic, I attempted to help them understand what I had conceived in the arrangement. At the end of the day, while trying to make my way to my car in the parking lot, a young black woman stopped me. She said to me, "Dr. Thomas, that song…that song… That song makes me feel *so* black!" I looked at her and hugged her neck, and said, "it makes me feel black, too." I looked up and said a silent thank you, Mr. Hairston!

It is not enough to know simply the music. One must know the culture of that folk music as well as the history of its people, but most importantly, the music must be sung with a respect of that culture. It is my hope that this book will provide for the choral conductor, singer, and interested person an historical background of this great music, performance considerations, a selected discussion of arrangers, and a look at how I approach several spiritual arrangements. I hope that it will assist choral conductors in reaching an informed performance of the music and hopefully create within their experience an experience for their African American singers that is an ennobling one, and, for their non-African American singers, one that cultivates a respect and appreciation of this music of the slave.

It is said that it is amazing that out of man's inhumanity to man should come forth America's greatest art form—the Negro spiritual.

ACKNOWLEDGEMENTS

I wish to thank the following people, without whose help this book could not have been completed.

Matthew Garrett and Craig Zamer, research assistants at Florida State University, whose work on the compilation of the appendix of spiritual arrangements contributes greatly to the value of this book!

Marilynn Summers, Choral Program Assistant at Florida State University, who spent many hours tracking down arrangers and composers.

Geoff Lorenz, for his vision and encouragement of this project.

Larry Pugh, President of Music Publishing at The Lorenz Corporation, and Mary Lynn Lightfoot, Choral Editor of Heritage Music Press, for their assistance in this project.

Judith Willoughby and Anton Armstrong, my friends and contributors to this book.

Special thanks go to my literary editor, Kris Kropff, and my wife, Portia, for not only their encouragement and support, but for the many hours spent in the last phases of this project.

Finally, a sincere debt of gratitude to the many arrangers of spirituals!

PART I

UNDERSTANDING THE SPIRITUAL

1

SINGING IN A STRANGE LAND

The Origin and Development
of the Spiritual

For there they that carried us away captive required of us
A song; and they that wasted us required of us mirth, saying,
'Sing us one of the songs of Zion.'
How shall we sing the Lord's song in a strange land?
—PSALM 137: 3–4

The Beginning of Slavery

In 1619 a Dutch Man of War brought to this country the first group of Africans. The ship landed on the coast of Virginia. This importation continued for more than two hundred years, with most of the Africans hailing from the West Coast of the continent. Eileen Southern states that perhaps the most important delineation was the separation of peoples into groups, specifically the Akan, Fon Yoruba, Ibo, Fanti, Fulani, Ashanti, Jolof, Mandingo, Bakongo, and Baoulé.[1] The number of Africans in America rapidly increased with each shipment of people. Some authors suggest as many as fifteen million Africans were transmitted to the Americas during this period.

The conditions that the slaves endured on these ships were indeed inhuman. Slave traders took as many slaves as could be stuffed into a ship, knowing that some would not make it to their final destination. One slave ship, *The Brookes,* was originally built to carry a maximum of 451 people but was carrying over 600 slaves from Africa to the Americas. James Walvin tells us that by the seventeenth century a slave could be purchased for twenty-five dollars and sold upon arrival for about $150.00. This price rose sharply after slave trade became illegal.[2] Many slaves died in route either from disease or starvation. None could speak English and the variety of tribes represented prohibited many from communicating with each other.

Olaudad Equiano was a captured slave who wrote about his experiences:

> The first object which saluted my eyes when I arrived on the coast was the sea, and a slave ship, which was then riding at anchor, and waiting for its cargo. These filled me with astonishment, which was soon converted into terror, when I was carried on board. I was immediately handled, and tossed up to see if I were sound, by some of the crew; and I was now persuaded that I had gotten into a world of bad spirits, and that they were going to kill me.

> I was soon put down under the decks, and there I received such a greeting in my nostrils as I had never experienced in my life; so that, with the loathsomeness of the stench, and crying together, I became so sick and low that I was not able to eat, nor had I the least desire to taste anything. I now wished for the last friend, death, to relieve me; but soon, to my grief, two of the white men offered me eatables; and, on my refusing to eat, one of them held me fast by the hands, and laid me across, I think, the windlass, and tied my feet, while the other flogged me severely.

> The white people looked and acted, as I thought, in so savage a manner; for I had never seen among my people such instances of brutal cruelty. The closeness of the place, and the heat of the climate, added to the number in the ship, which was so crowded that each had scarcely room to turn himself, almost suffocated us.

> The air soon became unfit for respiration, from a variety of loathsome smells, and brought on a sickness among the slaves, of which many died. The wretched situation was again aggravated by the chains, now unsupportable, and the filth of the necessary tubs, into which the children often fell, and were almost suffocated. The shrieks of the women, and the groans of the dying, rendered the whole a scene of horror almost inconceivable.[3]

Although the slave was separated from his home and, in many cases, his family, then stripped of all human dignity, he would be the building stone of a new nation. Hildred Roach writes, "Little did he know that his musical nature and spiritual stimuli would be so important in the development of the new world."[4]

Origins of the Negro Spiritual

The Spirituals are purely and solely the creation of the American Negro; that is, as much so as any music can be the pure and sole creation of any particular group... The Negro brought with him from Africa his native musical instinct and talent, and that was no small endowment to begin with.[5]

—JAMES WELDON JOHNSON

The Africans on the slave ships were proud people for whom music was an integral part of their entire society. Every great event was celebrated with dance, song and music, and the master musicians were held in high esteem by the people.[6] Bruno Nettl offers the following about the importance of music in the African society:

> It cannot be denied that Africans, on the whole, do participate in musical life much more—and more actively singing, playing, composing, dancing—than do members of Western civilization. ...Music in Africa can be said to have a greater or more important role than it does in Western civilization.[7]

But now these proud peoples for whom music was so vital were captives! According to slave narratives by Fredrick Douglass and Sojourner Truth, the Africans were forced to sing both on ship and on land. But out of these painful experiences would grow forth one of America's greatest art forms—the Negro spiritual.

In fact, it is the interaction and synthesis of the two cultures—the African culture with that of white southerners—that formed the basis for the emergence of the spiritual as a distinctive musical form. Richard Newman shares this view, and quotes Benjamin May, former president of Morehouse College, "The creation of the spirituals was no accident. It was a creation born of necessity, so that the slave might more adequately adjust himself to the conditions of the new world."[8] James Weldon Johnson felt strongly that the fusing of the spirit of Christianity with the slaves' African music gave birth to the Negro spiritual.

The result was a body of songs voicing all the cardinal virtues of Christianity—patience—forbearance—love—faith—and hope—through a necessarily modified form of primitive African music.[9]

Most scholars agree that whatever combination of elements came together, African Americans created a significant genre of music.

The Term, "Spiritual"

Although the spiritual is enjoyed and loved by performers and listeners alike, many are confused about its definition. And while some may be quick to silence their own questions out of a sense of embarrassment, it is worth noting that most of the scholarship on the spiritual does not bring a great deal of clarity to this discussion. Rather than seeking out a concise, dictionary-like definition of "spiritual," it is perhaps most helpful to explore several key components of the spiritual.

Several notable scholars offer insights into the folk song nature of the spiritual. Krehbiel writes, "Folk songs are echoes of the heartbeats of the vast folk, and in them are preserved feelings, beliefs and habits of the vast antiquity." Vaughan Williams writes that folk songs grow out of the needs of the people and that the people find a "fit and perfect" way to satisfy those needs.[10]

When we look at the needs of slaves, certainly a people enslaved needed a tool to express themselves. Singing and expressing one's emotion was a part of the West African tradition and became a lifeline to the African American slave. The spiritual, and the larger genera referred to as the slave song, embodied this lifeline and provided the slave an outlet for his emotions and his everyday concerns.[11]

These folk songs created in slavery frequently used religious subjects for much of their expression. Many spirituals contain themes from Jewish (Old Testament) religious traditions, with Moses, David, Daniel, Ezekiel, and Elijah making frequent appearances. Christian (New Testament) themes were also used. Furthering the connection to religion, Hildred Roach quotes arranger/composer Harry T. Burleigh in stating that the spiritual was the "spontaneous outbursts of intense religious fervor which had their origin chiefly in camp meetings, revivals and other religious exercises."[12]

It might also be useful to briefly mention what the spiritual isn't. It isn't gospel music. Arthur Jones attempts to explain the difference between the two forms by stating that gospel music is a composed form created in the twentieth century. (He does, however, acknowledge that it evolved from the spiritual tradition.)[13]

Other Related Forms

As with many genres of music, the spiritual is a part of a bigger genera, specifically the slave song. The slave song includes a number of other forms of music created by slaves during the Antebellum Period, which for purposes of this discussion includes the period from the arrival of the first slaves in 1619 through the freeing of the last slaves in the 1870s.

Most scholars agree that these songs found their way into performance in many different situations in plantation life, be it in work or play and, of course, in worship. As an example, after the regular services, a special dance/song called the *shout* took place. The following is an eyewitness description of the shout. It first appeared in *The Nation* on May 30, 1867:

> …But the benches are pushed back to the wall when the formal meeting is over, and old and young, men and women, sprucely dressed young men, grotesquely half-clad field hands—the women generally with gay handkerchiefs twisted about their heads and with short skirts—boys with tattered shirts and men's trousers, young girls bare-footed, all stand up in the middle of the floor, and when the "sperichil" is struck up begin first walking and by and by shuffling around, one after the other, in a ring. The foot is hardly taken from the floor, and the progression is mainly due to a jerking, hitching motion which agitates the entire shouter and soon brings out streams of perspiration. Sometimes they dance silently, sometimes as they shuffle they sing the chorus of the spiritual, and sometimes the song itself is also sung by the dancers. But more frequently a band, composed of some of the best singers and of tired shouters, stands at the side of the room to "base" the others, singing the body of the song and clapping their hands together or on the knees. Song and dance are alike extremely energetic, and often, when the shout lasts into the middle of the night, the monotonous thud, thud of the feet prevents sleep within half a mile of the praise house.[14]

James Weldon Johnson felt that the shout songs were not true spirituals, but he does agree with contemporary scholarship that perhaps the broader musical experience started with a spiritual and progressed into a monotonous chant, the repetition of which could extended itself for up to five hours. Together, the repetition and the movement of the shout produced an ecstatic state. He also stated that the more educated ministers and members banned the ring shout.

Like other scholars, Johnson points to the shout's existence as evidence of the African tradition in America, suggesting it was perhaps the survival of a primitive African dance. He also felt that this practice was primarily associated with the Atlantic and coastal regions of the United States. Eileen Southern suggests that the spirituals most closely associated with the shout in this region were "Oh, We'll Walk Around the Fountain," "I Know, Member, Know the Lord," "The Bells Done Ring," "Pray All the Members," "Go Ring That Bell," and "I Can't Stay Behind."[15]

Other non-spiritual forms also existed on the plantation. The field holler is one example. Its songs were sometimes simply a call for water or food, or served to let another worker know that the singer was present in the field. The children likewise created songs. The Creoles in Louisiana created a number of dance songs. These secular songs were often associated with Carnival. Moses Hogan, with his setting of "Mr. Banjo," was the first of the modern-day arrangers to begin to set these songs in a choral form. Example 1.1 below shows one of the first transcriptions of the original dance song; example 1.2 is a portion of Mr. Hogan's treatment of it.

136.   **MUSIEU BAINJO.**

Voyez   ce mu-let   là,   Musieu Bainjo,   Comme il est in-so-lent.

{ Chapeau   sur   cô-té,   Musieu Bain-jo,
La canne   à   la   main,   Musieu Bain-jo.
Botte qui   fait   crin, crin,   Musieu Bain-jo, }

1.1 "Musieu Bainjo," No. 136 from *Slave Songs of the United States*

1.2 From "Mister Banjo," arr. by Moses Hogan

Role of the Slave Song

In addition to its place in worship, the spiritual also accompanied other activities in the plantation life. Often the up-tempo ones accompanied the slave while working, or the tempo of a particular song was adjusted to fit a specific activity. For some activities, secular songs were created. Eileen Southern gives examples of several songs associated with various activities. Of those songs, she suggests "Rise Up In Due Time" for harvesting. Of the corn songs, which are a set of work songs utilized while shucking corn, she gives as an example "Roun' de Corn, Sally." Southern also reports that the editors of *Slave Songs of the United States* point out that some songs were sung at every sort of work. She suggests that "Poor Rosy" was utilized in this manner.[16]

The text of the spiritual—so important to its expression—also served a double meaning. Take for example, "Keep Your Lamps Trimmed and Burning." The message to be prepared as Jesus can deliver you at any time is an important one. But slaves also sang this spiritual to communicate secretly with one another, be it to alert their fellow slaves to the possibility of escape or to pending danger.

The Spiritual as Art Music

While in America, composer Antonín Dvořák studied many forms of folk music and hymnody and concluded that the Negro spiritual was the only genuine folk music in America from which a national music could be developed. Frederick Delius also concurred with Dvořák's conclusions.[17]

As you might imagine, Dvořák's comments spurred a strong reaction from many in the music community. While there was a group of American composers who took Dvořák's comments to heart and embraced the Negro spiritual (most notably George W. Chadwick, Henry Schoenberg, and Edward R. Kroeger) others found it difficult, at best, to give credit to Negroes for the creation of a "species of song in which an undeniably great composer had recognized artistic potential."[18]

It was the criticism of the Negro music that gave Henry Krehbiel the impetus to write his book, *Afro American Folksong*, which stands as a seminal book on the spiritual, and one that highlights the struggle for recognition of the spiritual as art music. A case in point: in his preface, Krehbiel makes reference to Dvořák's comments, but he also notes that while Dr. Dvořák composed a symphony, string quartet, and string quintet in which he utilized characteristic elements he discovered in Negro song, only the symphony, with its *From the New World* title, points to this influence.

The Lasting Impact

African Americans continued to involve singing and dancing in every aspect of their lives during this difficult period of American history. Although all forms of the slave song are important, certainly none have equaled or surpassed the musical or sociological interest that both researchers and laymen have in the Negro spiritual.

In his book *Black Song*, John Lovell touts the Negro spiritual as a true folk song. And one that was successful in blending the experiences and imagination of one folk group, and created songs for the universal heart. He goes on to say that the longevity of interest in the spiritual gives evidence to the depth that this form has dug into the universal heart.[19]

The sheer known number of existing spirituals is astounding. Richard Newman reports that in 1998 the Library of Congress had on record more than six thousand spirituals or fragments of spirituals.[20] For many arrangers, this is an almost limitless amount of material, and for the lover of the spiritual, it conveys so much that this wealth of music has endured the test of time. Universal is its message that although the slave's experience was bitter, his heartfelt voice is still heard today!

2

FROM THE ORAL TRADITION TO THE PRINTED PAGE

Selected Collectors of the Spiritual

The heartfelt voice of the slave resonates today thanks in large part to the efforts of several collectors who sought to preserve the spiritual. Among the most important are four anthologies from the nineteenth century. Viewed chronologically, they clearly show a development from simply capturing the melodies to the crafting of actual arrangements of these melodies.

As with *Urtext* editions of Renaissance music, there is much to be gained from an awareness of these collections. With further study, the eager arranger of these songs will discover a vast source of untouched materials, as well as a verification of the melodies of familiar songs.* But perhaps their greatest value is in the glimpse

---

* Here I offer a special note to arrangers or budding arrangers—avail yourself of this source material. Consult the early collectors and transcribers; you'll find a wealth of deserving material that has yet to be touched. Referencing the transcriptions can also save you from an inadvertent infringement of copyright law. Many of the arrangers discussed herein introduced their own melodic fragments within the arrangement; some even altered slightly the transcribed spiritual, thereby moving the work out of the public domain.

they provide into the performance of this music in both social and religious situations on the plantation.

Slave Songs of the United States (1867)

The earliest attempts to notate the improvised songs of the slaves began in the 1830s. The first collection of plantation songs to be printed, *Slave Songs of the United States*, edited by William Allen, Charles Ware and Lucy McKim Garrison, came some three decades later, in 1867.[†] It includes spirituals, shouts, work songs, and some purely secular songs of the slaves.[1]

This folk music was collected in interviews with slaves and newly freed slaves.[‡] It is interesting to note that the editors felt they had a finite amount of time to collect this music, sharing in the preface their feelings that many of the slaves were hesitant to sing these old spiritual songs and that the spiritual would soon be superseded by the new style of religious music that was imitative of white people.

Allen, Ware and Garrison paid very close attention in the transcribing of the dialect. They also did an excellent job of attempting to explain the dialect use of the slaves and its variation from plantation to plantation and state to state. Further, *Slave Songs of the United States* offers explanation of the variants in melody and text. To that end, both text and music and text only are included; however, there is not careful consideration to text underlay. As you can see in "Roll, Jordan, Roll" (ex. 2.1 on page 14), they attempt to set one verse and assume that the reader will be able to fit the words of the remaining verses appropriately. As one of the editors wrote, "One must make them fit the best he can, as the Negroes themselves do."

---

† It should be noted that some of these collectors had published some of these same songs in earlier journals. For example, Lucy McKim published "Roll, Jordan, Roll" and "Poor Rosy" in the Nov. 8, 1862, *Dwight's Journal of Music*. The preface of *Slave Songs of the United States* includes a complete list of prior publications.

‡ Although the Emancipation Proclamation went into effect January 1, 1863, it only served to free slaves in rebellious states. Consequently, freedom did not come to each of the states at the same time and some were still enslaved at the time these collectors were conducting their interviews.

1.   ROLL, JORDAN, ROLL.

1. My brudder sit-tin' on the tree of life, An' he yearde when Jor-dan

Var.

roll;____ Roll, Jor-dan, Roll, Jor-dan, Roll, Jor-dan, roll!

O march de an-gel march, O march de an-gel march; O my

soul a-rise in Heaven, Lord, For to yearde when Jor-dan roll.

2 Little chil'en, learn to fear de Lord,
And let your days be long;
Roll, Jordan, &c.

3 O, let no false nor spiteful word
Be found upon your tongue;
Roll, Jordan, &c.

2.1 "Roll, Jordan, Roll," No. 1 in *Slave Songs of the United States*

There is not an attempt to represent the embellishment associated with these songs, likely because of the difficulty inherent in notating/transcribing these melodies. Miss McKim writes, "It is difficult to express the entire character of these Negro ballads by mere musical notes and signs. The odd turns made in the throat, and the curious rhythmic effect produced by single voices chiming in at different irregular intervals, seem almost as impossible to place on the score as the singing of birds or the tones of an Aeolian Harp."[2]

Tempo indications are also absent from the collection. This was probably because the tempo would change depending upon usage. There was also no attempt to harmonize any of the melodies. These editors did not believe that what they heard was harmonization. However they do describe a procedure that the slaves called *base*:

…the leading singer starts the words of each verse, often improvising, and the others, who "base" him, as it is called, strike in with the refrain, or even join in the solo, when the words are familiar. When the "base" begins, the leader often stops, leaving the rest of his words to be guessed at, or it may be they are taken up by one of the other singers. And the "basers" themselves seem to follow their own whims, beginning when they please and leaving off when they please, striking an octave above or below…or hitting some other note that chords, so as to produce the effect of a marvelous complication and variety, and yet with the most perfect time, and rarely with any discord.[3]

Another helpful feature in this collection is a section by the editors with instructions as to how to sing the collected melodies. The editors have also divided the collection into four parts, grouping the song geographically. Part I is the South-Eastern Slave States, specifically South Carolina, Georgia and the Sea Islands. (This section represents the largest part of the collection.) Part II is the Northern Seaboard Slave States. These include Delaware, Maryland, Virginia, and North Carolina. Part III is the Inland Slave States, consisting of Tennessee, Arkansas and the Mississippi River area. Part IV is the Gulf States, including Florida and Louisiana, along with any remaining songs, which fall under the heading of miscellaneous.

Although not a source of repertoire per se, *Slave Songs of the United States* is invaluable as a reference book. Its section on language usage is crucial in understanding both the dialect incorporated in performing not only spirituals but also the secular music. For the arranger, it further offers a wealth of source material, much of which has yet to be set for the concert stage.

Fisk Jubilee Singers (1878)

This very important book is valuable in a dual way. The first half of the book, by J.B.T. Marsh, provides a glimpse into the formation and development of the famous Fisk Jubilee Singers. Mr. Marsh carefully guides the reader through the development of the Jubilee Singers and through their domestic and foreign tours. He clearly describes the peaks and valleys along the path of success for the ensemble. Mr. Marsh is careful to give a brief biographical sketch of each member of the group, and those immediately connected to the singers.

The second half of the book is devoted to the spirituals performed by the Fisk Jubilee Singers. This brings us closest to the first performances of these songs outside of the plantation experiences, and it is here where the spiritual took on its new character as art music. Professor T.F. Seward of New York was the first to write down the arrangements of the Jubilee Singers. It is his "Preface to the Music" that forms the second part of this seminal work.

Prof. Seward is quick to acknowledge the appeal of this music to audiences. He writes:

> The excellent rendering of the Jubilee Band is made more effective and the interest is intensified by the comparison of their former state of slavery and degradation with the present prospects and hopes of their race, which crowd upon every listener's mind during the singing of their songs. Yet the power is chiefly in the songs themselves, and hence a brief analysis of them will be of interest.[4]

Of the one hundred and thirty-nine songs included in the book, Seward writes that these songs were never composed, at least not by a composer in the usual way. Rather, the spiritual emerged from the religious fervor of its creators.

Different from the transcriptions contained in *Slave Songs of the United States*, the examples in *Fisk Jubilee Singers* suggest musical indications, such as the use of fermata in example 2.2 below. Also, harmonizations are written out. As is typical of the songs in the collection, the harmonization is quite simple and diatonic, often on refrains or choruses only. Some of the spirituals are in unison. The textual underlay is clear and the part writing remains, for the most part, in the medium ranges.

No. 2. Swing low, sweet Chariot.

2.2 "Swing Low, Sweet Chariot" from *Fisk Jubilee Singers*

Although these arrangements seem quite simplistic when compared to today's standards, they were powerful and took a rustic folk song from the plantations to European royalty.

Cabin and Plantation Songs (1874)

This collection brings something unique to the literature. First published in 1874, *Cabin and Plantation Songs* illustrates some of the first efforts towards enhancing the folk song or arranging it in a fashion to attempt to transmit what was lost in the genuine oral experiences of hearing the slaves. In this way, it stands in contrast to the efforts of earlier collectors who attempted only to notate the melody then later followed with rather block-style harmonization.

In the example below, we see more than four-part hymn-like harmonization with slight imitation between the voices and antiphonal writing between the bass voice part and the tenor, alto, and soprano parts being represented. Instead, this writing looks very much like the arranging of these songs that will later develop, so much so that this collection may be considered the beginning of a long line of arrangers of the Negro spiritual.

2.3 From "Some o' dese Mornin's" from *Cabin and Plantation Songs, 1st Edition*

Cabin and Plantation Songs, which bears the subtitle "As sung by the Hampton Students," underwent three editions. Thomas Fenner arranged the first edition. He also served as the conductor of the Hampton Students, and is the arranger of the above example. The second edition, arranged by Mr. F. G. Rathbun, includes several additional songs, including some from the Native

American tradition and other nationalities, as well as a few selections from the Tuskegee collection. The Tuskegee additions were arranged by Mr. Hamilton, himself a graduate of Hampton and one of the original members of the Hampton Singers.[5]

The third edition, published in 1901, adds an additional forty songs collected and arranged by Miss Bessie Cleaveland, who became a musical instructor at Hampton in 1892. Among the new songs was a hymn titled "General Armstrong: The Negroes' Battle Hymn," as well as a song sung as grace before a meal for the Hampton students.

Befo' De War Spirituals (1933)

The folk songs in this collection were ~~transcribed by Mr. McIlhenny,~~ with the ~~assistance of Mr. Henri Whermann.~~ These transcriptions were ~~gathered from and confirmed by the former slaves who had sung them.~~ Like the editors of *Slaves Songs of the United States*, McIlhenny and Whermann ~~felt an urgency to transcribe these songs, fearing that they would soon disappear into history as former slaves tried to distance themselves from the experience of slavery and, by extension, the songs of slavery.~~ This approach ~~resulted in a collection valuable in part for its authentic look at the slaves' lives on the plantation and the role folk music played in this environment.~~ Further, it offers some hints into the rustic performance practices of the slaves and includes many spirituals that are unfamiliar to today's audience.

Musically, the ~~harmonies in *Befo' De War Spirituals* are deliberately simple.~~ The writers were also ~~very careful to spell euphonically the Negro dialect,~~ as illustrated in example 2.4 on the facing page, and they made no attempt to change any text into standard American English.

COME AN' GO WIT' ME

2.4 "Come An' Go Wit' Me" from *Befo' De War Spirituals*

It is important to note that readers desiring to explore this collection must be prepared to slog through Mr. McIlhenny's frequent justifications of his family's practice of slavery on their sugar plantation on Avery Island in Louisiana. For example, he repeatedly insists that his family treated their Negroes well, writing, "the attitude of our slaves to their white owners was one of happy friendliness, without any bitterness, and this is the attitude of their descendants towards my people today."[6] Read today, in a time when most people agree that slavery in any form is inhuman and cannot be justified, it is nearly impossible not to have a visceral reaction to these words, but care should be taken to keep that reaction from diminishing the historical importance of this collection.

3

BEYOND THE PRINTED PAGE TO SHAPING AN ART

Selected Arrangers of the Spiritual

At the turn of the twentieth century, a group of musicians began using the folk music of the slaves as the foundation for choral works. These gifted composers and arrangers cultivated a genre of choral music that inspired future generations, who themselves went on to tend and innovate the concert spiritual, and inspire the modern and contemporary arrangers who are writing today, more than a century later. To understand their lives and musical influences and goals is to better understand their music.*

EARLY NATIONALISTIC ARRANGERS (1866–1896)

The early arrangers of the spiritual were indeed musicians of the highest quality. All of those examined in the section that fol-

---

* Editor's note: The arrangers discussed in this chapter are grouped stylistically. For clarity's sake, those groupings are delineated by the birth years of the arrangers in each. Within each group, the arrangers are presented in chronological order by birth year. Because the output of each came at different times in their lives, the chronology of works may be somewhat different.

lows were educated and trained as composers in the Western art tradition. In fact, many of these arrangers were composers, but they found that during the time at which they lived, acceptance of their non-spiritual work was extremely limited.

Undeterred, these arrangers forged new ground in the treatment of the spiritual. They did not seek to re-create the music of the slaves. Instead, they utilized the slave music in their new creations. The resulting arrangements began to take on a different character, but one that is not dissimilar from the Western art tradition. After all, their use of the folk songs of the slaves was not unlike the way Bartók and Kodály used Hungarian folk music in their works.

Harry T. Burleigh (1866–1949)

Harry T. Burleigh is one of the earliest arrangers of spirituals. From early childhood he had a love of music that was recognized by his mother. She was an employee of Mrs. Russell and arranged for Burleigh to work as the doorman when there were concerts at the Russell home. His grandfather had been a slave and it was through him that Burleigh learned the plantation songs.

In 1892, at the age of 26, Burleigh moved from his hometown of Erie, Pennsylvania, and entered the National Conservatory of Music in New York. He studied voice, harmony and counterpoint, and played in the orchestra. It was also there that he got to know Victor Herbert and Edward MacDowell. MacDowell's mother, an acquaintance of Mrs. Russell, had been influential in securing a scholarship for Burleigh.

HARRY T. BURLEIGH

Antonín Dvořák was the director of the Conservatory during Burleigh's tenure as a student, and it was Burleigh who introduced him to the spiritual. They became friends and often Burleigh would copy manuscripts for Dvořák. When Dvořák arranged the song "Old Folks at Home," Burleigh was the soloist for the performance in Madison Square Garden. This concert, held on January 23, 1894, utilized an all-black chorus, many of whose members came from the St. Philip's Colored Choir.

A successful recitalist and composer, Burleigh was quick to give a helping hand to his contemporary black musicians. Among those musicians he was in close contact with were Nathaniel Dett,

James and Rosamond Johnson, Eva Jessye, ~~Jester Hairston,~~ Edward Boatner, John Work, Clarence Cameron White, and Afro-British composer Samuel Coleridge-Taylor.

Burleigh was the ~~first to set these plantation songs as art songs.~~ His solo settings became very popular with the singers of the day, both black and white. ~~Whereas some black writers struggled to get their compositions published, by 1901 G. Schirmer, Inc. had published a collection of seven songs arranged by Burleigh, titled~~ *Plantation Melodies Old and New.* By 1905 nine songs were published by the William Maxwell Company. Burleigh developed a close relationship with George Maxwell, William's brother, who was subsequently hired as managing editor for G. Ricordi and Company. George would go on to become the first president of the American Society of Arrangers, Composers and Publishers (ASCAP), but while at Ricordi, he hired Burleigh, first as a freelance editor and eventually as a full-time employee.[1]

The popularity of groups following in the footsteps of the Fisk Jubilee Singers, groups like the sixteen-voice Williams and Walker Glee Club, Amphion Club of Melrose, Massachusetts, the Orpheus Club of Philadelphia, the International Singers of New York, and the Lotus Quartette of Boston, along with the 200- and 300-voice choirs that were also popular, ~~generated much of the demand for Burleigh's choral arrangements. To meet the needs of so many different ensembles, Burleigh often arranged the same spiritual in multiple voicings,~~ beginning a practice that is commonplace today. As an example, in 1913, he crafted an SATB setting of "Deep River" (the first such setting of this spiritual). The following year, TTBB and SSA settings were published. Similarly, his 1917 treatment of "Swing Low, Sweet Chariot" is set for SATB, TTBB, SSA, SA, or TB chorus.

Although Burleigh ~~set most of his spiritual arrangements for *a cappella* chorus, he did set some for accompanied chorus.~~ "Behold a Star," for example, written in 1928, is set for SATB chorus and organ. "Sometimes I Feel Like a Motherless Child" (1949) is written for SSA and piano, and "Heav'n Heav'n," (1921) is written for SATB and piano. Within his choral arrangements there is great inconsistency in the use of Negro dialect. Burleigh covers the extremes, from no dialect, as in "Were You There?," to extensive use, as in "My Lord, What a Morning." Further, when he did elect to use dialect, he was inconsistent in its use.

In the Burleigh arrangements, we find finely crafted settings of these slave songs. There is no attempt other than the use of dialect to recreate the sound of the slaves. The settings are straightforward and voice leading is impeccable. As James Weldon Johnson wrote, "Mr. Burleigh was the pioneer in making arrangements for the spirituals that widened their appeal and extended their use to singers and the general music public."[2]

More than anything else, in Burleigh's arrangements we see the musical realization of his reverence for this music. The high esteem in which he held it is best expressed by Burleigh himself:

> Spirituals are the only legacy of slavery of which the race can be proud. Into the making of these spirituals was poured the aspirations of a race in bondage whose religion, intensely felt, was their only hope and comfort. They rank with the great folk music of the world.[3]

John Rosamond Johnson (1873–1954)

John Rosamond Johnson and his famous brother James Weldon Johnson were both born in Jacksonville, Florida. Rosamond Johnson's early musical training began with his mother. Later, he enrolled in the New England Conservatory of Music and studied piano, organ, composition, and voice. He then went to London for additional training. In 1917 Atlanta University bestowed upon him an honorary M.A.

Johnson began his career as a music teacher in the public schools of Jacksonville, Florida, eventually becoming supervisor of music for the Jacksonville Public Schools. Later, he became the music director and trustee at the Music School Settlement for Colored People in New York.[4]

JOHN ROSAMOND JOHNSON

Rosamond Johnson collaborated with his brother James Weldon, a poet, and Bob Cole to form Cole and the Johnson Brothers. Together, they produced more than two hundred songs, some of which were included in several musicals by white composers. Also among their output were two successful operettas that ran on Broadway with all-black casts. Johnson also wrote three additional musicals with other collaborators.

The two brothers are perhaps best known for writing the text and music to "Lift Every Voice and Sing." This hymn, which became known as the Negro National Anthem, was sung in most black congregations in the United States and was performed before nearly all civic meetings held at any black church. Now, we hear it predominately during Black History Month.

Rosamond Johnson's major contribution as an arranger of the Negro spiritual came in the collaboration with his brother on *The Books of American Negro Spirituals*. Rosamond Johnson was responsible for most of the musical arrangements of these songs. He set them for solo voice and piano, with piano parts that are interesting but do not overpower the melody. Further, he was "true not only to the best traditions of the melodies but also to the form. No changes have been made in the form of songs. The only development has been in harmonizations, and these harmonizations have been kept true in character."[5]

Unlike Burleigh's choral settings, Rosamond Johnson's are primarily SATB with piano accompaniment. These settings are appealing to the average listener and exemplify the idiom of nineteenth-century Romanticism that was present in most of the music of the arrangers and composers who were active during the 1930s.

R. Nathaniel Dett (1882–1943)

In the person of Nathaniel Dett is encapsulated a composer, conductor, arranger, and educator. Nathaniel Dett was born October 11, 1882, in Drummondville, Ontario, Canada. His musical prowess was noted in his early years. He had a love for the piano and a tremendous ear. Because of the lack of finances, only his two older brothers were allowed to take piano lessons; however the younger Dett could attend the lessons with his brothers. Dett recalls:

R. NATHANIEL DETT

On the rare occasions when the teacher happened to leave the room to get more music I would slide from my chair, fly to the piano stool, and play until warned by my brothers that "teacher" was returning. After one such absence she became curious as to who the performer was, saying that the music was "better playing than my brothers did." When they told her who it was that had been playing, she asked me to play for her, but I was too shy. Finally, she hid herself one day behind the curtains at the window and my brothers persuaded me to play some of the things I had heard her play. The result was that she offered to give me free lessons.[6]

In his early years, Dett did not have an appreciation for the spirituals. He had heard his grandmother singing them, but they had no meaning to him.[†] He later shared these feelings, writing in *Musical America:*

> The Negro people as a whole cannot be looked to as a very great aid in the work of conserving their folk music. At the present time they are inclined to regard it as a vestige of the slavery they are trying to put behind them and to be ashamed of it. Moreover, the prevailing manner of presenting Negro music to the public—the "coon" song of vaudeville or the minstrel show—has not tended to increase appreciation of it, either among the Negro or white races.[7]

This attitude soon gave way to a sincere appreciation of the slave music of his ancestors. It was during his study at Oberlin that he began to embrace the folk music of his ancestors. It was on an occasion at Oberlin that Dett heard a performance by the Kneisel Quartet of the slow movement from Dvořák's *American Quartet.* Anne Key Simpson conjectures that this was perhaps the first time that Dett really assimilated in his thinking the use of traditional folk tunes in serious music. Of this epiphany, Dett writes:

> Suddenly it seemed I heard again the frail sweet voice of my long-departed grandmother, calling across the years; and, in a rush of emotion, which stirred my spirit to its very center, the meaning of the songs, which had given her soul such peace, was revealed to me.[8]

One of the earliest examples of Dett incorporating the spiritual into his composition process is in a work he performed on one of his senior recitals: "Nobody Knows the Trouble I See," arranged for violin and piano.[9] Although Dett wrote for various instrumental combinations, it is in his works for piano, voice and chorus that he achieved the greatest success. Among his well-known works for piano is the suite *In the Bottoms.* Its movement "The Dance (Juba)" continues to be performed by pianists today, and in its day, the piece was so popular that arrangements of it were made for band and orchestra. Dett himself made an arrangement for choir.

After graduation from Oberlin College, Dett began his teaching career at Lane College in Jackson, Tennessee. He later became the director of music at Kansas City High School and also Lincoln Institute. In 1913 he began his work at the Hampton Institute. It was at this institution that his choral writing flourished and he developed a chorus that became internationally famous.

---

† In many ways, my feelings as a young man about the spiritual, which I shared in the Preface, mirrored Dett's.

Dett's choral writing is steeped in Neo-Romantic tradition, is predominately *a cappella*, and features limited use of dialect. Beyond these generalities, his choral arrangements utilizing the spiritual can be organized into two main categories. The first includes those where he attempted to write harmonizations that are simple and authentic, based on the singing of these songs by the Hampton students since 1868.[10] "Were You There When They Crucified My Lord?" (example 3.1 below) typifies the arrangements in this category.

Were You There When They Crucified My Lord?

3.1 From "Were You There When They Crucified My Lord?"

In spite of his intentions to keep these arrangements simple and authentic, Dett's treatments were still met with criticism by some members of the musical community who felt he was obscuring the folk song. For example, George Pullen Jackson, while referring to *Religious Folk-Songs of the Negro: as Sung at Hampton Institute*, wrote:

> R. Nathaniel Dett has done excellent editing of the textual material he inherited from the earlier Fenner Hampton compilation (1874) of songs recorded from oral tradition and borrowed from the Fisk collection; and his tunes are musically handled—perhaps too musicianly, for with their inappropriate and over-generous Italian expression, directions, and other artifices, one sees that they are polished up for the technically refined concert stage, a treatment which makes the song less valuable to those who would learn something of Negro folk music as it really was.[11]

The second category into which his spiritual arrangements fall includes those where Dett utilizes the spiritual theme as a basis on which to build his composition. One of his most popular compositions, "Listen to the Lambs," illustrates this compositional approach. Although the theme—the spiritual—is African American, the composition (an example of which is provided on page 28) clearly has Romantic characteristics. Also notable about this work is that although Dett felt that Negro schools, rather than Negro churches, were the best place for the preservation of the spiritual, under the title of this piece he wrote, "A Religious Characteristic in the form of an Anthem."

3.2 From "Listen to the Lambs"

A composition of Dett's that uses more of the spiritual theme is "I'll Never Turn Back No More." This composition is written for SATB chorus with tenor or soprano solo. As illustrated in example 3.3 below, the tessitura on the solo is quite high. Further, Anne Key Simpson identifies this composition as a good example of Negro long-meter (four-line stanza in iambic measure), and applauds Dett's success in observing the long-meter limits.

3.3 From "I'll Never Turn Back No More"

Nathaniel Dett did write two extended choral works that utilized the spiritual. The first is *The Chariot Jubilee*, published in 1919 and written for Professor Howard Lyman and the Syracuse University Chorus. Written for eight-part mixed chorus, tenor solo and orchestra, the work was well received by the audience and critics. During the 1932–1933 school year Dett completed his second extended work, *The Ordering of Moses*. This work was in fulfillment of his master's degree at Eastman School of Music. After three revisions, it was published in 1937 and received its premier at the Cincinnati May Festival. The work was dedicated to George Foster Peabody and is scored for SATB chorus, five soloists and orchestra. It received very positive reviews.

Hall Johnson (1888–1970)

Hall Johnson was educated as an instrumental musician but soon turned his attention to choral music. In this arena, he would go on to establish himself as a hugely important and influential conductor, composer, and arranger, and as one of history's most zealous advocates for the Negro spiritual.

HALL JOHNSON

Johnson, like others of his generation, felt that the spiritual traditions were dying and would be lost completely when he and his contemporaries—those old enough to really remember the sound of the early spiritual performances—passed away. Consequently, creating an authentic aural record which would preserve this art form was very important to him. To this end, on September 8, 1925, Johnson organized The Hall Johnson Negro Choir. The first professional all-Negro choir in the United States, Johnson was adamant that this choir's goal was not to entertain. Rather, it was to carry on the tradition of this music, or, as he shares in his own words:

> We wanted to show how the American Negro slaves—in 250 years of constant practice, self-developed under pressure but equipped with their inborn sense of rhythm and drama (plus their new religion)—created, propagated and illuminated an art form which was, and still is, unique in the world of music. The slaves named them "spirituals" to distinguish them from their worldly, "everyday" songs. Also, their musical style of performance was very special. It cannot be accurately notated but must be studied by imitation.[12]

More than just the melodies, Johnson felt it was imperative to create a true aural image of the spiritual. (Johnson felt that earlier attempts to do this, including some by the Library of Congress, were well meaning, but he was ultimately critical of the results, stating that the researchers picked up "all kinds of sporadic dribble of Negro folk-singing," and that although interesting, they had nothing at all to do with the "grand old spiritual."[13]) Johnson's first recording efforts came in 1928 with RCA Victor. Unfortunately the dozen or so songs he recorded with his choir are no longer available (Johnson maintained that after WWII the songs disappeared from the catalog), but thankfully we have not only an aural representation of The Hall Johnson Choir, but a visual one as well.

In 1930 Johnson was appointed music director for the Broadway production *The Green Pastures*. This show was so successful that it was made into a film in 1936; Johnson and his choir were invited to California to participate. (A successful endeavor, Johnson would go on to direct choruses in the films *Lost Horizon*, *Way Down South*, and *Cabin in the Sky*.) Although the choir sang the spirituals in the orchestra pit or off stage in the Broadway production, they were front and center in the film version of *The Green Pastures*. Still available today, this film is a magnificent record of Johnson's idea of the spiritual and an excellent resource to turn to when performing the spiritual arrangements of Hall Johnson.

The bulk of Johnson's spiritual arrangements were written specifically for his choir. Most are scored for SATB chorus, *a cappella* (with just a handful including piano accompaniment). Some utilize a soloist, typically in the soprano or tenor part, although there are occasional solos for baritone or alto. Johnson did craft some settings in multiple voicings, and there are also arrangements written exclusively for female and male voices. Stemming largely from Johnson's strong convictions about capturing the authentic sound of the spiritual, we see a strong use of dialect in his arrangements, as is illustrated in example 3.4 below.

Some of Johnson's most popular settings of spirituals include "His Name So Sweet," "I've Been 'Buked," "Honor, Honor," and "Scandalize My Name." Another very popular composition of Johnson's is "Ain't Got Time to Die." Although it is often called a spiritual, this is not the case, for the words and music were written by Mr. Johnson (albeit in the style of a spiritual).

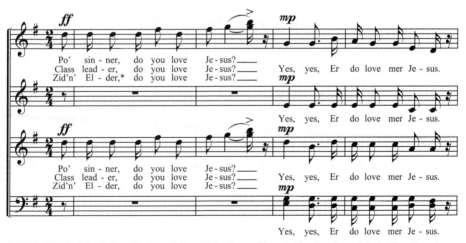

* "Zid'n' Elder" is dialect for "Presiding Elder," an officer in the Southern Methodist Church.

3.4 From "His Name So Sweet"

Eva Jessye (1895–1992)

Eileen Southern refers to Eva Jessye as "a pioneer among women choral conductors." This strong Kansan woman attended Western University in Kansas and later attended and graduated

EVA JESSYE

from Langston University in Oklahoma. She then began her career as a teacher and, in 1922, decided to go to New York. With strong determination and character she achieved what many, black or white, man or woman, could not—conduct her own professional choir, be an active part of New York musical life, and earn international distinction.

A wonderful example of her determination is recounted by Eileen Southern from an interview that she had with Ms. Jessye. Upon arriving in New York, Ms. Jessye found it difficult to find any employment in music; out of desperation, she applied for a position as a dietician in a hospital. A doctor came to her apartment to interview her and noticed that she was a musician. He inquired as to why she was applying for the dietician position and not seeking her dreams. He told her, "Whatever your profession is, if you have been trained in it and you know what you are doing, stick with it and make it pay." Jessye never forgot this statement and it marked a turning point in her career.[14]

Jessye went on to form her own chorus, which quickly found international acclaim and recognition. In 1933 she was asked to be the choir director for a production of *Four Saints in Three Acts* by American composer Virgil Thompson. In 1935 George Gershwin chose her to direct the Eva Jessye Choir in his *Porgy and Bess*, and later, King Vidor chose her as music director of his film *Hallelujah*.

In addition to her success as a conductor, Jessye made several important contributions to the concert spiritual repertoire. Her writing is tonal, Romantic and principally for SATB chorus. Most settings are accompanied. Of particular interest are her folk oratorios *Paradise Lost and Regained* (1934) and *The Life of Christ in Negro Spirituals* (1931). Two additional separate spiritual arrangements, "When the Saints Go Marching" and "Who is That Yonder?" (1965), clearly illustrate her arranging style.

William Grant Still (1895–1978)

William Grant Still is one of the most honored and recognized African American composers of his generation. Often referred to as "Dean of Negro Composers," no less than the great conductor Leopold Stokowski adds to the case that Still is better labeled "Dean of American Composers," saying of him in 1945 that he is "One of our greatest American composers. He has made a real contribution to music."[15]

WILLIAM GRANT STILL

Still began his college education at Wilberforce University in Ohio as a student of medicine. He dropped out of school at Wilberforce, married, then continued his education at Oberlin, this time as a music student. His Oberlin education was interrupted in 1918 to serve in the U.S. Navy, after which he returned to his studies, this time at the New England Conservatory.

A well-rounded musician, Still, who studied the violin as a young man, joined the String Quartet at Wilberforce and eventually taught himself to play all of the instruments of the string family, as well as the oboe, clarinet, and saxophone. Still put these skills to use, playing oboe for W.C. Handy in the pit band for the musical *Shuffle Along*. He also worked for Don Voorhees, Sophie Tucker, Paul Whiteman, Willard Robison, and Artie Shaw, and arranged and conducted the Deep River Hour on CBS and WOR.

As a conductor, Still can proudly claim many "firsts." He was the first Negro to conduct a major symphony orchestra in the United States (Los Angeles Philharmonic Orchestra, 1936), the first to conduct a major symphony orchestra in the Deep South (New Orleans Symphony Orchestra, 1955), and the first to conduct an all-white radio orchestra in New York City. He was also the first to have an opera produced by a major company in the United States; the year was 1949.[16]

Of his 150 compositions, it is his orchestral works that best showcase his compositional gifts, and his citations and honors for these works are immense. Among his prestigious awards are Guggenheim and Rosenwald Fellowships, as well as numerous commissions, including those from the Columbia Broadcasting System, the New York World's Fair, and the Cleveland Orchestra. Still also composed several extended works for chorus and orchestra, most of which owe their success to his ability to orchestrate so exquisitely.

Still's choral settings of spirituals are not abundant, although he did craft a number of spirituals for solo voice and piano that were performed by the artists of the day. Like the other early nationalistic arrangers explored in this section, most of Still's choral settings are in the Neo-Romantic style. Written primarily for SATB chorus and piano, some of them have a solo part indicated. Perhaps one of his most beautiful yet simple settings is "The Blind Man," an excerpt of which is below. As the great American composer Howard Hanson wrote in his preface to this work, "[Dr. Still's] music does what, I believe, most of us feel music should do, it communicates."

3.5 From "The Blind Man"

MIDDLE PERIOD ARRANGERS (1897–1927)

Under the guidance of this group of arrangers, who continued many of the traditions established by their predecessors, the popularity of the spiritual continued to flourish and reach even larger audiences.

Edward H. Boatner (1898–1981)

Like Nathaniel Dett, Edward H. Boatner was a composer, arranger, conductor, and teacher. Born in New Orleans, Louisiana, Boatner attended Western University, received his B.M. from from Chicago College of Music (now known as the School of Music at Roosevelt University), and also attended New England Conservatory and Boston Conservatory. Boatner served as Professor of Music at Samuel Huston College in Austin, Texas (now known as Huston-Tillotson University). From 1925 to 1931 Boatner served as the Director of Music for the National Baptist Convention. He later settled in New York and taught privately.

EDWARD H. BOATNER

Boatner was very active as a solo singer and crafted more than two-hundred solo settings for voice and piano. His solo arrangements, which were performed and encouraged by tenor Roland Hayes, outnumber his choral works and were better received. His choral works did have one very important advocate, though—Nathaniel Dett.

Most of Boatner's choral settings are for SATB chorus, *a cappella*. Some of these settings include a soloist. There are also some SATB settings with piano. His *a cappella* spiritual settings are similar to Dett's in both writing and harmonic style, and in the limited to nonexistent use of dialect in the settings, as illustrated in example 3.6 on the next page.

3.6 From "Who Is That Yonder?"

Also like Dett, the spiritual held a special place for Boatner, as his comments in *The Story of the Spirituals: 30 Spirituals and Their Origins* illustrate:

> For many years after emancipation, blacks turned their backs on the slave-created spirituals. Perhaps it was too bitter a reminder of the past. Today there is more ready acceptance of this part of our musical heritage. We certainly should not forget that ragtime, jazz, blues, swing, gospel, rhythm, and rock and roll all have stemmed from the spiritual! Although there have been many Afro-American contributions to the forms, styles and trends of American music, the original and the most beautiful remains the spiritual.[17]

The earliest of the Middle Period Arrangers, it is not surprising that Boatner's work shows a strong similarity to the works of the Early Nationalistic Arrangers, particularly in its adherence to Neo-Romantic traditions. The strength of his work was recognized not only by important performers of the day but also by the broader musical community, who bestowed on him the Holstein, Harmon, and Wanamaker awards.[18]

William L. Dawson (1899–1990)

William Dawson was born in Anniston, Alabama. His mother's family had extensive land holdings and his mother was educated. Some speculate that his father, George W. Dawson, was born into slavery. Dawson became aware of his musical heritage quite early. According to Mark Malone, as a child Dawson was taken to a concert in Anniston featuring the Jubilee Singers from Fisk University. There, he exclaimed, "Oh, Mama! I know those songs."

WILLIAM L. DAWSON

As a young man, Dawson attended the Tuskegee Institute. Tuskegee was a wonderful place that nurtured the growth of an avid and eager musician, and Dawson was involved in the choir, the band and the small groups, including a quintet of singers. After graduation, Dawson held a one-year position as bandmaster at Kansas Vocational College in Topeka, Kansas, after which he began his graduate studies at Horner Institute of Fine Arts in Kansas City, Missouri. This same year, 1922, Dawson became bandmaster and conductor of the choir at Lincoln High School in Kansas City. In this position, Dawson conducted a one-hundred and fifty voice choir that specialized in Negro folk songs, many of which Dawson arranged. It was the performances of this choir that gave impetus to publication of Dawson's choral compositions.

Dawson graduated from the Horner Institute of Fine Arts in 1925 with a B.M. In 1927 Dawson graduated with a master's degree in composition from the American Conservatory in Chicago. For the next three years Dawson would hold numerous jobs. He was first chair trombone in the Civic Orchestra of Chicago and served as editor and arranger for Gamble Hinge Music Co. He also worked for the H.T. FitzSimmons Co.

In 1930 Dawson accepted an invitation to become the Director of the Tuskegee Institute's School of Music. This began the golden era known as the "Dawson Years." Under his direction the choir would achieve international acclaim. And it was during this time that the bulk of Dawson's most popular arrangements were written.

In Dawson's catalog we find one of the greatest amounts of single publications of these Negro folk songs, as he would prefer to call them.‡ The majority of his settings are for SATB, yet a significant number of SSAA and TTBB settings exist as well. Most of the arrangements are *a cappella,* however he did set some of them with piano accompaniment.

Although he is principally known as an arranger of the Negro folk song, Dawson did find success with some of his instrumental compositions, including his *Negro Folk Symphony,* which achieved the attention of musicians and critics. After its premier in 1934 by the Philadelphia Orchestra under the direction of Leopold Stokowski, one critic from the *New York Times* wrote "that the Dawson work had 'dramatic feeling, a racial sensuousness and directness of melodic speech, and a barbaric turbulence.'"

Hildred Roach defines Dawson's style as Romantic, using tonal centers, and various overlapping and syncopated and irregularly accented rhythms. She gives as an example his setting of "I Wan' to be Ready" for mixed choir, pointing specifically to the use within of pedal points, other suspended tones, and polytonality.[19]

---

‡ Dawson was adamant that these Negro folk songs be called just that, "Negro Folk Songs," not spirituals.

3.7 From "I Wan' to be Ready"

This setting also shows the use of subtle dialect, specifically the dropping of the "t" in "want" to "wan'." Unlike many of the earlier arrangers, Dawson freely incorporated dialect, sometimes going so far as to change words. As an example, "My Lord What a Morning" becomes "My Lord What a Mourning" in his arrangement.

Malone, in his work *William Levi Dawson: American Music Educator,* notes that on some compositions Dawson is credited as arranger while others are attributed to him as though he were the composer or had discovered them. Malone continues:

> When asked, Dawson will tell you that he approaches each piece as a composer. Some arrangements are obviously more his by compositional design. Changes in melodic and harmonic structure give a piece an entirely new flavor, almost a new identity.[20]

Dawson is not alone in his approach to setting these folk songs. The very fortunate thing is that today's listeners have the recording of the Tuskegee Institute Choir under his direction. This recording, *Spirituals: Tuskegee Institute Choir,* William L. Dawson, Director, provides for the current conductor an idea of the preferences of this great musician.

John Wesley Work III (1901–1967)

John Wesley Work III was born into a family already distinguished for its musical contributions. His grandfather, John Wesley Work, was a church choir director in Nashville; some of his choir

JOHN WESLEY WORK III

members were members of the original Fisk Jubilee Singers. His father, John Wesley Work Jr., is often credited as the first black collector of Negro folk songs thanks to his involvement with the 1901 collection *New Jubilee Songs as Sung by the Fisk Jubilee Singers*, a collaboration with his brother Frederick Jerome Work. Work Jr.'s most famous setting of a spiritual for voice and piano is "Go, Tell It on the Mountain," issued in 1901. His subsequent collection in 1915, for which he served as the only collector, is *Folksongs of the American Negro*.[21]

Like his grandfather and father, John Wesley Work III had an affiliation with Fisk University. His early musical training was at the Fisk University Laboratory School, then on to the Fisk High School, and finally to Fisk University, where he earned a B.A. in 1923. He earned a master's degree in 1930 from Columbia University, writing a thesis entitled *American Negro Songs and Spirituals*. He also studied at the Institute of Musical Art (now known as the Juilliard School) and at Yale University.

Following his mother's death in 1926, Work took over as the trainer for the singing groups at Fisk University. He remained at Fisk until 1966. In addition to being the director of the Jubilee Singers and Fisk Men's Glee Club, he served as theorist and composer, and, for five years, as chairman of the Department of Music. Work was away from Fisk during the years of 1931 and 1933. In both of those years, he was awarded Julius Rosenwald Foundation Fellowships and elected to take leave from Fisk to earn a B.M. from Yale University.

Like many of the Early Nationalistic Arrangers, we see two styles of choral writings. In his collection *American Negro Songs and Spirituals: 230 Folk Songs, Religious and Secular*, we see Work functioning as a collector, setting these folk songs in a very simple and diatonic way. As shown in example 3.8 on the facing page, the text settings de-emphasize the use of dialect, with only hints at it in the text.

MY SOUL'S BEEN ANCHORED IN THE LORD
(SECOND VERSION)

3.8 From "My Soul's Been Anchored in the Lord" from *American Negro Songs and Spirituals*

In his settings of spirituals for solo voice and chorus, which comprise the largest part of his output, we see a style that is a bit more ambitious, as illustrated in example 3.9 below.

3.9 From "Rock, Mount Sinai"

In John W. Work III we find not only a choral director and arranger, but indeed an advocate for the folk music of African Americans. The depth of this advocacy is exemplified by his contributions to the Library of Congress/Fisk University Mississippi Delta Collection. Begun in 1940 as an effort to document the folk culture of Coahoma County, Mississippi, this two-year field study was conducted by Work, his Fisk University colleagues Charles S. Johnson and Lewis Jones, and Alan Lomax, the head of the Archive of American Folksong at the Library of Congress. Together, they recorded secular and religious music, sermons, children's games, jokes, folktales, interviews, and dances. The resulting collection includes some 521 manuscript pages and 96 phonographic discs.[22]

Jester Hairston (1901–2000)

Perhaps no other arranger has been more responsible for inspiring and invigorating choral groups throughout the world utilizing the Negro spiritual than Jester Hairston. More than educator, conductor, composer/arranger, or actor—though he was all four—Hairston was a multi-faceted personality whose accolades stretch from serving the U.S. State Department as Ambassador of Goodwill to honoree of the National Association of the American Choral Directors Association in Louisville, Kentucky, in 1987.

JESTER HAIRSTON

The grandchild of former slaves from the Hairston Plantation at Belews Creek, North Carolina, Hairston was educated at and graduated from Tufts University. His major was music. He began his teaching career at a school in Harlem and later went on to become a member of and assistant director for Hall Johnson's Choir. Hairston traveled with that choir to Hollywood to make the film *Green Pastures*, and continued to train choirs for radio and Broadway after returning to New York. In 1937, he collaborated with Dmitri Tiomkin on the score for *Lost Horizon*. Hairston also formed his own choir and wrote music that was used as underscore in movies and television programs, including *Duel in the Sun*, *Portrait of Jenny*, and *Friendly Persuasion*.[23]

Hairston's acting began first on radio as part of the popular *The Amos 'N Andy Show*, which was a radio show before it was a television program. Of this experience and the Screen Actors Guild (SAG), Hairston states:

> When I worked on *The Amos 'N Andy Show*, I couldn't let it bother me that the other black characters were [voiced] by whites because what could I do? It offended me, but the only way that a black man could get a role was to go ahead and take whatever the white man would give him because the pictures and studios belonged to him. I didn't make any fuss. If I had, they would have called me a communist and ran me out of Hollywood. There weren't many blacks in SAG when I joined, but I had to join if I had any intention of staying out here.[24]

Hairston became an active (some sources say founding) member of the Screen Actors Guild and remained active as an actor throughout his entire lifetime. He appeared as the singing voice of Sidney Poitier in the film *Amen* and as the butler in *Lady Sings the Blues*. He also had roles in the television series *That's My Mama* and *Amen*.

As a choral arranger of the spiritual, Hairston's settings are very tonal and accessible for the singer. Like many of his predecessors, Hairston loved the folk music of his ancestors and devoted considerable time to lecturing on the topic and serving as a choral clinician in schools, churches, and concert halls all over the world. No matter where you go, if you find a singer that has been under his direction, a sincere appreciation of the man and his culture dominates all conversation. Mr. Hairston was undeniably a personality that touched the lives of all that were in his presence.

Undine Smith Moore (1904–1989)

A prolific composer and arranger, the works of Undine Moore number over seventy-five for various media. Moore received a degree from Fisk University and earned an M.A. and the Professional Diploma in Music from Columbia University. She also did advanced study at Eastman School of Music and Manhattan School of Music.

Given that Moore called herself, "a teacher who composes, rather than a composer who teaches," it is no surprise that she taught for forty-five years at Virginia State College. In addition to her work there, she was frequently invited to lecture at many colleges, including Carleton College in Northfield, Minnesota, Howard University, and Fisk University. Throughout her career, Moore was committed to music written by black composers. This led her to co-found and co-direct the Black Music Center at Virginia

UNDINE SMITH MOORE

State, through which she was able to bring many of the leading black composers to campus.

Although Moore wrote in many media, it is for her choral music that she is best known. Her writing is clear, concise and predominately tonal, with some use of chromaticism. There is a combination of homophonic and polyphonic textures. Perhaps her best-known spiritual setting is "Daniel, Daniel, Servant of the Lord," an excerpt of which is provided on the facing page.

Moore was awarded honorary degrees from Virginia State and Indiana University and was nominated for a Pulitzer Prize for her cantata *Scenes from the Life of a Martyr: To the Memory of Martin Luther King.*[25]

3.10 From "Daniel, Daniel, Servant of the Lord"

William Henry Smith (1908–1944)

Although the work of William Henry Smith continues to be popular, little is known of his life. He was born in Massachusetts and received musical training in Boston and in Chicago. For a time, he did some teaching in Texas. His most well-documented position was as director of music at the Olivet Baptist Church in Chicago, Illinois under the tremendous leadership of pastor Dr. Lacey Kirk Williams.

An historic church that had its beginnings in the 1850s, by 1915 Olivet Baptist Church had a membership numbering over four thousand. Four years later, the church called Dr. Lacey Kirk Williams as pastor. He would become president of the National Baptist Convention in 1924, but before that, he led Olivet Baptist to national prominence. Under his direction, the church was the largest African American church and, according to church records, was also the largest Protestant Church in the world at that time.

Most of the arrangements Smith wrote during his short life, only forty-six years, were completed in 1937. Evelyn White states that William Henry Smith visited camp meetings and other singing groups, listening and learning the music from the oral tradition and then arranging this music for his choirs.[26]

In his spiritual settings, accessibility and singability are clearly visible in his part writing. He had the wonderful ability to keep the writing simple but rhythmically interesting. Most of his settings are for *a cappella* voices and there is little use of dialect or dissonance. His two most popular arrangements are "Climbing up the Mountain" (1937) and "Ride the Chariot" (1939), which was arranged for both SATB and TTBB. As shown in example 3.11, found on the facing page, Smith clearly possessed the ability to craft a TTBB setting that is as successful as its SATB counterpart.

Ride the Chariot
T.T.B.B.

NEGRO SPIRITUAL
Arr. by Wm. Henry Smith

3.11 From "Ride the Chariot" (TTBB)

Roy Ringwald (1910–1995)

Of the arrangers included in this section, Roy Ringwald exemplifies the successful self-taught composer. Ringwald was born in Helena, Montana, and resided in Palos Verdes Hills, California, at the time of his death. His formal musical training was limited to what he received in parochial and public schools. Following high school, he immediately began his professional career, establishing a relationship with Andre Kostelanetz (a name identified with easy listening music) and other active popular musicians.

ROY RINGWALD

In 1935, Ringwald began an association with Fred Waring and the Pennsylvanians, writing arrangements of patriotic, folk, and holiday songs, both accompanied and *a cappella*, for them. Because he was arranging for a particular group, his arrangements were written specifically for the strengths of that group and ultimately reflect the sound of this distinctive ensemble.[27]

For many Americans, the recordings and broadcasts of Fred Waring and the Pennsylvanians were their main exposure to the African American folk song, particularly the Negro spiritual. In this way, Ringwald was instrumental in shaping how much of the general public conceived of this music.

His most significant contribution to this genre is *God's Trombones*. In this work (see excerpt on the facing page), Ringwald took the poems of James Weldon Johnson's work of same name and added his arrangements of spirituals, creating a cohesive extended choral/orchestral work utilizing the spiritual. This work continues to have numerous performances.

In addition to *God's Trombones* Ringwald arranged many other settings of spirituals, both *a cappella* and accompanied. Among them are setting of "Sometimes I Feel Like a Motherless Child," "Were You There When They Crucified My Lord?" "Mary's Baby," and a very popular setting of "Deep River."

IV. The Judgment Day

3.12 From "IV. The Judgment Day" from *God's Trombones*

Leonard de Paur (1915–1998)

A conductor, composer, and administrator, Leonard de Paur's contributions to music are immense. De Paur received his music education at the University of Colorado, Juilliard School, Columbia University, and L'Universite Laval. He did additional private study with Henry Cowell, Sergei Radamsky, Pierre Monteux, and Hall Johnson, for whom he became assistant conductor in 1932. In 1936 de Paur became the musical director for Orson Welles's production of *Macbeth*. Set in 19th-century Haiti, this critically acclaimed work is often referred to as the "Haitian" *Macbeth* and is among the headlines of de Paur's impressive career. That same year he became the director for the New York City Negro Unit of the Federal Theater.

LEONARD DE PAUR

The next phase of de Paur's career took him to the armed forces. He joined in 1942 and was immediately assigned as the choral director of the Army Air Force's Winged Victory show. Soon thereafter, he was assigned to take over a group that began with a quartet of singers but evolved into a glee club. This fifty-five voice glee club so impressed military officials that it was soon detached and sent to battle areas to boost morale. Negro regimental bands and choruses had been an integral part of the army during World War I and II, but it wasn't until 1943 that the first Negro units of the USO shows toured in the European theater. Hildred Roach reports that between 1947 and 1968, de Paur created and conducted more the 2,300 concerts in foreign tours.[§] In those performances, and in the on-base entertainment programs he organized, de Paur always included Negro folk songs. The presentation of these songs was always dignified.

This glee club continued to perform long after the war came to an end, although it was renamed the De Paur Infantry Chorus, and later the De Paur Chorus. Even after this chorus was disbanded in 1957, de Paur remained active as a conductor and guest conducted a number of orchestras, including the Cincinnati Symphony Orchestra and the Minnesota Symphony. He also reconnected with his love of the theater, conducting one of the national

---

§ Although this number has been disputed, with some articles written after de Paur's death suggesting that the number of foreign performances was closer to 1,300, the fact remains that no matter the true number, de Paur was a frequent performer abroad.

tours of *Purlie* and founding and touring with the De Paur Opera Gala. Late in life, de Paur served as the Director of Community Relations at the Lincoln Center for the Performing Arts, and as a consultant to many organizations.[28]

Because of his varied interests and the diverse needs of his choirs, de Paur arranged folk songs from many traditions. His arrangements, which include SATB and TTBB settings, show a consummate understanding of the male voice. Perhaps his most well-known setting for male voices is "Marry a Woman Uglier Than You," which continues to be a favorite of male choruses. In de Paur's spiritual arrangements, there is minimal use of dialect. And as illustrated in the example below for SATB chorus and tenor soloist, the harmonic writing is appropriate and interesting but not adventurous.

Jesus Hung and Died

3.13 From "Jesus Hung and Died"

Mitchell Southall (1922–1989)

Mitchell Southall earned his M.A., M.F.A. and Ph.D. from the University of Iowa in music theory, composition, and conducting, respectively. He earned his B.A. from Langston University in Oklahoma, a school to which he would later return as Chairman of the Music Department and choir director. In addition to Langston University, Southall also held positions at Southern University in Louisiana, Rust College and Miles College in Georgia, and Lane College in Tennessee, an institution that boasts Nathaniel Dett and Marvin Curtis as former faculty members.

During his lifetime, Southall's spiritual arrangements enjoyed success and were frequently performed. Although a fine pianist, his choral arrangements of spirituals were predominately *a cappella*. Hildred Roach describes his setting of spirituals as "consistent with modern rhythmic features including syncopation and slight deviations from the traditional framework."[29] These characteristics are on display in example 3.14 on the facing page. Southall is best known to today's audiences for his composition "In Silent Night" for mixed chorus.

3.14 From "There's No Hiding Place Down There"

Alice Parker (b. 1925)

Alice Parker has distinguished herself as one of America's preeminent choral arrangers thanks in large part to her work with the Negro folk song, which she continues to arrange. Initially, her

ALICE PARKER

spiritual arrangements were for and in collaboration with Robert Shaw, a teacher of Parker's at Juilliard. This collaboration lasted almost twenty years and produced two albums that feature spirituals exclusively as well as many other albums that include one or two spiritual arrangements.

The first two spirituals that Parker and Shaw set were "Swing Low, Sweet Chariot" and "Deep River." Chosen in part because they were familiar, Parker and Shaw called upon people's memories as a basis for inspiration and melodic ideas. Soon after delving into this genre, though, Parker discovered the wonderful collection of spirituals in the New York Public Library and with it, a world of new possibilities. By arranging these less-familiar spirituals, Parker and Shaw helped rejuvenate many folk songs that had fallen out of contemporary performance.

Parker freely admits that her first spiritual sketch for Robert Shaw was a disaster. Recently removed from composition and theory classes, she tried to utilize all that she had learned in that first sketch. In response, Shaw suggested she continue to sing the melody until it was satisfying to her without accompaniment, then allow the resulting melody to form the basis for what should go around it, letting the arrangement build as a somewhat contrapuntal idea as opposed to being constructed on a harmonic foundation. The result of this approach is seen in measures 9–15 of "John Saw duh Number," shown on the facing page.[30]

While she was arranging these pieces, the Shaw Chorale was also preparing many other great works from the Western art tradition. This exposure to the choral writing of master composers certainly influenced her own early writing.

John Saw duh Number

For Full Chorus of Mixed Voices

a cappella

Negro Spiritual

Arranged by Alice Parker
and Robert Shaw

3.15 From "John Saw duh Number"

Parker's writing now is in a new tradition inspired largely by her work as a teacher of vocal improvisation in the style of the jazz improvisation of New Orleans in the '50s. Some of her newer arrangements reflect this use of jazz improvisation, among them "Come On Up," "Cert'nly Lord," "Take Me to the Water," "Stayed on Jesus," and "I Know the Lord." Parker describes these arrangements as one singer has the melodies and others are providing answers, creating a kind of polyphony. By her own admission, these settings are harder to read than her earlier arrangements but sound improvised in performance. A good example of this more polyphonic approach is in her 1988 arrangement "By an' By" (example 3.16 on the facing page).

Although Ms. Parker pursued this newer avenue in her later settings, she has not abandoned traditional forms. For example, she still utilizes call and response.

Albert J. McNeil (b. 1925)

Today's audiences know Albert McNeil primarily as the conductor of the Albert McNeil Jubilee Singers. In addition to serving as the conductor of that ensemble, though, he was Professor of Music at University of California – Davis where he was the Director of Choral Activities and head of the music education program, and taught courses in ethnomusicology.

ALBERT J. MCNEIL

McNeil is also in demand as a clinician, having served as clinician for the American Choral Directors Association, International Federation of Choral Musicians, Music Educators National Conference, and numerous other professional organizations. He has also been a guest conductor for a host of organizations and choirs, including past performances with the Mormon Tabernacle Choir.

In his settings of spirituals we find well-written examples with a conservative harmonic language. Most are for mixed chorus and a solo voice, typically soprano or, as he notates, (Soprano or Tenor).

Throughout his long and distinguished career, McNeil has fostered the careers of many young composers and arrangers of the spiritual.

3.16 From "By an' By"

MODERN ARRANGERS (1928–1958)

In this group of arrangers we see a greater diversity in the treatment of the Negro folk songs. There is an increase in the use of accompaniment, from piano to full orchestrations. The harmonic language has grown and hints of twentieth-century harmony begin to permeate some of the compositions, as do the influences of jazz and gospel. Some of the composers also began using the spiritual tune as the basis of an original composition rather than crafting an arrangement of the spiritual.

Betty Jackson King (1928–1994)

Like many of her predecessors, Betty Jackson King wore many occupational hats, including educator, choral conductor, composer,

BETTY JACKSON KING

performer, and organization leader. A native of Chicago, Illinois, King received her bachelor and master's degrees, in piano and composition, respectively, from Roosevelt University in Chicago. In fact, it was in partial fulfillment of the master's degree for which she wrote her oratorio *Saul of Tarsus*.

As an educator and conductor, King was employed at Wildwood High School in New Jersey, Roosevelt University, University of Chicago Laboratory School, and Dillard University in New Orleans, Louisiana. Hildred Roach notes King was also frequently engaged as a choral conductor by numerous groups, including the Grace Notes Pre-Professional Choral Ensemble, the Congregational Church of Park Manor, and the Riverside Church School Choirs.

King was also very active in two organizations that supported the work of Negro musicians. In 1975, she joined First Water, an organization developed to promote the classical works of black artists. The following year, she became the president of the National Association of Negro Musicians, an organization that remains vital and active today.[31]

Most of her spiritual arrangements are *a cappella* and for mixed voicing. Her two most well-known arrangements for male and female voices, respectively, are "Stan' the Storm," (SSAA/S with piano) and "Ole Ark's a-Moverin'" (TTBB/B). Perhaps King's most unique compositional contribution to the spiritual is her setting "Sinner, Please Don't Let This Harvest Pass (With African

Lyrics)." As illustrated in example 3.17 below, it incorporates an African lyric within the text of the spiritual.

3.17 From "Sinner, Please Don't Let This Harvest Pass"

Lena Johnson McLin (b. 1928)

Lena McLin is one of the more prolific arrangers discussed in this chapter. A member of the National Association of Negro Musicians and the Music Educators National Conference, McLin received her B.A. from Spelman College in Atlanta, Georgia. Her M.A. is from the American Conservatory.

LENA MCLIN

For many years McLin served as the choral director and director of music at Kenwood Academy High School in Chicago. She brought distinction and excellence to the program, and the legacy she established during her tenure continues today.‖ McLin also served as the director of the Chancel Choir at Southfield United Methodist Church. It was for these two immediate needs—school and church choirs—that much of her music was written. And her compositional process was certainly aided by having both choirs at her disposal, for they could perform her compositions and provide immediate feedback.

‖ In my adjudication of the Kenwood Academy Choir under Ms. McLin's direction, they clearly demonstrated their ability to sing music outside the African American tradition and certainly gave definitive performances of the music of their teacher.

In McLin we find a composer not afraid to set the spirituals with a piano accompaniment, even if the arrangement harkens back to an older style. This is the case in her "Glory, Glory, Hallelujah," excerpted below. Her settings are effective and can easily make the shift from concert hall to church. She never felt limited as an arranger or composer, crafting a significant amount of music that does not utilize the spiritual. In addition to her writing, she produced the twenty-five minute film *Origin of the Spiritual*.

GLORY, GLORY, HALLELUJAH

Traditional
Negro Spiritual

arr. Lena McLin

3.18 From "Glory, Glory, Hallelujah"

Brazeal Wayne Dennard (b. 1929)

Brazeal Dennard is one of the leading interpreters of the choral arrangements of the Negro spiritual. He is also a champion for the music of African Americans, serving as President of the National Association of Negro Musicians and performing and recording extensively with his choir, The Brazeal Dennard Chorale, which was founded in 1972. He was also the recipient of The Maynard Klein Award in recognition of artistic excellence in the field of choral music, presented by the Michigan Chapter of the American Choral Directors Association.

BRAZEAL WAYNE DENNARD

A product of the Detroit Public Schools, Dennard built his life in this city, first as a successful high school choral conductor and later as supervisor of music for the Detroit Public Schools. He has since retired from that post and currently serves as adjunct faculty at Wayne State University and on the Board of Directors of the Detroit Symphony Orchestra.

Dennard has arranged a handful of spirituals, choosing those folk songs that not only have a personal significance to him, but also those that will be appealing to both singers and listeners. For him, the focus of any music must be its message. To that end, he keeps his writing simple and as close to the original as possible.[32] These elements are beautifully demonstrated in his setting of "Lord, I Want to Be a Christian," an excerpt of which is presented on the following page.**

** The Spirituals Project interviewed Mr. Dennard in 1999 at length regarding his thoughts on and approach to performing the spiritual. A recording and transcript of this revealing interview is posted at the Web site *Sweet Chariot: The Story of the Spiritual* (http://ctl.du.edu/spirituals/Present).

3.19 From "Lord, I Want to Be a Christian"

Wendell Phillips Whalum (1931–1987)

Robert Shaw, in a conversation with this author, referred to Dr. Whalum as the "keeper of the music of the African American tradition." Shaw felt that no one better understood the music or could articulate and perform it with as much honesty as Whalum.

Whalum graduated from Morehouse College of Atlanta, Georgia, in 1952 and joined its faculty in 1953 where he remained until his death in 1987. While teaching at Morehouse, Whalum continued his education, earning an M.A. at Columbia University and a Ph.D. from the University of Iowa.

WENDELL PHILLIPS WHALUM

Perhaps best known as the conductor of the famed Morehouse Glee Club, Whalum directed this ensemble in many prestigious performances, including a tour of Africa sponsored by the U.S. State Department. As one might suspect from a conductor of a glee club, Whalum wrote a significant number of arrangements for male voices, but he likewise created some wonderful mixed-voice settings.

Whalum's arrangements are simply conceived and are tonal in nature. His arrangements also extend outside the African American tradition. For example, he arranged the West Indian carol "De Mornin' Come" and "Keresimesi Qdun De O," a Nigerian Christmas song. Whalum's most famous non-spiritual setting is "Betelehemu," which remains the signature piece of the Morehouse Glee Club and is a highlight of their annual Christmas Carol Concert.

Eugene Thamon Simpson (b. 1932)

In Eugene Thamon Simpson one finds a musician of great versatility. Active as an educator, administrator, choral conductor, composer/arranger, vocal accompanist, pianist, vocalist, and studio singer, Simpson further displays great comfort in many genres of music, be it folk, commercial, popular, or classical.

EUGENE THAMON SIMPSON

His musical training began at Howard University, where he received a B.M. He continued his studies at Yale University, earning a B.M. and M.M., and at Columbia University, where he received his Ed.D. Simpson has held numerous positions in academia, including posts at Fort Valley State College (Georgia), the New York public schools, Virginia State College, Bowie State College, and Glassboro State College in New Jersey. He also is or has been an active member with a number of professional organizations, including the Music Educators National Conference, American Choral Directors Association, the American Guild of Television and Radio Artists, Phi Delta Kappa, Pi Kappa Lambda, and Phi Mu Alpha Sinfonia.[33]

Simpson, like Nathaniel Dett and others, has an interest in the spiritual and folk music. Of particular interest to him is Hall Johnson. In addition to a 1970 article for *The Choral Journal* about Mr. Johnson's legacy, Simpson authored a book, *Black Genius: The Life, Spirit, and Music of Hall Johnson*, about this legendary figure. It is through Simpson's interpretations of Johnson's settings, as well as those of William Dawson, that we learn about his own ideas, many of which are reflected in a 1970 recording Simpson made with the Virginia State University Choir.

The most popular of Simpson's settings is "Hold On," published in 1974. Most of his settings use traditional harmonies and a moderate use of dialect, including "Sister Mary Had-A But One Child" (excerpted on the facing page). According to Simpson, this arrangement was inspired by his recollection of tenor Roland Hayes singing the song in a recital at Howard University when Simpson was an undergraduate there. Simpson goes on to say, "I also recall attending Mr. Hayes's 75th Anniversary Concert at Carnegie Hall and I'm not sure that he didn't also perform the song then. It was one of his favorites and in his performance, he brought to it a beauty, sincerity and intimacy rarely achieved. His voice remains in my ear 55 years later."[34]

3.20 From "Sister Mary Had-A But One Child"

Robert Harris (b. 1938)

Robert Harris has distinguished himself as a conductor, clinician, and lecturer, and as a composer and arranger. As it pertains to the former group, he is currently Professor of Conducting and Director of Choral Organizations at Northwestern University in Evanston, Illinois. Prior positions include Assistant Professor of Music at Wayne State University in Detroit and Associate Professor of Composition and Director of Choral Activities at Michigan State University. It is notable that in both of those positions, he was returning to institutions where he himself studied; his B.S. in music is from Wayne State and his Ph.D. in composition is from Michigan State. Harris's extensive work as a guest conductor has taken him to Argentina, China, Korea, and South Africa where he led master classes in several cities, including Cape Town, Durban, and Bloemfontein. He has also served as choral panelist for the National Endowment of the Arts, twice as co-chairman.

ROBERT HARRIS

As a composer and arranger, Harris is quite prolific, having written more than sixty choral works. Although his works provide a challenge for the good chorus, they are accessible and extremely well written. Stylistically, Harris challenges the harmonic comfort zone of singers who are well entrenched in nineteenth-century harmonies. But his part writing is such that the choir feels successful as he broadens their harmonic language.

Harris's spiritual arrangements are few but highly effective. His setting of "Go Down Moses" for mixed chorus, for example, is challenging but deserving of many performances. Particularly effective are his spiritual arrangements for treble voices; one outstanding example is "This Little Light of Mine" for two-part treble and piano, from *Three Spirituals*.

Robert Morris (b. 1941)

Robert Morris is an educator and conductor, and a champion for the preservation of the Negro spiritual. He has taught at Hampton University, Winston-Salem State University, Jackson State University, and Macalester College. In 1990 he coordinated a choral tribute to William L. Dawson for the Southern Division Conference of the American Choral Directors Association. He conducted a similar tribute to Mr. Dawson at the 1991 National Convention of the American Choral Directors Association.

Morris's spiritual settings are predominately for mixed voices, *a cappella* and with limited use of dialect. One of his most popular settings is "I Thank You, Jesus" for mixed voices, *a cappella*. Dr. Morris refers to this work as his "high school exercise." When asked which of his settings is his favorite, "my favorite is whatever setting I'm working on at the time," is his reply. Most of Morris's settings were written for a specific choir that he was conducting and were utilized as pedagogical lessons to teach that choir a technique, be it balance/blend, pitch and intonation, expressiveness (phrasing and dynamics), or the ability to follow the gestural language of the conductor. Morris states, "In fact, I can site what I was trying to achieve in a choir with each of my settings."

ROBERT MORRIS

It is often difficult for composers to synthesize their own writing style, but when asked, Morris points to his varied background in Chicago as a significant influence, particularly the many churches he attended, which included United Methodist, Baptist, and Church of God in Christ. He also cites as an influence his time as a student at a Catholic college, where he sang for midnight masses, as well as his exposure to the Jewish high holiday services, for which he was also a singer. Morris further points to the influence of the quartet style and the *Wings Over Jordan* choir, which was heard on the radio program of same name when he was a boy.

Morris clearly acknowledges the change in spiritual performance as it moved from the slave experience to the urban setting and finally to the concert setting. It is as part of the latter category that he feels his settings should be evaluated and performed.[35]

Roland Carter (b. 1942)

Roland Carter is a leading figure in the preservation of the folk song of African Americans. The founder and CEO of Mar-Vel Music Company, a publisher specializing in the music of African American composers and their traditions, he also serves as the music director for the Chattanooga Choral Society for the Preservation of African American Songs.

Born in Chattanooga, Tennessee, Carter returned to his hometown to accept the position of Ruth S. Holmberg UC Foundation Professor of American Music in the Cadek Department of Music at the University of Tennessee at Chattanooga. Previously, he served as Chairman of the Music Department at Hampton

Institute, the same university where he earned his B.A. (Carter received his M.A. at New York University.)

ROLAND CARTER

Most of Carter's spiritual arrangements are for mixed voices with limited use of dialect. A signature example, and perhaps his best-known spiritual arrangement, is "You Must Have That True Religion." Carter's body of work also includes non-spiritual works, most notably his arrangement of the James and Rosamond John song "Lift Every Voice and Sing." Called the Negro National Anthem by many, choirs frequently sing Carter's arrangement of this powerful hymn.

Not exclusively a choral composer, Carter has written organ arrangements of many of his choral works. In recent years, he has also started writing for orchestra. Carter's first orchestral composition, *Common Ground*, which draws its themes from Negro spirituals, was premiered by the Chattanooga Symphony during their 2001–2002 season. That same season, his *Hold Fast to Dreams* was performed by the Atlanta Symphony and the Plymouth Music Series of Minnesota (now VocalEssence).

Larry Farrow (b. 1950)

Larry Farrow came to the attention of most choral musicians through his work as an arranger and composer with the Albert McNeil Jubilee Singers, a group he joined when he was just sixteen. Four short years later, when he was just twenty, Far-

LARRY FARROW

row became a rehearsal pianist for the great Josephine Baker. He continued to build on this popular music foundation, serving as conductor and arranger for the group Friends of Distinction as well as Harry Belafonte, Nancy Wilson, Joe Williams, Gloria Lynne, Della Reese, and the Jacksons. Farrow has had numerous engagements as guest conductor for pops concerts with symphony orchestras throughout the United States. As a commercial musician, he has worked for Disney, the California Miss America Pageant, and ABC, as associate musical director for Bill Cosby's show *COS*. Farrow brought this experience to the academic arena as Assistant Professor of Commercial Music at the College of Music at Florida State University.

The arranger of a handful of spiritual settings, Farrow's background in commercial music has certainly been an influence. When asked about his spiritual arrangements, Farrow said that his goal is to honor those great musicians that came before him using the traditional settings, but also to reflect contemporary music and offer a "new vision" in a contemporary media environment.[36] It is clear by looking at the harmonic language in example 3.21 below, with its strong jazz and contemporary influence, that he is achieving his goals for these arrangements.

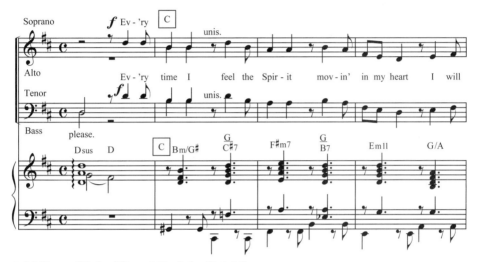

3.21 From "Ev'ry Time I Feel the Spirit"

Marvin Curtis (b. 1951)

Born in Chicago, Illinois, Marvin Curtis has the distinction of being the first African American composer to write a work for a Presidential Inauguration—his "City on the Hill" was performed for the inauguration of President Clinton on January 20, 1993. That same year, Curtis went, as a Ford Foundation Fellow, to the National Council for Black Studies Conference in Accra, Ghana, where he studied at the University of Ghana at Lagon.

In addition to these impressive achievements, Curtis has also served on the faculties of California State University – Stanislaus, Virginia Union University in Richmond, Virginia, and Lane College. Curtis's current position is Assistant Dean of the College of Humanities and Social Science

MARVIN CURTIS

and Choir Director at Fayetteville State University in North Carolina. (Curtis holds a B.M. from North Park College in Chicago, Illinois, an M.A. from the Presbyterian School of Christian Education, and his doctoral study was at the University of the Pacific.)

Curtis is the composer of numerous choral works, including cantatas and octavo selections. Most are for mixed choir with piano, although he also has utilized organ, brass, handbells, and full orchestration for his accompaniments. His arrangements of spirituals are accessible, *a cappella*, and limited in their use of dialect.

One of those incorporating more dialect is "Home In-a Dat Rock," which is accompanied by piano. When asked about his own guidelines when arranging a spiritual, Curtis states:

> In arranging a spiritual, my primary objective is to keep the spirit of the words and the melody alive. I will look for historical, biblical, or social references that make the work relevant. It is important for me to remember where these songs have come from and make them accessible in a musical form so that they can continue to be shared with generations.[37]

One of his most popular settings is "Great Day," which Curtis feels reflects the triumphant spirit of the African American culture. To further enhance that spirit, he purposely set the original's second and third verse in reverse order: *This is the day of Jubilee, The Lord has set his people free—God's gonna build up Zion's walls!* An original work, "Sit at d'Lamb's Table" is written in the style of a spiritual, with the folk-like quality of the melodic material and the use of Negro dialect serving to enhance that impression.

Although the bulk of his compositions are choral in nature, his orchestral works have been performed by the Richmond Symphony, the Minnesota Orchestra, the Stanislaus Symphony Orchestra, and the Petersburg Symphony Orchestra.

André J. Thomas (b. 1952)

André Thomas was born in Wichita, Kansas, and was educated in the Wichita Public Schools. He received his B.M.E. from Friends University, his M.M. in piano performance from Northwestern University, and his D.M.A. in choral conducting from the University of Illinois Champaign - Urbana. He has been employed as a teacher in the Wichita Public School system, where a love for the adolescent voice was kindled. He has served on the faculty of the University of Texas at Austin, and is currently the Owen F. Sellers Professor of Music and Director of Choral Activities at Florida State University in Tallahassee.

A love of African American music and choral music was born early on in Thomas, who, when he was just four years old, would sit at the piano and play by ear the songs he heard in church. This love is clearly reflected in his works, most of which are either arrangements of spirituals or compositions utilizing the spiritual tune as the basis of the compositional process. Of his non-spiritual arrangements, most have a connection to the African American tradition. Specifically, the poems of Langston Hughes are featured in "I Dream a World" and "Hold Fast to Dreams." "The Drinking Gourd" is based on the African American map song "Follow the Drinking Gourd" and "Goin' Up to Glory" is loosely based on the field holler "Sun Up to Sun Down." (Of his almost two dozen pieces, "Barbara Allen" and "Fences" are the only pieces without an African American connection.)

ANDRÉ J. THOMAS

There is no one consistent compositional style in Thomas's spiritual arrangements; each setting is individual and often reflects different influences. For example, there are gospel influences in his setting of "When the Trumpet Sounds" and "Go Where I Send Thee." In his setting of "I'm Gonna Sing," there are jazz influences. Some of his settings, such as his well-known "Keep Your Lamps!," stay much closer to the original spiritual, reflecting the influence of his mentors Jester Hairston and William Dawson. Thomas pays homage to these two great men in his setting of "Rockin' Jerusalem." The first ten measures, which begin with a male ostinato followed by the women entering in triads, parallel the opening of Jester Hairston's setting of "Elijah Rock." The last ten measures pay tribute to William Dawson with their use of imitation.

The accompaniment employed for each setting usually mirrors the stylistic influence. The more traditional settings are often *a cappella* (although sometimes piano is employed). The gospel-and jazz-influenced settings usually have a (at times demanding) piano accompaniment. Some are arranged with full orchestral accompaniments. These include "Band of Angels," "Here's a Pretty Little Baby," "Go Where I Send Thee," and "Beautiful City."

In addition to his acclaim as a composer and arranger, Thomas is in demand throughout the world as a choral conductor and clinician and is active in numerous professional organizations.[††]

[††] For a complete biography of Dr. Thomas, see About the Author on page 271.

Moses Hogan (1957–2003)

Moses Hogan, more than any other of the Modern Arrangers, is heralded as the composer/arranger who revitalized the performance of spirituals. A graduate of the New Orleans Center for Creative Arts (NOCCA) and Oberlin Conservatory of Music in Ohio, Hogan also studied at New York's Juilliard School and Louisiana State University in Baton Rouge. In his short life, he published over seventy arrangements of spirituals, most of which are *a cappella* and for mixed voices. These arrangements became further entrenched in the repertoire—and public consciousness—thanks to Hogan's work as director of several choral ensembles.

MOSES HOGAN

Hogan founded and conducted three ensembles that performed primarily his arrangements. The first, the New World Ensemble, was formed in 1980. In 1994, the second ensemble, the Moses Hogan Chorale, performed for the Southern Division of the American Choral Directors Association. This incredibly received performance was followed by invitations for the Chorale to perform at other ACDA regional conventions and the National convention, as well as at the International Federation of Choral Musicians at the World Symposium held in Sydney, Australia.

The Moses Hogan Chorale was an exceptional group, but Hogan nonetheless felt the need to develop an ensemble of professional singers, and did just that after the Chorale completed its final touring season in 1999. This new ensemble, the Moses Hogan Singers, was nationally auditioned and all were professional musicians. He conducted this group until he fell ill. The hundreds of performances and recordings by the Moses Hogan Singers solidified his arrangements in the choral repertoire.

When asked about his spiritual arrangements, Hogan first points to his upbringing in the African American Baptist Church. His uncle was the choir director so Hogan learned and heard many spirituals during his childhood. He was particularly interested in and intrigued with the *a cappella* settings of the spirituals that he heard as part of his religious worship experience. When he later penned those spirituals, he worked to preserve the melody and meaning but was not necessarily concerned with replicating the sounds that he heard at church. Rather, his arrangements were the result of a combination of his classical and Baptist training.[38]

In addition to his writing, ~~Hogan served as editor of the *Oxford Book of Spirituals*~~, an expansive collection of spirituals published by Oxford University Press.

CONTEMPORARY ARRANGERS (1959–PRESENT)

Although there are many young composers who could fit into this category, the following eight composers/arrangers have emerged with distinct musical voices in their settings of the Negro spiritual. All eight have chosen to set not just spirituals but also other African American folk forms as well as original music in the Western art tradition. Rollo Dilworth, Rosephanye Powell, and Victor Johnson have the largest output of published choral works, followed by Stacey Gibbs, David Morrow, Jeffery Ames, Damon Dandridge, and Mark Butler.

David Morrow (b. 1959)

David Morrow is a graduate of Morehouse College in Atlanta, where he received a B.A., and the University of Michigan, where he earned a M.M. in choral conducting. He holds a D.M.A. in choral conducting from the University of Cincinnati College Conservatory of Music.

DAVID MORROW

Morrow joined the Morehouse faculty in 1981 and since 1987 he has been the conductor of the acclaimed Morehouse Glee Club. In addition to conducting this organization, he is also the director of the Atlanta University Center Community Chorus, director of Onyx Opera Atlanta, and co-director of the Spelman-Morehouse Chorus. The Glee Club under his direction has appeared at the National Convention of the American Choral Directors Association and was broadcast nationally from the Kennedy Center when Robert Shaw received the 1991 Kennedy Center Honors.

Like his predecessor at Morehouse, Wendell Whalum, Morrow's arrangements are predominately for male voices. When asked about his arranging style, David Morrow offered the following:

> Much of what I know regarding arrangements of spirituals comes from my association with Wendell Whalum and

Uzee Brown. They, as I, were or are fond of the music of the African American folk tradition. It is always my hope that the arrangements of spirituals that I create still have the style and mood of how they might [have been] done in the folk tradition. The gentle use of a lilt in the music and the use of heterophony, imitation, and syncopation are very important in that [they help] the pieces sound as though parts were improvised in the folk style. The use of musical gestures that are of gospel influence is very subtle and is done just to add a contemporary flair to the arrangements, not to reinvent the music or develop it in a different style. It is very important to me that the melody be recognizable and that the harmonies I chose are simple enough to support it and colorful enough to illuminate the text and mood of the spiritual.[39]

Stacey V. Gibbs (b. 1962)

Gibbs is unique among this group of arrangers in that his full-time employment is not in music; he has been a manager in the hospitality industry for over fifteen years. As a young man in Flint, Michigan, he was active in music and attended Beecher High School. He later attended Kentucky State University where he met the legendary William Dawson, a man whose compositions he had long admired. At this meeting, Mr. Dawson said to Gibbs, "Always embrace the spiritual with pride and humility." These words stayed with Gibbs and are a profound influence on his arrangements.[40]

Regarding his compositional style, Gibbs points to Hall Johnson's rhythmic approach to the spiritual as a strong influence. This is clearly demonstrated in most of his arrangements, particularly "Lord If I Got My Ticket" and "I Don' Feel No Way Tired." Most of his arrangements, which number twenty-six, are for mixed chorus, *a cappella*. His harmonies tend to be traditional and, like Dawson, dialect is utilized. Because of their rhythmic interest and singable part-writing, Gibbs's arrangements are becoming very popular among choral musician. To date, the Paul A. Smith Singers, Albert McNeil Jubilee Singers, Brazeal Dennard Chorale, and the Boys Choir of Harlem have performed his arrangements.

Rosephanye Powell (b. 1962)

Dr. Rosephanye Dunn Powell has become a popular composer and arranger among choral conductors, with works that are in great demand at choral festivals nationally and internationally and frequently appear on the conventions of the American Choral Directors Association.

Holding a B.M.E. from Alabama State University, an M.M. in vocal performance and pedagogy from Westminster Choir College, and a D.M.A. in vocal performance from Florida State University, Powell currently is an Associate Professor of Music at Auburn University. She previously served on the faculties of Philander Smith College in Arkansas and Georgia Southern University. She is a member of the American Society of Composers, Authors, and Publishers, American Choral Directors Association, College Music Society, National Association of Teachers of Singing, and Music Educators National Conference. She has been included in *Who's Who Among America's Teachers* and *Outstanding Young Women in America.*

ROSEPHANYE POWELL

Powell's spiritual settings use a Neo-Romantic harmonic language with little dissonance. Most are *a cappella* and, as you would expect from such an exceptional singer, the vocal lines are very singable. There is moderate use of dialect in the settings. Her settings range in difficulty from accessible to moderately challenging.

Both she and her husband, Dr. William Powell, have found success setting music reflecting the African culture, and she has crafted several original compositions in the style of the spiritual. (Her non-spiritual settings outnumber her settings of Negro spirituals.) A wonderful and popular work in the style of the spiritual is her composition for women's voices "Still I Rise." In addition to her endeavors as a composer and singer, Powell is the editor for *William Grant Still: An Art Song Collection,* published by William Grant Still Music.

Rollo Dilworth (b. 1970)

Rollo Dilworth is an educator/conductor who has experienced success teaching at the elementary, secondary, and university levels. He received his B.S. in music education from the Case Western Reserve University. He continued his education at the University of Missouri – St. Louis where he studied composition with Robert Ray and received his M.E. in secondary education. He received his D.M.A. in conducting from Northwestern University where he studied composition and conducting with Robert Harris. Dilworth has had additional composition study with Pauline Oliveros and Marta Ptaszynska.

Currently an Associate Professor of Music and Director of Choral Activities and Music Education at the North Park University School of Music in Chicago, Illinois, Dilworth's perform-

ROLLO DILWORTH

ing endeavors have taken him to Europe, Asia, Africa, and Australia. He is a frequent conductor of honor choirs and was the co-conductor of the National Multi-Cultural Honor Choir at the American Choral Directors Association 2007 National Convention in Miami, Florida. Dilworth is also a contributing author to a general music textbook series and other elementary teaching resources. Dilworth is an active member of the Music Educators National Conference, National Association of Negro Musicians, American Choral Directors Association, and Chorus America.

It is the sincerity of the man and his music that has helped to make Dilworth so successful in his endeavors. As an example, one of his more extensive works is his *Trilogy of Dreams*, for children's voices. This piece utilizes the poetry of Langston Hughes to honor the slain civil rights leader Martin Luther King Jr., a man Dilworth calls "one of the greatest visionaries ever to live." He goes on to say:

> One of the things I have to do whenever I travel to a city is find Martin Luther King Drive. I've never seen one in which the street wasn't cluttered with litter and the houses in shambles We have not made the legacy of Martin Luther King clear enough to this generation. …The "I Have a Dream" speech has been done so many times it just gets stale and old. We have to think of new ways to make this dream more real, or [children] are going to forget.[41]

So deeply felt is his commitment that Dilworth has no intention of re-voicing *Trilogy of Dreams* for mixed voices as he feels it loses its power when not performed by children.

Dilworth, who has been particularly successful writing for young voices, has a compositional style that is fresh and appealing. His spirituals often reflect gospel influences in their harmonizations and piano accompaniments, as shown in example 3.22 on the facing page.

3.22 From "Walk in Jerusalem"

Mark Butler (b. 1963)

Mark Butler is a young composer and arranger who received his public school education in Quitman, Georgia. He received his B.S. degree in music education from Florida A&M University and completed his M.M.E. from Florida State University.

MARK BUTLER

Butler taught for twelve years at Dougherty High School in Albany, Georgia, where he was the conductor and founder of the Dougherty High Chorale. Under his direction this ensemble received sixteen consecutive first places and overall sweepstake wins at national choral festivals throughout the United States. They were also selected three times as performing representatives for the state of Georgia at the Black Caucus National Convention in Washington, D.C. Mark is currently the Choral Director at Osborne High School in Marietta, Georgia.

Although he has arranged few spirituals, he has developed a distinctive musical voice. His spiritual arrangements are heavily influenced by the writing style of Moses Hogan.

I remember as a child hearing the historic black college choruses sing the Negro spirituals. They would have such a unique musical presentation and performance approach—one of a kind. It seemed to have been the audience's (whites' as well as blacks') favorite part of the concert. I always wondered what made them so different from the spirituals I would hear in church. The church singing would have the same text, but was not quite as unique and interesting. Later, as I became involved in music, I realized that [the black choruses were singing] choral arrangements written to be performed by trained vocalists.

Hall Johnson, William Dawson, Jester Hairston, and others have all made such a strong impact on my style of writing. Thank God for Moses Hogan, whom I had the pleasure of meeting only once. I teased him by saying that he and I were twin arrangers; God had placed the same thoughts in our ears and minds. Mr. Hogan made it possible for this new, fresh, yet still traditional method of [arranging] to be accepted by choruses and directors in the U.S. and abroad.[42]

Jeffery L. Ames (b. 1969)

Jeffery Ames is the Associate Director of Choirs at Baylor University in Waco, Texas. He is a native of Virginia and earned a B.M., with a double major in vocal performance and piano accompanying, from James Madison University in Virginia. He received his M.M.E. and his Ph.D. in choral conducting/music education from Florida State University.

Ames is the first recipient of the ACDA 2004 James Mulholland Choral Music Fellowship. Prior to his appointment to the faculty of Baylor University, he taught high school music for seven years in the state of Florida. Choirs under his direction appeared at the Florida ACDA conferences and twice at Carnegie Hall. His gospel choir was selected to give a special concert for former Secretary of State Colin Powell. The National ACDA Conference, the Southern Division ACDA Conference, the Florida American Choral Directors Association, and the Florida Music Educators Association have all premiered Ames's choral music.

JEFFERY L. AMES

Although his publications are few, all have been favorably received by choral conductors. Of his three selections in the African American tradition, the first, "Let Everything That Hath Breath," is a gospel song. "I've Been in the Storm," for mixed chorus and soli, was arranged in homage to the victims of Hurricane Katrina. The harmonic language is tonal and there is no use of dialect. In his setting of "Peter Go Ring-A Dem Bells" for two-part treble chorus, piano, and handbells, Ames does incorporate some moderate use of dialect. He based that use on the text used by Thomas Fenner in the first printed publication of this spiritual. Ames also makes a case that this spiritual is closely related to the Underground Railroad. Consequently, he incorporates references to Harriet Tubman and quotes the folk songs "Steal Away," "Follow the Drinking Gourd," and "Wade in the Water." The other unique feature about this setting is the use of handbells. Ames's SSAA *a cappella* arrangement of "Ezekiel Saw the Wheel" (as yet unpublished) is another fine example of the craft of this young composer/arranger.

Damon Dandridge (b. 1977)

Damon Dandridge is an enthusiastic young composer and arranger. He received his B.S. in music education with choral/voice emphasis from South Carolina State University and completed his M.M. in choral conducting from Florida State University. Dandridge has taught in the public schools in his hometown of Detroit and is currently the Director of Choral Activities at Cheyney University in Pennsylvania.

DAMON DANDRIDGE

His spiritual settings, like his personality, are energetic and youthful. The harmonic language is Neo-Romantic and the writing style utilizes some imitation. Dandridge writes for mixed, men's, and women's choruses and describes his writing style as "contemporary choral techniques fused with a traditional Baptist sound and form."[43]

Victor C. Johnson (b. 1978)

Although the youngest of the contemporary arrangers, Victor Johnson already boasts more than thirty published choral arrangements. The first of these, "African Noel," was published when he was just a sophomore in high school.

VICTOR C. JOHNSON

A native of Dallas, Texas, Johnson attended the University of Texas at Arlington where he majored in music education with a concentration in organ. While attending UTA, he served as student conductor of the university's choral ensembles and opera workshop accompanist. In 1997, he was named "Outstanding Music Freshmen" and also "Outstanding Musician" in 2001. Johnson currently teaches at the Ft. Worth Academy of Fine Arts and is the director of the Children's Choir of Texas. He also serves at the First Baptist Church of Hamilton Park, Richardson, Texas, as organist and director of the Women's Chorus and Children's Handbell Choir.

The crux of Johnson's compositional efforts lies in the Western art tradition but his four spiritual arrangements are excellent additions to the repertoire, particularly if seeking accessible arrangements of spirituals for the adolescent voice, which can often be a challenge. Most of Johnson's arrangements have been set in multiple voicings, including SATB, SAB, TTB, SSA, and three-part mixed. The folk tune or tunes are clearly apparent to the listener. All feature piano accompaniments that are accessible for the average pianist and never overwhelm the vocal parts. And as illustrated in example 3.23 on the following page, Johnson's part writing is always logical and predictable, helping to ensure quick success for the young singer.

When asked to share his thoughts about his spiritual arrangements, Johnson offered the following:

> In arranging spirituals, I focus mainly on how I can make the arrangement suitable and interesting to a school-aged singer, while at the same time remaining true to the Negro folk song. Since the original slave songs were sung unaccompanied, another challenge is to create an accompaniment that complements the spiritual. I try to incorporate interesting harmonies that give the spiritual a somewhat-contemporary feel. Although some spirituals don't easily lend themselves to being accompanied, a well-written accompaniment adds depth to the musical texture and helps create a successful performance.

> I don't necessarily keep spirituals in their original dialect because, at times, the original language can confuse the performer and the listener. Instead of enjoying the arrangement, listeners find themselves trying to understand what the choir is singing. In turn, they may enjoy the music, but not understand the message and meaning of the text.[44]

3.23 From "Song of Freedom"

ADDITIONAL ARRANGERS

The composers and arrangers highlighted in this chapter are but a small collection of those who work or have worked with the Negro spiritual. There are many additional writers who could have been discussed, including those listed below. The settings of these arrangers certainly merit investigation by anyone seeking a concert spiritual.

Chester L. Alwes (b. 1947)
Peter Bagley (b. 1935)
Marshall Bartholomew (1885–1978)
Kenneth Billups (1918–1985)
Margaret Bonds (1913–1972)
Uzee Brown, Jr. (b. 1942)
Wallace McClain Cheatham (b. 1945)
Edgar Rogie Clark (1913–1978)
Salone Clary (b. 1939)
Lee Cloud (1950–1995)
Robert De Cormier (b. 1922)
Carl Rossini Diton (1886–1962)
Vera Edwards (b. 1959)
Roger Emerson (b. 1950)
James Furman (1937–1989)
Ruth Helen Gillum (1906–1991)
Adolphus C. Hailstork III (b. 1941)
Jack Halloran (1916–1997)
William C. Handy (1873–1958)
Mark Hayes (b. 1953)
Augustus O. Hill (b. 1948)

Ralph Hunter (1921–2002)
Richard Jackson (1964–2001)
Joseph Joubert (b. 1958)
Thomas Kerr (1915–1988)
William Lawrence (1895–1981)
Norman Luboff (1917–1987)
Phillip McIntyre (1951–1991)
Gilbert M. Martin (b. 1941)
Warren Martin (1916–1982)
Harold J. Montague (1907–1950)
Evelyn Pittman (1910–1992)
Howard Roberts (b. 1942)
Leon Roberts (1950–1999)
Noah Ryder (1914–1964)
Robert Shaw (1916–1999)
Evelyn Simpson-Curenton (b. 1953)
Linda Spevacek (b. 1945)
Linda Twine (b. 1945)
Clarence Cameron White (1880–1960)
Julius P. Williams (b. 1954)

PART II

PERFORMING THE SPIRITUAL

4

FROM THE PRINTED PAGE TO THE CONCERT STAGE

Interpreting the Spiritual

The body of concert spirituals is vast and wonderfully diverse. It is a collection of music that simultaneously intrigues yet intimidates many choral conductors (particularly those without roots in the African American experience), often to the point of paralysis. Those who aren't paralyzed sometimes charge ahead without a clear vision of the piece, rendering a performance that fails to capture the intent of the arranger.

I remember a performance by a fine high school chorus of Moses Hogan's arrangement of "Joshua Fit the Battle of Jericho." The conductor consulted his students and allowed them input into the performance of this work. The result was a performance that included a distortion of the tonal quality toward a nasal production used by some gospel artists in the early 1990s, along with the utilization of "fall offs" (a jazz technique) at the ends of phrases and some extemporization in the vocal parts. It was a rendition far removed from the intent of Mr. Hogan.

Some conductors will impose rhythm and blues, gospel, and jazz techniques on all performances of spirituals in an effort to create a "black" sound (this generally being a sound concept inspired by their remembrance of a performance by a "black ensemble" or influenced by a young African American student who may give guidance based upon his or her church experiences). All of this may be full of good intention; the result, however, is often an experience fraught with stylistic abuse and, ultimately, a mockery of the intentions of the arranger.

When approaching these arrangements you must first let basic musicianship guide your interpretation. Remember, these concert spirituals were crafted by musicians trained in Western art music. The standard conventions of rhythm within a metrical framework, for example, still exist in these arrangements. As with any piece of choral music, the text is nearly always the determining factor in all matters of interpretation. The utilization of dialect is a seemingly unique consideration, but it isn't really much different from questions of diction in any choral piece in that dialect is how we are pronouncing the text. As for its use, the reasons for making adjustments to dialect are not different from those that dictate differences in pronunciation between an opera aria and a cabaret song. In the latter, just as in a spiritual with dialect, we are shifting to the vernacular of the people.

Within this framework of basic choral musicianship, we are functioning as interpreters of a concert arrangement of folk music. It is our responsibility to become informed about the heritage of the folk music and the life and musical intention of the arranger, and to share that information with our singers. Equipped with this information, our task becomes simple—strive to honor the spiritual's history and the arranger's intentions. As long as we do that, we ensure performances of the spiritual that are ennobling and uplifting to their singers and audiences.

General suggestions for dialect, text, tonal quality, and rhythm in the concert spiritual are offered in this chapter. I encourage you to use this information to expand your choir's palette of sounds and techniques. This way, rather than making the piece fit an existing palette, you can capture and enhance its individual character.*

Dialect

Literary figures have long utilized dialect in their writing. In the late nineteenth century, the great poet Paul Laurence Dunbar

---

* In the chapter that follows, *Reflections on Six Spirituals*, I flesh out my decisions of interpretations for six specific pieces and offer my rehearsal techniques for imparting them to a choir. It is my hope that seeing the concepts in practice will offer clarity and reinforcement to the general information presented here.

reformed the way dialect was written. Several decades later, Zora Neale Hurston, a leading figure in the Harlem Renaissance and frequent user of dialect, referred to it as the language of her people.

Just as the use of dialect in literature allows a writer to present a more complete picture of a character, the use of dialect within a concert spiritual helps to create a stylistically appropriate performance of these arrangements. It is similar to the use of German Latin when performing Latin texts set by Mozart. This was the language that was in Mozart's ear when he composed; why not try to recreate that? The spiritual is popular music in its truest sense—the music of people; why not make adjustments toward what it would have sounded like in common usage?

While there are no steadfast "rules" of dialect, one of the more common practices is the softening of the "th" sound to a "d" sound or a "t" sound. As the great Jester Hairston told me, the reason for this shift is because most African languages didn't include a "th" sound, so the Negro dialect developed with this adaptation.

Another common shift in dialect is the suppression of the "r" sound, especially on an unaccented syllable. In this case, the vowel that precedes the "r" would be pronounced as a schwa. An example: "never" is pronounced "nevuh." In many ways, though, this softening of the "er" is much more a part of American English than it is Negro dialect. In fact, this use of a schwa is in keeping with the rules in Madeline Marshall's *The Singer's Manual of English Diction*. I would suggest that her rules should, for the most part, be followed in all spiritual arrangements.

Phonetic decay, the practice of not completing a word, is another common element of dialect. An example is found in my arrangement of "Keep Your Lamps!" The text is *the time is drawing nigh*. With dialect, this text would be sung *duh time is drawin' nigh*.

This example also highlights another element of dialect: the shift from "the" to "de." As for pronouncing "de," James Weldon Johnson tells us that it should vary based on what follows it. Specifically, that it becomes "dee" before a word beginning with a vowel and "duh" before a word beginning with a consonant.[1] The shift to "de" is a more extreme use of dialect and is seen primarily in Dawson and others who more greatly utilize dialect.

Even with this knowledge, making decisions of dialect within a specific arrangement is not without its challenges. This is largely because most arrangers are frequently inconsistent with themselves in the use of dialect, sometimes even within a single arrangement. This problem is well illustrated by James Weldon Johnson in his preface to *The Books of American Negro Spirituals*:

> In setting down the words of the songs here included I have
> endeavored to keep them as true to the original dialect as is
> compatible with a more or less ready recognition of what the
> words really are. When a dialect spelling would puzzle and
> confuse the reader and actually throw him off, the regular
> English spelling has been followed.[2]

In other words, "I've included dialect unless I haven't." Further,
some arrangers include other folk elements but elect to exclude
dialect entirely, fearing it won't be done well. So what's a conductor to do?

If a work includes some instances of dialect but forgoes others, consider including, for example, phonetic decay in your performance even if it isn't notated. The best guide, if available, is a recording by the piece's arranger. Did The Moses Hogan Singers perform
the piece with dialect even if it wasn't written? Although not quite
"from the horse's mouth," the recording of another conductor who
is a well-regarded interpreter of the spiritual can serve as a model if
a recording by the arranger isn't available. In the case of an arrangement that doesn't include any elements of dialect, don't feel that
your interpretation must be limited to a straightforward singing.
Let the inclusion of other folk elements guide your interpretation,
as it often does mine, to the inclusion of some dialect.

If you are hesitant to include any dialect because, as I've heard
often from conductors, you "don't want to make blacks sound ig-
norant," "don't want to disrespect this culture," or "don't want to
embarrass or otherwise make uncomfortable the black students in
my choir," I offer a respectful, "just chill out, folks."

I think of dialect as adding a little seasoning to the piece. And
just as when making dinner, if the "seasoning" brings attention to
itself, it is probably too much. Along those same lines, the dialect
shouldn't be forced or overdone, and unwritten accents certainly
shouldn't be added on those words. Most importantly, though, all
of us strive to create positive experiences for our singers, so if anything I did ran counter to that, I would certainly stop. The first
hint of awkwardness I saw on a face singing dialect would cause
me to reinterpret the arrangement without a moment's pause.

When it comes to dialect, if we error in either direction, as long
as the intentions are good, the spirit of the piece will carry it forward. Even if someone puts a hard "t" on "chariot," the rhythm will
carry it on; it will still be recognizable as "Swing Down, Chariot."

Text

As choral musicians, text is paramount, and the significant factor to consider when deciding on interpretation and performance. The text is the composer's germ of inspiration when writing a composition for voices. He or she starts with a text and begins to translate it into sounds of music, into what the voices will do, all with the goal of exploiting the text. The composer is successful when the music is carefully, comfortably, and logically wedded to the text.

Just as it would be impossible to think of singing the art music of Brahms, Mendelssohn, Schubert, or Schumann without understanding every word, everyone involved in the performance of the spiritual—from the conductor to the singers to the listeners—needs to understand what those words *mean*. Not only must the words be clearly heard when performing the spiritual in concert formation (hence the importance of diction), it is vital that the text be understood in context.

My goal when performing any piece is for every choir member to personally touch and connect with the text. In some ways, it's easier to accomplish this with the spiritual than it is with Brahms, for example. The texts of these songs are inspired by the religious fervor of an itinerant preacher on a plantation and by the sheer emotional response to the everyday life of an enslaved people. The slave has already made this text personal. All we as conductors need do is make it personal to the choir.

What was the social situation of the slave who sang these words? What environmental factors influenced this song? What elements of life are reflected but perhaps lie just below the surface of the written words? Seeking the answers to these questions and sharing them with your choir is key to creating successful interpretations of the concert spiritual.[†]

Take, for example, the spiritual "Keep Your Lamps!" As with many of the slave songs, this song's impetus came from hearing a sermon, specifically one based upon the parable found in Matthew 25: 1–13. In this passage of scripture, Jesus tells the story of the wise and foolish virgins. They had been told that the bridegroom would be coming; thus, they got their lamps, trimmed them, set them burning, and went to the appointed place. The bridegroom,

---

† For those not familiar with the biblical stories, or seeking assistance understanding their relationship to these songs, Richard Newman, in his book *Go Down Moses: Celebrating the African American Spiritual*, gives individual commentary on a number of spirituals. As you bring these stories alive to your singers, be sure to assume their manner. If you want them to feel a lightness, for example, you need to have that lightness in your telling.

however, did not arrive at the appointed time and the foolish virgins had only enough oil for one night. It was while they were away getting more oil that the bridegroom arrived. Jesus then says to his disciples, you know neither the day nor the hour of my return. Be ye ready!

What a powerful song this parable stirred in the soul of one slave listener! Subsequent contemporary listeners were surely moved by the message, as Jesus was indeed a deliverer and a hope for the slave. But many historians also speculate that this song was sung often when there was a possibility of temporal deliverance. Slaves could not openly talk about escape, but they could certainly sing about its possibilities.

This depth and complexity of meaning that underscore the slave song should have a similarly powerful effect when performing "Keep Your Lamps!" in concert. To help convey this power to the choir, often I will have singers in their rows turn and face one wall and put their hands on the shoulders of the person in front of them. I then ask them to imagine that around their ankles are shackles and that the arms represent the chains that connect their legs to the legs of the slave in front of them. Then the group proceeds to move forward and sing. Immediately the group senses the heaviness and the dragging sensation that give energy to the vocal line. After experiencing the music this way—"through the eyes of the slave" is how I refer to it—the emotional impact of singing the song is forever changed!

Tonal Quality

Determining the appropriate tonal quality for any performance is an area in which choral conductors continue to seek answers. What is the appropriate sound for when and in what style a composition was written? How can tonal quality be achieved within the means of maintaining good vocal production? These same questions are frequently asked when interpreting the Negro spiritual.

If we look back to descriptions of the sound of the spiritual in its true folk state, we read phrases like "great billows of sound," "rich deep voices swelling through a forest," and "free use of falsetto in the male voices." Listeners recount a range of sounds, including screaming and yelling, all confined within a single performance.[3] Alice Parker, when describing the sound she heard as a child while visiting her grandmother in Greenville, South Carolina, describes the singers with mouths open wide and with a sound that seemed to go through the entire body and connect to the earth. According to Ms. Parker, this was not a manufactured sound.[4]

Once the spiritual left the realm of folk song, its sound quality changed, and continued to into the late nineteenth century, by which time it was artistically changed by the "refinements of the singer's training."[5] This training was on display in ensembles like the Fisk Jubilee Singers, whose sound one contemporary witness described as follows:

> The songs…possessed in themselves a peculiar power, a plaintive, emotional beauty, and other characteristics that seemed entirely independent of artistic embellishment. These characteristics were, with a refreshing originality, naturalness, and soulfulness of voice and method, fully developed by the singers, who sang with all their might, yet with most pleasing sweetness of tone.[6]

This quote is the cornerstone on which I build a sound concept. The constant thought in my mind is that the sound be full and strong, but still retain the "pleasing sweetness." Most importantly, though, the tone quality must match the message of the text and reinforce the arranger's intent. Because of the harmonic language involved in Moses Hogan's "Ev'ry Time I Feel the Spirit," for example, a brighter vowel might be utilized. A similar approach would be taken with Larry Farrow's setting of "Ev'ry Time I Feel the Spirit." This would be in absolute contrast to Stacey Gibbs's setting of "Way Over in Beulah Lan'." In this selection, a darker vowel would be better suited. In order to achieve that more earthy sound, some smearing into the pitch would be utilized.‡

Think about popular African American singers—from Nat King Cole to James Brown to Aretha Franklin to Beyoncé. The differences in the tonal quality of their voices are striking. That same variety exists within our great body of spirituals. Exploit that variety in your interpretations by letting there be meaningful contrasts influenced by the text.

Rhythm

There are various approaches to rhythm when making stylistic decisions regarding any piece of music. In French Baroque music, for example, one might employ *inégale,* the practice of turning sequential eighth notes into a triplet-quarter-eighth figure. A simi-

---

‡ It should be noted that when working in Europe, I've found that all of the vowels tend to be more forward than those sung by Americans. Even the schwa sound is brighter in Europe than in America. Having the singers imitate the conductor helps to move the vowels a bit further back, making them more American sounding.

lar practice is utilized in jazz when a performer is asked to swing sequential eighth notes.

Because the spiritual can be energetic and rhythmic, some choral conductors will implement this process of swing when performing spirituals. Although there are a few examples where the melody and text lend themselves to a swing feel, most spirituals do not and should not be performed this way. Again, it is important to consider the arranger's intention. Pointing to myself as an example, only my arrangements of "I'm Gonna Sing" and "The Drinking Gourd" employ swing, and on both occasions said treatment is indicated in the score.

In general, there is a feeling of rhythmic pulse in all of the spiritual songs. But it is important to not wear this rhythm on your shirtsleeve. Some conductors over-emphasize the syncopations in the rhythm, almost to the point of angularity. This results in an unconvincing performance at best and a caricature of the original at worst. In nearly all spiritual arrangements there is roundness to the rhythm—not unlike the smoothness you see in the dancing of blacks in the '50s and '60s—even when the tempo is fast.

Intent of the Arranger

When preparing a concert spiritual, it is important to remember that these works were arranged by musicians trained in Western art music. Each arranger has a distinctive style along with specific musical intentions for the work. This is why it is so important for the informed conductor to become aware of each arranger and his or her stylistic intentions. Just as when we conduct the Hungarian folk song arrangements of Bartók or Kodály, or the American folk music arrangements of Copland, we are interpreting the work of the arranger, when we conduct a spiritual arrangement, we are interpreting the work of its arranger. The conductor must evaluate each arrangement of a given folk song independently and determine the stylistic intent of each arranger.

Many arrangers insist that their music be performed exactly as written. One such arranger was William Dawson. Another was Moses Hogan. On the other hand, some arrangers include jazz or gospel elements in their arrangements of spirituals, opening the door to a possible expansion of these elements in your interpretation. A brighter tonal quality and the use of keyboard accompaniment would be the primary areas affected. Also, improvisation could be utilized. I wouldn't go all the way to free improvisation in the gospel style, but I will slightly bend any of the notes that come into the blues scale.

In general, I make more allowances in this direction and take more chances in the direction of the style in the hybrid arrangements because the arranger is already leaning in this direction. I feel bolstered in my decisions, too, by the tradition: when these folk songs were first transcribed, the transcribers struggled to notate the pitches because the slaves wouldn't land on a specific pitch.[§]

Just as we can turn to the writings of Thurston Dart and Robert Donington when we perform Renaissance and Baroque music, we have a body of writing we can turn to when performing concert arrangements of this folk music. Specifically, we have transcriptions of the melody and accounts of early performances. Conductors who reference these transcriptions and read these accounts cannot help but be influenced by them. Even better, we have recordings to reference.

Many notable composer/arrangers also conducted ensembles, most of which, not surprisingly, specialized in the performance of their conductor's music. It would behoove any conductor performing arrangements by these individuals to listen to recordings of their ensembles. Not only will it give you an idea of what's in the arranger's ear, you can look at what an arranger (or his or her editor) marks versus what an arranger performs.

The Hall Johnson Chorale performs throughout the 1936 film *The Green Pastures*. There are numerous recordings of the Albert McNeil Jubilee Singers, which illuminate not only Albert McNeil's arrangements, but Larry Farrow's as well. The RCA recordings of the Robert Shaw Chorale are still available and clearly demonstrate the musical intent of Robert Shaw and Alice Parker in their settings of spirituals during that era. Perhaps the most definitive example of Mr. Dawson's intent can be heard in his recording of his spiritual arrangements with his choir at Tuskegee. Although Moses Hogan has left us, his recordings with The New World Ensemble, The Moses Hogan Chorale, and The Moses Hogan Singers are still available. Many of the other composer/arrangers discussed in this book have also recorded their spiritual arrangements (or supervised the recording thereof).[||]

[§] As an arranger, I've at times attempted to capture this element of the original performances. One example is the use of D flat on beat 3 in m. 35 of "Swing Down, Chariot" (see page 116).

[||] An extensive discography begins on page 268.

Toward Authenticity

You may have noticed that nowhere in the last 95 pages have I used the word "authentic." So many conductors seem to get hung up by this issue of authenticity. Don't. It isn't necessary. I would suggest that what some hold up as "authentic" is, in fact, not authentic at all.

We're performing concert arrangements, not "authentic" folk music. Like any folk music, the minute the Negro spiritual was written down, it was no longer authentic. Some eschew the use of piano in the arrangements, using as their rationale the fact that there was no piano in the field. My response: no, but the slaves in the field weren't singing a fugue either. Further, because the Negro folk songs were transmitted orally, variations existed across plantations. And who can be assured that any of the versions were transcribed correctly?

Rather than asking, "can we create an authentic performance" (and perhaps choosing not to program an arrangement because you answer no), ask, "what can we create instead?" What we are beholden to create is our best representation of the sound that was in the mind of the concert arranger. As long as we are honoring and respecting that and the broader tradition, we should all move ahead, secure and empowered in our right to perform this music.

That isn't to say that the history and tradition of this music shouldn't influence our interpretation. Like most folk music, the singing, one would guess, would have been quite natural, devoid of *bel canto* singing technique. Without a doubt, an operatic sound produced with lifted soft palette was not the sound of the slaves. Often, those who herald the "authentic" sound are referring to the sound produced by the historic black colleges in the early years. This indeed would be the concept of the arrangers from that tradition, so endeavoring to capture it is a worthy goal, if your choir is able to match that tonal quality. On the other end of the spectrum, you may well hear "but that's not how we do it at church" from your students. Educating your choir about the concert spiritual should silence these comments.**

In what is often a related concern, some conductors express discomfort about performing this music of the slave because, to perform it well, one must talk about the slave experience. If you

---

** Educators working in the public schools may be challenged on their inclusion of this music because it employs a sacred text. As it the case with the countless sacred works in the repertoire, one needn't become a Christian to sing the music of the slave. Students must understand the text in the context of the life of the slave and sing it with respect of that experience. When asked, my short response is usually, "Concerts are not conversions."

aren't comfortable speaking about the slave experience directly, pull in Frederick Douglass's description of the experience. Tell a story from another person's perspective. Certainly sensitivity is required but conductors should feel comfortable moving beyond any hesitancy they may have.

I'm not Jewish, can I speak about the Holocaust? Can I relate to the atrocities of the Holocaust? Understand what they *meant* to the Jews who experienced them? To Stravinsky, as he watched the S.S. kill his friend? We can all relate to the slave experience. Again, I offer a respectful, "just chill out, folks." As long as we recognize the strength of the ancestry and honor and acknowledge that in a respectful way, only those who are looking for a problem will find a problem.

My ancestors have left an incredible legacy of music. Some have called it "perhaps America's greatest art form." It is my hope that the information in this book—not just the performance guidelines but the history of its origin and development and the glimpses into the life and work of many of its distinguished arrangers—is the beginning of more reading about this noble form of music. Further, I hope it will help contemporary choral conductors feel secure in their ability to produce informed performances of the spiritual that are inspiring and meaningful to singers and listeners.

That this music is close to my heart shouldn't surprise. And it is indeed with humility that I hope I've made some small contribution to its performance and preservation.

5

REFLECTIONS ON SIX SPIRITUALS

"SOON AH WILL BE DONE," ARRANGED BY WILLIAM L. DAWSON

Dawson's "Soon Ah Will Be Done" is one of a handful of definitive concert spirituals, having been featured on countless recordings and performances. It also poses one of the most enduring questions of interpretation in the repertoire of concert spirituals: should I take Dawson's marked tempo of ♩ = 104?

I tend to take this piece close to, albeit a bit slower than, the tempo Dawson indicated. My decision is based on two factors: 1) he wrote it that way and 2) this is a response to something that has occurred. To me, Dawson's tempo is okay because of the urgency of the folk song. This is a slave's reaction to his situation; an emotional outburst driven by the frustration at it all. I picture the slave pursing his lips, leaning forward, throwing his hands to the side, and saying, forcefully and quickly, *Soon I will be done with the troubles of this world!* This is what I think Dawson is trying to capture in his arrangement—the urgency and passion of that frustrated slave. One caveat is that if I'm in a very reverberant hall, I will probably take this slower so it has time to speak out and come back, otherwise the text is garbled. As with any piece, the size of the choir will also affect the tempo, as will the age of the singers.

As with any question of interpretation, there must be a rea-son for doing whatever one decides to do. Anton Armstrong, for example, on his recording with the wonderful St. Olaf Choir, be-gins this piece at ♩ = 40, then moves to 68 at measure 8.* There is always license in interpretation, and both renditions can clearly be effective. The most important issue is that conductors have a well-thought-through reason underlying their choices. That being said, I've heard stories of Dawson taking this piece much faster than 104. I wouldn't recommend that, as holding together the ensemble becomes very difficult.

When beginning this piece, it is very important to set up the correct rhythm with your singers. This arrangement absolutely should not be turned into a swing. Not only do the straight eighths give the piece much of its urgency, Mr. Dawson's arrangements do not reflect jazz influences. Performing them without imparting those influences honors his intentions. Initially, I would rehearse this slowly, both to ensure the opening rhythmic figure is well es-tablished and because it will help with the dialect.

To create the tone and quality of the sound I want for this piece, I'll say to the choir, "I want you to imagine you are an older person, little past 80, and your teeth are not quite in your mouth. You're mumbling, not really opening your mouth. Can you speak that back to me? Now, sing that." What happens is a hushed, cov-ered sound. This also helps keep singers from over-articulating. It is, however, necessary to use diction to propel the music so it doesn't plod. It just shouldn't be overdone.

I'll also ask singers to clap hands and send them forward, moving away from and back into the body, creating an ebb and flow that you'd have in a tidal wave. When we get to measure 9, though, there's no ebb and flow. Here, *Ah wan'* is connecting to the ground. Sometimes, if I don't get the strong *marcato* accent I want on *meet*, I'll ask singers to point their finger to me and shake it and, as they shake it, bring it back to the body very quickly.

The emotional intensity of the text also dictates the musical direction at the end of the phrase, each crescendoing into the next, particularly when it leads to *goin' home t' live wid God.*

Of all the arrangers, Dawson may have been the most exten-sive in his use of dialect. While it may appear at first overdone, with a few exceptions his indications are just as I would perform it, as they reflect common usage. That's certainly the case with the

---

* In Chapter 6, Dr. Armstrong discusses the reasons underlying his interpretation. While his approach differs from my own, I certainly understand his influences, as my family watched *Imitation of Life,* and heard Mahalia Jackson's rendition, every year when I was growing up, too.

shift from *I will* to *Ah will*. The shift from *with* to *wid* is another common change. Those areas where I would take exception when performing are as follows:

- I would negate the "r" in *No more (weepin' an' a-wailin')*, singing it as a schwa, as would be done in standard English diction.
- I would change *de* to *duh* when it precedes a word that begins with a consonant.
- I would be consistent in the "ah" pronunciation of "I" throughout, so would sing *Ah wan'*, even though it is written as *I wan'*.
- I would soften the "er" in *mother* to a schwa. Again, Mr. Dawson doesn't make this indication, but the rest of the arrangement obviously indicates a strong preference for dialect. We also see evidence of inconsistency (the "Ah" versus "I" mentioned above being a prime example) so we can feel secure in our decision.

Of course, securing a recording of Mr. Dawson leading a performance of this arrangement is highly recommended, and my usual first step when preparing any arrangement by Dawson, Moses Hogan, or the others who've left recordings as part of their legacy.

Soon Ah Will Be Done
For Mixed Voices

William L. Dawson

*Soon I
**a-with

I wan' t' meet my moth - er.

I wan' t' meet my moth - er.

I wan' t' meet my moth - er, I'm goin' t' live wid God.

I wan'_____ t' meet my moth - er, I'm goin' t' live wid God.

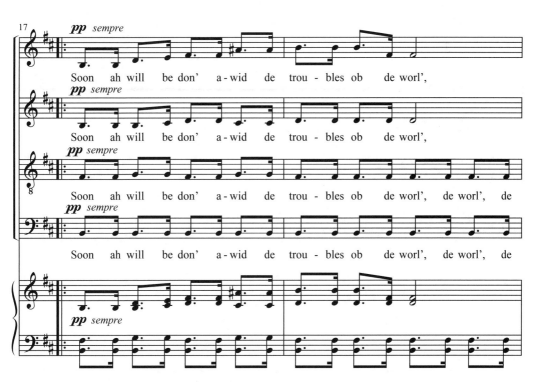

Soon ah will be don' a - wid de trou - bles ob de worl',

Soon ah will be don' a - wid de trou - bles ob de worl',

Soon ah will be don' a - wid de trou - bles ob de worl', de worl', de

Soon ah will be don' a - wid de trou - bles ob de worl', de worl', de

"SWING DOWN, CHARIOT," ARRANGED BY ANDRÉ J. THOMAS

"Swing Down, Chariot" is one of two famous spirituals inspired by a story of the prophet Ezekiel (the other being "Ezekiel Saw the Wheel," best known in the setting by William Dawson). This particular arrangement was written for The Ohio State University Men's Glee Club in honor of their director, James Gallagher. Although I also crafted a setting for mixed voices, I am partial to the TTBB arrangement for that is how I heard and conceived it. Consequently, that is the arrangement I've chosen to discuss here. Most of the rehearsal suggestions will easily translate to the mixed edition, though.

My first thinking on this text took me back to my childhood days, hearing the visiting gospel quartets sing at the church. From that point of inspiration, I aspired to bring the early quartet experience into the concert world by turning the glee club into the gospel quartet. Several elements resulted: I needed to have a lead-in by the basses; hence you have *Oh – oh – oh – oh, Swing*. This part reoccurs frequently, interrupting the other parts. Also typical in the gospel quartets (and in the barbershop quartets they influenced) was the placement of the melody in the second tenor. I have followed that practice here. When I conduct this piece, I'll often go a step farther and have a soloist sing the melody on the verses. Of course, these decisions are always dictated first and foremost by the available forces. The call and response element of the arrangement will come through in either rendering.

Textually, it is the personalization of this story that is notable—the way we go away from the story and bring it into everyday life. *Swing down, chariot, stop and let me ride.* This is an "I" statement, even a plaintive cry—I wanna get out of here! But there's also a bit of humor in this personalization, as the slave connects his vision of heaven to the real world. Ezekiel wanted to leave so bad, he didn't care how the chariot looked or felt, he just wanted a ride out of there—and fast. That humor is translated in the arrangement in the gregariousness of the *Oh – oh – oh – oh* bass part. To me, this is just laughter, so much so that I'll ask basses to "give me Santa Claus" if it isn't coming through as laughter.

Also inherent in this spiritual is the promise of another home, meaning a place in heaven. This is an important theme throughout the entire body of folk music, whether it's referred to as home or heavenly land or Beulah Land. The slave was fixed on having this other existence, for it brought comfort, encouragement, even optimism.[†] Those elements, along with the humorousness in the personalization, drive this spiritual, shaping (and demanding) the musical energy.

Once this jovial quality is established, the next step is to get a buoyancy and lightness in the voices. Classically trained singers, in an attempt to ensure rhythmic accuracy, will often sing this piece in a very marked and rigid way. To help counter this tendency, I return to the inspiration of the gospel quartet and introduce a kinesthetic element. I ask the singers to stomp their foot along with the pulse and slap their thigh on the offbeat. Two things happen: the rushing stops, because the singers are doing too many things to rush; and the voices lighten up, because we've established a physical connection to the style, helping the singers to lift up off the beat.

As the rhythmic components gel, we can look toward other musical elements, including dynamic variety. As touched on earlier, this piece is voiced with the melody in the tenor II part. That should guide overall balance throughout, as well as in a place like the pickup to measure 66, where an *mf* is given for tenor II and a *p* is indicated for the rest of the ensemble. Care should be taken to ensure that these hums are performed very quietly. A word of explanation about the hums is also in order. Again, thinking about the sound concept of the gospel quartets, these hums should be sung as the word *hum*, actually speaking the word and closing quickly to the "m." This is true each time the word is given. Note that the chromaticism in the hums further reflects the gospel quartet influence.

Yet another element of the gospel quartets is found in the last measure: the smear from D flat to D natural. The play between major and minor is a trait found in all African American music dating back to the folk music and exploited heavily in the jazz and blues traditions. Given the overall sound concept, its inclusion here seemed natural. Again, this should be performed within the style (so some elongation), but not exaggerated. Similarly, there are a few places where tones from the blues scale should be slightly bent. The D flat on beat 3 of measure 35, for example, provides a wonderful place to introduce a little color.

The other color addition comes through a softening of the "t"s to "d"s throughout. Often, this occurs naturally. If, as I listen to a particular group perform the piece, there are a lot of sharp conso-

---

† It's interesting to note that some writers say this idea of two homes—one in the spirit world and one in the physical world—is a part of the African tradition, a tradition which obviously fits very comfortably into the Christianity that was introduced to the Africans when they were brought here.

nants, I'll simply say, "Change all the "t"s to "d"s and sing it again." I don't call it dialect and I don't make a big deal of it, and yet this quick comment is usually all it takes to achieve the sound concept.

Two other elements that deserve quick mention are the tempo relationships moving from chorus to verse and back again and the evenness of the eighths. Be sure that you are true to the ♩ = ♩ relationship that exists as you move from the $\frac{2}{2}$ chorus into the $\frac{4}{4}$ verse. Often, directors are guilty of overthinking it; step back, get out of the way, and it will happen very naturally. The use of swing only when indicated was discussed at length earlier, but here we can reference a specific example: this arrangement should not be swung; straight eighths are written and nowhere is a swing indication given.

Commissioned by the Ohio State University Men's Glee Club, in honor of our conductor,
Professor James Gallagher, on the occasion of his retirement.

Swing Down, Chariot

TTBB Chorus, a cappella*

Trad., alt.

Traditional Spiritual
Arranged by André J. Thomas

Ranges: Tenor I   Tenor II   Baritone   Bass

Spirited ♩ = ca. 108

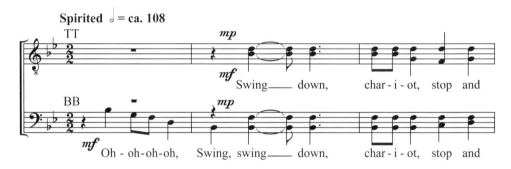

Duration: approx. 3:05
*Also available for SATB (15/1798H).

JD

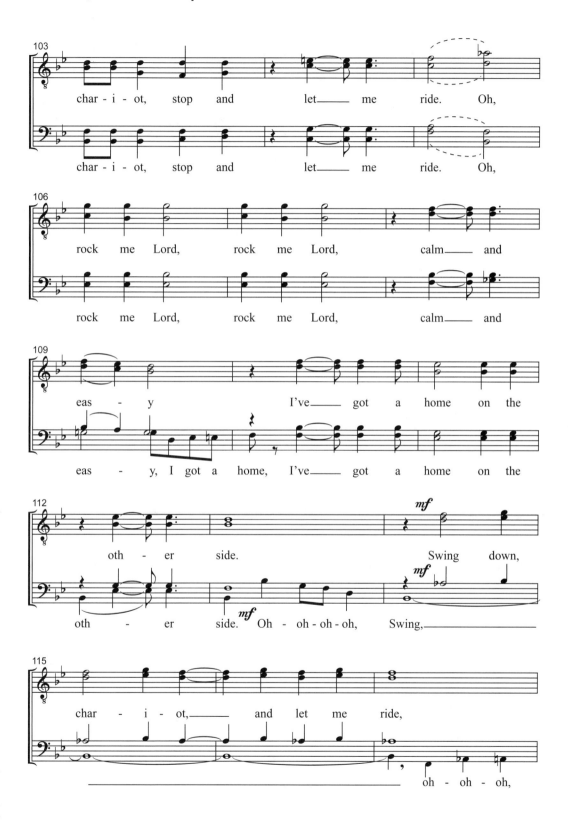

"Way Over in Beulah Lan'," arranged by Stacey V. Gibbs

The slave likely would have known of two meanings for Beulah Land, both of which would have held deep significance in his life. John Bunyan, in his 1678 work *Pilgrim's Progress* (which, at the time of slavery, was as widely read as the Bible), co-opted the term to mean Promised Land, or heaven. Biblically, Beulah Land is drawn from Isaiah 62:4.

> Thou shalt no more be termed Forsaken; neither shall thy land any more be termed Desolate: but thou shalt be called Hephzibah and thy land Beulah: for the LORD delighteth in thee, and thy land shall be married.

Here, Beulah embodies the new relationship God has with his people as they return from exile to embrace their homeland.

As in so many spirituals, we again see the slave attaching to the promise of another home, but here we have the added element of a connectedness to a physical land. So while we are thinking of Beulah Land with a hope, a sense of "Ooh, that's the place I want to go" (with its golden streets and its good wine), we are also rooted in the earth. Finding a way to connect this spiritual to the ground even while looking upward becomes a necessity of interpretation.

Coming out of the introduction, I really need the music to capture this—to really hit the earth—even though the tempo moves a bit. When rehearsing this section, I have the choir stomp as if they are digging into the earth and feeling the essence of this music. We then progress from stomping to moving: stepping strongly with the right leg and touching with the left, then stepping with the left and touching with the right, moving from side to side with the upper body pulled up, even leaned slightly, with the back and strong shoulders leading the way. The resulting sound so matched my concept for this piece (which was shaped by listening to early recordings, including those by Hall Johnson) we carried this movement into performance and added a forward lean on *we gonna have a good time*. Ultimately, it was as if the choir was processing through a church, really feeling the weight of the piece.

I'm not one to do a lot of movement in performance, but in the case of this particular arrangement it helped to establish and reinforce the appropriate rhythmic pulse and energy. Sometimes these elements are light; sometimes they are heavy. In this arrangement, the pulse and energy are heavy, but it's important to make sure there is contrast to this weight or the piece will bog down. For example, while we are pressing to the accent, we must also release off the accent; I teach this as coming up off the stomp.

Stacey writes in a traditional manner, so most of his settings are *a cappella*, and include antiphonal singing throughout with some layering. The echo effect, call and response, layering—all are phenomenal in this piece. He also has a real ability to build momentum, which is on full display in this arrangement. The introduction helps to do this and provides a point of contrast for what's to come. He writes two different tempi: the introduction is marked freely at ♩ = 56, then we move to ♩ = 104, where it is marked in a steady 2. Here, I went with my instincts, conducting the opening section in 4 and moving to 2 at measure 9. It's important to establish the pulse as ungiving and consistent; the rhythm comes all around it but the pulse never gives in. Why? Music was used to coordinate the slaves' work, so the pulse had to be steady. Once that's established, the music vibrates and is quite majestic.

Some dialect is indicated to help color the sound, but when my choir began to perform it, they still sounded like a graduate choir performing spirituals. In other words, even with the altered pronunciation, they sang a very open "ah" in *gonna*, a forward "ouh" in *good*, as well as an elongated dipthong treatment in *time*. In the end, what I heard fell short of my sound concept for this piece; it needed a bit more color, a bit more seasoning:

- In *gonna*, I close quickly to the "n," with a pure "o" with a slight "a" coloration preceding it. We also put a bit of a pop on the re-articulation of "na," particularly in the introduction.
- I ask the sopranos to do a slight smear into A-flat on *have* in measure 2, and a bend into the C on the downbeat of measure 3.
- At the downbeat of 4, the rest of the voices sing *time* with a brighter "i."
- I made a lot of the accent on *way* on the downbeat of 5.
- In measure 7, we left "Beu" immediately, gliding into the "oo" and making it very rhythmic, almost accenting the "oo."
- We sang *Lan'* as indicated, with a close to the "n," but we made that close *very* sharp.
- I wasn't comfortable with *chilun'* so elected to perform it as *childrun*, with a schwa.

This set up a really great color, and we kept this treatment consistent through the arrangement.

The reaction of our audience to "Way Over in Beulah Lan'" was the best of what we hope for when interpreting the spiritual—ears perked, eyes wide, and a thought of "Ooh, what a color shift." A lot of that was the text, and the use of movement. For my singers, most of whom are training to be opera singers, it was a chance to open up. In general, choral singing is difficult for them because they need to limit the full bore of their sound as well as their vibrato. But here, the sound was full and the vibrato prominent.

I took advantage of the strong voices at my disposal and performed measures 121–122 and 129–130 as a duet. (Stacey gives us the option of duet or small group.) Getting into this duet section, I did feel that holding the choir at the marked *forte* (given at measure 116) was too much. Instead, I reinforced the *decrescendo* that will naturally occur because the line is descending by asking the choir to add a *decrescendo* into the *mezzo piano* at measure 123. You will need all the strong voices at your disposal at the end of the piece, which gets very, very high.

for Paul A. Smith and
The California State University Northridge Singers

Way Over in Beulah Lan'

SATB *divisi, a cappella*

Traditional Spiritual
Arranged by Stacey V. Gibbs

*Duet or small group

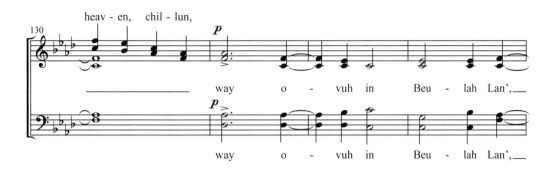

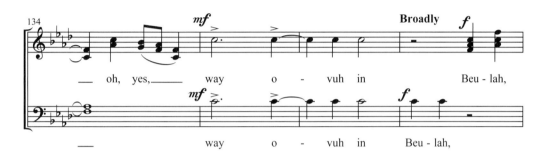

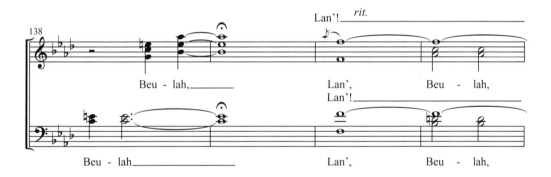

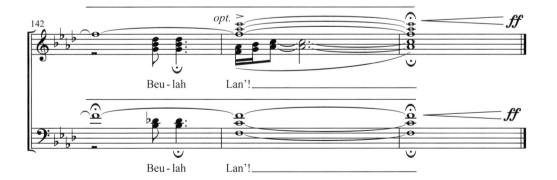

"BEAUTIFUL CITY," ARRANGED BY ANDRÉ J. THOMAS

This arrangement was heavily influenced by a concert given in tribute to Marian Anderson. Kathleen Battle and Jessye Norman were singing. James Levine was conducting the Metropolitan Opera Orchestra, along with the *Porgy and Bess* chorus, prepared by Robert De Cormier. Ms. Battle sang "Oh, What a Beautiful City." It was the lightness and beauty of her voice that was in my ear as I began this setting.‡

Two spirituals are included in this arrangement. "Oh, What a Beautiful City," first quoted in measures 8–12, although with a slight alteration from the folk song, is the melody. "In Bright Mansions Above" is introduced in the pickup to measure 24 in a very simplistic setting, not unlike what you might find in the early Fisk settings (with the exception of the piano accompaniment, of course).

The common thematic element between these two spirituals is their description of heaven. For the slave, these songs would likely have come as a reaction to the description of heaven in the book of Revelations, with its streets of gold and golden slippers. While they still include the prominent theme of being comforted by the prospect of another home, here the focus is on how different this place is from their lives. Yes, the plantations had a certain beauty, but even the road leading to the big house was just a dusty, dirt road. Here we have streets of gold. Wow! I make a lot of that contrast as we connect with the text.

A complementary aspect of the text is the feeling the believer would have when confronted with heaven. Some may have doubts or fears, but not the believer. He is confident; just bopping along through heaven, smiling and thinking, "Wow, isn't this a cool place?" That contented smile, that sense of "cool" should permeate the opening. Often, I'll ask singers to simply move their head from shoulder to shoulder, just bopping, bringing the cool.

When we reach *Oh, what a beautiful city!* in measure 8, I'll spend a little time concentrating on the "o" vowel. My usual approach is, "I don't want an Ohio "o," I don't want a Florida "o," I want a Minnes–oh–ta "o."" That is generally all that's required to lengthen and deepen the vowel.

The statement of "In Bright Mansions Above," which begins with the pickups into measure 24, should be pure legato, with long

---

‡ This remarkable concert was given in New York City on March 8, 1990. It aired on PBS and was released on the Deutsche Grammophon CD *Spirituals in Concert*.

vowels and very linear. Again, we let the social context of the spiritual guide our interpretation here: the slave was always aware of the master's presence, so would sing in a hushed manner to himself.

When we get to *My mother lives up in glory*, the character changes yet again. Here, we need to capture the exaltation that happens in a church service; they've gone on ahead but you get to join them too. Let that line explode.

The beautiful city, city of God! motive that begins at measure 47 is yet another character shift, this time to a sound inspired by the rhythm and blues I heard growing up—the Four Tops, the Temptations, the O'Jays, the Spinners. All of these groups had set moves they did together, and let's face it, they were cool. We need to make some cool here, too, and not unlike the beginning, we can use a kinesthetic tool to help. I'll go through the following in rehearsal:

> How can we make some cool here? We can make "city" really long. Pretend you have taffy in your hands; when we get to city, pull that taffy apart, moving from the center of your body outward.

This usually gives me the style I want; then we work on the inflection: "You wouldn't say 'Beautiful **city. City** of God.' No, it's '**Beautiful** city. City of **God**.' And sing again, please." It amazing how these simple exchanges almost instantly create my desired sound concept.

The character shifts that occur throughout this piece invite reinforcement through the use of dynamics. Although marked *mf*, when the women enter in trio at measure 49 (and in all of the similar entrances that follow), I'll have them enter at *p*, but grow. I might also bend these slightly (but just slightly). Note also that in the second phrase of this section, *Beautiful city!* at measure 51, I'll use "Beau" as a glide, moving the singers quickly to the "oo." At measure 57, everything gets soft, but the basses should enter at a good *mf* on *Oh, yes!* (The savvy reader will no doubt recognize the influence of the gospel quartet once again.) From here, we build to the end where, in the penultimate measure, I add a fermata and hold it until the singers start turning blue, then, we hit the downbeat for the release of the chord!

To close, I offer a few words on rhythm and diction. As with any piece, the rhythm of this arrangement must be internalized and have direction. It cannot be reaction. Too often in highly rhythmic pieces we are reacting to the rhythm rather than anticipating it. Further, this arrangement demands a precision of rhythm, but we cannot lose that roundness. Take care not to make the dotted eighths too short or clipped, thus becoming too angular.

In matters of diction, I do ask for a deep-set vowel on "I," so, *Ah want to live there too*. Again, I'll refer to Madeline Marshall's guidelines for pronouncing *sister* and *number*, so they become *sistuh* and *numbuh*, respectively. *In-a* is the only written dialect, however I do soften most of the "t"s to "d"s simply so they sound more normal. (In hindsight, I wish I'd notated this, as not everyone is comfortable taking this liberty.) One example of dialect that I don't employ is the shift of *three* to *dree*; I don't believe it would have been sung like this, even by the slave.

The most frequent mistake of diction that I have to address with this piece actually has nothing to do with dialect. Rather, it's the shifting pronunciation of *the* depending upon whether it precedes east or west. Per standard English diction, it should be *thee east* and *thuh west*. Repetition is the best technique for fixing this problem.

Beautiful City
SATB

André J. Thomas
Quoting the spirituals:
Oh, What a Beautiful City, and
In Bright Mansions Above

Duration: approx. 3:40

LT

Three gates in - a the south! Twelve gates— to the cit - y,— Hal - le -

lu.— Oh, what a beau-ti - ful cit - y!

Oh, what a beau-ti-ful cit - y! Oh, what a beau-ti-ful cit - y!

man-sions a-bove, Lord, I want to live up yon-der, in bright man-sions a-bove.

Three gates in - a the east! Three gates in - a the west!

Three gates in - a the north! Three gates in - a the south!

"RIDE ON, KING JESUS," ARRANGED BY MOSES HOGAN

This piece was commissioned by Norma Raybon, the director of the Glee Club at Spelman College, the women's college located in the quad area of Atlanta that is home to several other historic black colleges, including Morehouse. Although originally written for women's voices, it is the setting for mixed voices that is discussed here.

As discussed earlier, I begin my preparation of any choral music with the text. In this case, that means reaching for my Bible, as I know this is religious music. I turn to John 12:12–13:

> On the next day much people that were come to the feast, when they heard that Jesus was coming to Jerusalem, Took branches of palm trees and went forth to meet him, and cried, Hosanna: Blessed *is* the King of Israel that cometh in the name of the Lord.

How would the slave have heard this story? What would he have heard? Literally and in his heart? What does that mean for me as an interpreter of this spiritual arrangement? What is my personal connection to this story?

Scholarship tells us that the slave would have heard this story from an itinerant preacher, preaching the story of Jesus riding on a donkey, ever the humble man. But we also know that Jesus was *the* big hero in the life of the slave, the person that transcended the slave from earthly life to heavenly life. Because of his importance, the slaves wouldn't let Jesus ride a donkey. No, Jesus needed to ride on a milk-white horse, and ride on proudly. And thus the song is born.

For me, the connection to church experiences of my youth is immediate: I can visualize a congregation responding to such preaching with shouts of "Ride on, King Jesus! Ride on!," shouts of joy and energy, of exuberance and pride. All of that helps to form my sound concept for this arrangement, and by sharing this with the choir, I immediately affect how they are going to sing this text. Will it be staid and formal, or will be sung with energy as if to say, "yeah, man, you're doin' it"?

Another textual element that I like to share with choirs is the contrast of the referential with the personal. Spirituals include both the personal telling of stories and sharing of emotions and the reactions of a community in reference to the personal. When we sing, *I was but young when I begun*, we're singing the personal. We're singing the words of an old woman who continues on, *but now my race is almost done*. The choir's answer of *No man can a-hinder thee* represents the referential. Capturing how these words would have functioned originally is all part of representing and respecting the meaning of the text.

The use of dialect in "Ride On, King Jesus" is very typical of what you'll find in most arrangements. Phonetic decay is indicated on *conquerin' king*. In measures 30 and 31, Moses gives us *The ribber of Jordan*, the softening of the "v" to a "b" being mentioned specifically by Johnson and others. This, however, is the only dialect included in the arrangement. What does this tell us? Firstly, it tell us that Moses is but one of the many arrangers who were inconsistent in their use of dialect within a given piece. Secondly and most importantly, it tells us that the arranger was open to dialect, therefore granting us license to introduce it elsewhere as appropriate.

Other appropriate utilizations of dialect in this arrangement include:

- A softening of the "d" in *Ride*
- A dropping of the "r" in *hinder*, although as is often the case this is as much a schwa treatment as it is dialect. I should note here that that I would not sing *(hinda) de*. Again, as interpreters we must look to the intention of the arranger. Here, we can glean that intention from the recordings of Moses Hogan's groups, which do not include "de."
- When singing *Lord*, I would follow standard rules of English diction which treat the "r" it as a schwa. Note that I would not sing the "r" coloration that is sometimes done.

The rhythms of this arrangement also require a little preparation. Take the opening figure in measures 3 and 4: Both the downbeat *Ride* and the syncopated *on* that follows are marked with accents, but *Ride* should be brought out more than *on*. Why? Two reasons: 1) this is metric music, so the downbeat should be given more stress; and 2) it is important that the syncopation be present but not exaggerated or forced. Too often, conductors, in an attempt to bring out this rhythmic element, will exaggerate the syncopation to the point of angularity. Think about the smoothness of black dances from the '50s and '60s—the Temptation Walk, for example. I'll go so far as to ask choirs to do the Temptation Walk with me, moving from side to side as we sing. Once we've established this beginning passage, I'm careful to do it the same way throughout.

Sometimes an arranger will indicate that something different from the usual interpretation is desired. In this case, Moses has done that in measure 8, adding an accent on the "and" of 1 on the second syllable of *Jesus*. Again, this shouldn't be exaggerated, but care should be paid.

Because this is such a big piece, I work very hard to make sure the choir gives me dynamic contrast. The *piano* sections are *really piano*, for instance. Further, I will make a few adjustments to match the stylistic interpretation. The bass entrance in measure 8 provides a great example. I voice this so that the basses are predominant. To me, this is a direct lift from how this song would have been sung by the early quartets, with the bass leading the way.

My final alteration comes in the penultimate bar. Moses gives us a breath mark between beats 2 and 3. I take the mark, but with a *fermata* while having the sopranos sing through it. And I really take my time!

A final thought regarding this piece is to be careful with the tempo. I would suggest thinking of the marked ♩ = 132 as the upward limit for this piece. Once established, take care not to rush, and not to jump to the rhythm or anticipate the syncopation. It is essential that the performance be grounded in a steady, underlying rhythm. If singers are struggling, slow it down. Find a tempo at which the group can execute the syncopation successfully and speed up from there, taking care to secure the group at each faster tempo. In part because of the tempo, but also because it reflects the strong classical background and training of Moses Hogan, this arrangement demands a talented pianist.

Commissioned by Spelman College
Dedicated to Dr. Audrey Forbes Manley, President of Spelman College
Premiered by the Spelman Glee Club, Dr. Norma Raybon, Director

Ride On, King Jesus

For SATB div. and Piano
Performance Time: Approx. 2:30

Traditional Spiritual
Arranged by Moses Hogan

"I'M GONNA SING," ARRANGED BY ANDRÉ J. THOMAS

One of the central considerations facing conductors when performing the spiritual is the use of swing. As discussed at length in Chapter 4, most spirituals should not be swung, and certainly as a conductor interpreting an arrangement I would avoid swing unless the arranger made such a designation on the piece. There are some spiritual arrangements, though, that do utilize swing. One example is my "I'm Gonna Sing."

Generally, if swing is applied, there is an overall jazz influence in the arrangement itself; this influence stemming from the early jazz musicians in New Orleans performing the spirituals in Dixieland bands. That sound certainly served as an inspiration to me in this arrangement. Also, the flow of the text of the folk song suggested, to me, a swing-type sound.[§]

In this arrangement, I chose to notate the swing rhythm (with quarter-eighth triplets) rather than simply writing "Swing" at the top. Provided the music is read accurately, this ensures that the piece swings where it should and doesn't where it shouldn't. This also prevents conductors from indiscriminately applying swing, and helps those who don't have an understanding of swing. (Should you find yourself performing an arrangement where swing is indicated rather than notated, I would suggest you consider the axiom if in doubt, less is more when it comes to matters of interpretation.)

When I perform this piece, I almost always add a bass player and a drummer, again, harkening to the jazz combo. Although there aren't notated parts, this addition is quite simple, particularly if you have players who are familiar with jazz. The bass plays the bass part of the piano, transposed to a comfortable range. The drummer will play a swing feel throughout, even against the ascending even-eighths in the piano in measures 70 and 71. (Most trap players won't need music for this; the instruction "play with a swing feel throughout" will suffice.)

The use of instruments changes the way the piano accompaniment will be played. Just as in a jazz combo, the piano provides the melody and harmony. The bass is the foundation; you don't want to double those lines in the piano. Experienced jazz pianists will be able to revoice these on the fly. The inexperienced player may,

---

§ Even though I heard swing in this folk song, and chose to exploit that in my arrangement, not every arranger did. Again, we must remember to honor the intent of the arranger and not just think, "André Thomas's 'I'm Gonna Sing' swings, so this arrangement of 'I'm Gonna Sing' should, too."

for the most part, double what's in the right hand in both hands, but lightly so the bass predominates. For the solid chords in measures 10–15 (and elsewhere), the right-hand part should be played as written, but only the top note of the left-hand part should be played. The trap player will have all the special rhythms, and will provide the underlying pulse that keeps it pumping. One of the conductor's main responsibilities in this rendering of "I'm Gonna Sing" is controlling the combo, particularly during the more reverent *I'm gonna pray...* verse. You must remind them of their function as the accompaniment.

Like many arrangers of the concert spirituals, I've added an introduction and other motific material of interest based on the spiritual itself. Specifically, the swing acclamation *Sing on! Dance on! ...Pray on! ...Shout on till the spirit says sing!* This serves not only as an introduction, but the acclamation bridges the verses as well.

Beginning at measure 9 is the traditional spiritual, set very clearly and simply in unison voices. This straightforward presentation is important to me because I feel a spiritual arrangement is successful only if the audience can easily identify the folk song, and further, that it is the lasting musical impression of the piece. Is the original tune in their ear? Do they leave the performance humming it? Consequently, on subsequent verses, even though I vary its presentation, the melody stays present.

After the acclamation following the second verse, I've added another section of new material (measures 40–47). It was inspired by my experiences in church seeing a sister on the right-hand side of the church stand up and say "sing on, brother," and being answered by a man on the other side of the church who jumps up. These declarations should be energetic. Their sound—and the sound concept for the entire arrangement—should be clear. In this setting, I'm not trying for darker or richer.

In measure 51, we return to the unison presentation of the spiritual. Even though the arrangement builds to the end and the newly composed acclamation returns, I want the listeners to have this final exposure to the folk tune. It is important that it not be obscured, so the piano (and bass and drums, should you elect to use them) should be kept simple; there's a reason the accompaniment is half notes!

Because of its jazz influences, I consider this arrangement a hybrid. It, like any piece that uses the melody and text from a Negro folk song, is a spiritual, just one that moves beyond some of the more traditional four-part *a cappella* settings. Within the range of hybrid arrangements, "I'm Gonna Sing" is certainly on the traditional end, though, with a work like Larry Farrow's "Ev'ry Time

I Feel the Spirit" being at the more contemporary end. In a piece like that, which features ninth and thirteen chords and changes in the piano part, much of what we discussed here is still applicable. Swing should only be performed if indicated, and even then, less is more. When the folk tune is presented, care should be taken to bring it out. (Farrow's "Ev'ry Time I Feel the Spirit" also includes "Great Day" which, too, should be highlighted.) One difference in the more contemporary hybrids is that I would approach the sound concept more like vocal jazz—brighter, clearer, and cleaner with no coloration; otherwise the harmonies won't come through clearly.

I'm Gonna Sing

SATB Chorus and Piano*

A.J.T. and trad., alt.

Traditional Spiritual
Arranged by André J. Thomas

Duration: approx. 2:15
*Also available for SSA (15/2024H).

JD

shout and o-bey the spir-it of the Lord!

Sing on!__ Dance__ on!__ Sing on!__ Pray__ on!__

Sing on!__ Shout__ on!__ Sing! Pray!

6

OTHER PERSPECTIVES

Interviews with Dr. Anton Armstrong
and Prof. Judith Willoughby

One of the greatest resources conductors have at their disposal is other conductors. I am fortunate that Dr. Anton Armstrong (the Harry R. and Thora H. Tosdal Professor of Music and Conductor of the St. Olaf Choir) and Prof. Judith Willoughby (the Wanda L. Bass Professor of Conducting and Choral Music Education at Oklahoma City University), two exceptional conductors with a vast range of experiences who are also frequent interpreters of the concert spiritual, agreed to share their responses to the following questions with me and, in turn, you.

- What are the most important things you look for in selecting a spiritual arrangement?
- When performing a spiritual arrangement, what changes do you make to the composer's printed instructions and why?
- How do you utilize dialect when it is written in an arrangement?
- How do you handle the utilization of dialect when it is not indicated?

- What are your thoughts about a "black sound"? What modifications do you make to create it?
- What unique challenges do you find when conducting spirituals outside the United States?
- How do you respond to critics who say, "Singing spirituals is detrimental to good vocal production?"
- Regarding tone, what elements do you change when working with an African American chorus?
- What do you do to establish rhythmic energy with your choruses when singing spiritual arrangements?
- Do you ever encourage movement or body percussion while performing a spiritual?
- Who are ten arrangers whose works you have performed and that you would suggest to your colleagues?

Their responses further illuminate much of what's been offered herein yet also shed new light, as they include additional and even contradictory opinions.

What are the most important things you look for in selecting a spiritual arrangement?

Willoughby: The composer/arranger must have a unique voice that first connects, for me, on an emotional level. The arrangement or newly composed work must have integrity. In other words, it must feel like an organic marriage with the text and/or the meaning or multiple meanings of the text.

I prefer *a cappella* spiritual arrangements, as they speak to me in a more authentic voice. I grew up hearing spirituals in the African Methodist Episcopal (AME) Zion Church where I was baptized. And my earliest memory was of hearing spirituals performed unaccompanied, and often with a rather simple elegance, but also unpretentious. This is a deep memory and I am sure that it affects the choices that I make when picking spiritual arrangements for my choruses to study and perform. I also remember singing spirituals in Sunday school (including "This Little Light of Mine," "Swing Low, Sweet Chariot," and "Mary Had a Baby") and I have a distant memory of my mother singing spirituals to me when I was very young. I asked her recently if I imagined this or if it really happened. She assured me that, in fact, she used to sing to me before I went to bed.

I am sure that the simplicity of these beautiful songs is deep in my psyche, so I appreciate arrangements that are clean, balanced, and rhythmically alive, regardless of whether they are fast or slow. I also look to arrangements where the melodic and harmonic treatments are sympathetic to each other, even in their tensions. There should be balance between the melodic structure and harmonies, as well as with the rhythmic and harmonic energy, be it quiet or active. I also look for harmonies that work appropriately with the melody, and a musical setting of the text that complements the voice. Excellent spiritual arrangements provide great opportunities, pedagogically, to explore various vocal colors that illuminate the text—the joy or pathos, the sorrow or expectation. I am not particularly drawn to spirituals whose settings embrace the latest pop culture style. The settings that I have reviewed which are written in this style seem false to me.

I don't have the same criteria for spiritual arrangements that are composed with elements of gospel style, which I call hybrids. These works often include clapping and significant keyboard accompaniments, and even other instruments. When spirituals are set in gospel style (the hybrid), I evaluate each arrangement on a case-by-case basis. Over time, one develops certain expectations for the works of composers who embrace hybrid styles and finds favorites among composers of this compositional genre.* It makes me feel particularly comfortable when a composer actually states the intent of his or her piece, or, through the compositional process, makes it very clear that he or she was endeavoring to create a hybrid arrangement. That stated intent grants, for me, a measure of authenticity to the hybrid form.

Although you didn't specifically ask this question, I want to say a word about spiritual songs which become the compositional "meat" for a strictly constructed, contemporary, classical motet. (Some of Adolphus Hailstork's choral works come to mind [e.g. *Crucifixion*].) I am very liberal in my thinking about these works and apply the same criteria in evaluating them as I would for any other traditionally composed work. I look for a work that is structurally well written, text sensitive, vocally appropriate, and artistically compelling.

Armstrong: First of all, I look to the setting and its use of the slave song—the actual spiritual. (I frequently see pieces called spiritual arrangements, yet they will barely use any fragment of the spiritual song.) Not only must the slave song be present, the setting must have a certain transparency. The basic integrity of the spiritual/slave song must remain intact.

---

* Composers who sometimes write in this style include André Thomas, Paul Caldwell, and [almost exclusively] Rollo Dilworth.

I gravitate towards works by those arrangers who seem to understand the basis of African song, particularly that melody and rhythm are paramount aspects. So much of African song that I have studied and experienced includes the layering of those melodies, which creates a specific type of harmonic foundation, structure, and texture.

I have tended to find that these characteristics are present more frequently in settings done by African American composers, as I feel they display a greater sensitivity to certain elements of African American musical composition and tend to have a certain flavor. That said, there are many people outside of the African American background who created settings with great integrity. Arrangers like Alice Parker and Robert Shaw come to mind, as do Jack Halloran, especially his "Witness," Paul Caldwell and Sean Ivory, and Larry Fleming, the founder and conductor of the National Lutheran Choir who has a set of triptychs about Jesus.

When selecting a spiritual arrangement, I also try to be aware of what I call extraneous styles of writing. So often when arranging the slave songs, people cross forms. They create more of a jazz or even a gospel sound. To a lesser extreme, some arrangers, including André Thomas and Moses Hogan, will include piano accompaniments in their arrangements. For me, this raises the question of authenticity, yet I find many of these settings compelling. I think that comes from the integrity of presentation that I believe is inherent in these arrangements.

Part of this integrity comes from arrangers presenting the songs in their most simple and accessible form. I can appreciate Michael Tippet's use of the spiritual as the staple points in "A Child of Our Time" in much the way Bach used the chorale for his *Passions*. But I don't often program his setting as an example of the spiritual because I think Tippet's arrangement has removed the spiritual from the cultural context, therefore removing its integrity.

I also made a very conscious decision when I recorded the settings of William Dawson (at the behest of Neil Kjos Music Co., who now owns the editions) not to perform many of the later revisions. It is my feeling that Dawson, for his own personal reasons and perhaps in an attempt to validate the spiritual form, heavily revised these works. In the process, I feel they lost some of the basic integrity of his earlier arrangements, which I find much more compelling and much more real.

When performing a spiritual arrangement, what changes do you make to the composer's printed instructions and why?

Willoughby: I treat the composer arranging a spiritual with the same care and respect I would grant to any other composer. Conductors are, after all, the composer's advocate, as well as re-creators of the music. So the answer to this question depends upon the composer and my accumulated knowledge about his or her predilections. For example, I am aware that John Wesley Work Jr. wanted the chorus to sing what was on the page—period. (John Work and Igor Stravinsky would have made great companions in this regard.)

I do not change what has been written unless I have actually talked with the composer about it. If I don't have access to that information, and I cannot find someone who has reliable knowledge of the composer's intent, I may turn to another composition with a similar mood, strength, or tenderness. This rigor with my own approach comes from hearing so many bad spiritual performances led by conductors who have no information about the performance practice. (They treat the spiritual like a pop tune!)

We are fortunate, in this century, to have bodies of work from composers who are meticulous in their notation. (Moses Hogan comes to mind.) There is no reason to change a single note. One would be so lucky as to successfully execute every marking on the page—especially in what I call Mr. Hogan's "allegro" spirituals, those that are fast, dense, and pianistically conceived.. There are many caring, careful composers who notate their scores with great attention to detail; there is plenty of information to follow in the score.

This is true, as well, for spiritual composers/arrangers from the early and mid twentieth century, including Nathaniel Dett, William Dawson, Hall Johnson, Jester Hairston, Wendall Whalum, Undine Smith Moore, Robert Morris, Roland Carter, and others. If one simply follows the markings in the score, and understands the cultural context, there is still plenty of room to be interpretively sensitive. Some of the most powerful spiritual interpretations that I have been privileged to experience have been *a cappella* spirituals performed by esteemed concert singers in performance. I am sure that this informs my choices to always ere on the side of a clean performance which is vocally and rhythmically colored according to the requirements of the text.

Armstrong: In my first interpretation, I really try to respect the arranger's intent, which isn't particularly challenging because I often choose a particular setting because I feel an affirmation of what that arranger has done. In those instances where I have taken issue with an arranger/composer, it is usually in the area of tempo. I sometimes find that the indicated tempos, even of the very revered arrangers, are too fast. This is body-based music; if it is performed too fast, the rhythms won't be presented in the most prominent and effective way.

This is the case in my performances of Dr. Thomas's "Keep Your Lamps!" After doing my own research (which was later confirmed by Dr. Thomas), I learned that this spiritual was body-based music. Knowing the context of this music—that this was how this music functioned in the lives of the slaves—and seeing the impact of tempo in Renaissance and Baroque dance music, I take the piece more slowly.

To date possibly my most striking example of changing a tempo is in Dawson's celebrated setting of "Soon Ah Will Be Done." As others before me, I was highly influenced by Mahalia Jackson's singing of this spiritual at the end of the film *Imitation of Life*. Her rendition truly becomes a lament yet it also reflects a paradox of the spiritual—yes, it is dealing with the sorrow, the pain, the torment of this earth, but there is a hope of life thereafter. When I heard it, the text finally made sense to me. And for me, Dr. Dawson's tempo did not present a full meaning of the text as I experienced it. (Quite honestly, when I've heard choirs perform this piece, it often comes off as a minstrel song, almost a parody, and certainly a poor imitation of what I would like to see and what I felt.) In my renditions, and with great admiration for Dr. Dawson's setting, I treat the refrain more as a lament, taking a much slower tempo. The verses, which have a sense of folk, I allow to be faster and closer to what I believe Dr. Dawson indicated.

How do you utilize dialect when it is written in an arrangement?

Willoughby: This is a thought-provoking question. But it is less tricky for me than it was twenty years ago. I say this because I have since learned about the difficulties some African cultures (in particular West African) had in pronouncing certain sounds such as "th." For this reason, the word *the* might have become *duh* or *de* in spoken dialect. I am even more sensitive to these challenges in light of the Africans' plight—brought to the United States, left to make sense of that trauma, the new continent, a new language, and a new life (if one could call it that).

Dialect, properly set, can help the rhythmic energy of a choral work, as it does in William Dawson's "Soon Ah Will Be Done." I do, however, stay away from texts that sound like "coon language." There are enough excellent spiritual arrangements from which to choose (and the numbers are growing all the time) that it is not necessary for me to even consider a song with a text treatment that is not informed by an understanding of the roots of the African American folk tradition or is written without deep understanding of the cultural context of the many genres of spirituals. Sometimes dialect, or the absence of it, affects the rhythmic or interpretive vitality of the work. For example, dropping a final, active consonant (e.g. "g" or "d") or, as previously stated, changing *the* to *de* or *duh.*

Armstrong: In dealing with dialect, there is a wider question: to use or not to use? There are three schools of thought on dialect: 1) use standard English; 2) adopt a hybrid approach; or 3) use slave dialect.

The use of standard English is favored by the older generation, so as to not show disrespect, and is often the approach taken outside the U.S. In the hybrid approach, much of the dialect is almost vernacular in nature. The goal of this approach, which is used by many contemporary conductors, composers, and arrangers, is to give a flavor of the folk song without expecting that all people will be able to approximate the language of the slave. Those who attempt to bring the greatest integrity and some aspect of authenticity to the performance seem to favor the use of slave dialect. This position is well captured by our colleague Marvin Curtis, who wrote in a 1991 article, "Dialect is an integral facet of the languages."

As one who has attempted to sing the slave song with more and more use of dialect, I do use the whole concept of phonetic decay in many of my interpretations of language in the spirituals, especially on certain final consonants. I return to "Keep Your Lamps!" and offer as an example the dropping of the final "g" in many of the words, so *burning* becomes *burnin'* and *drawing* becomes *drawin'.*

How do you handle the utilization of dialect when it is not indicated?

Willoughby: As noted in the previous answer, I may make a minor change in a word (e.g. modifying the final consonant or changing a word to reflect the pronunciation patterns that would have been used by displaced West Africans trying to pronounce the English language). Otherwise, I don't use it.

Armstrong: I tend to use dialect in my interpretation of the spirituals. In addition to the use of phonetic decay outlined in answer to the previous question, we have to recognize that certain sounds common in the English language are absent in many of the African dialects. This is especially true in the dialects of the West African tribes from which many of the slaves were drawn and brought to this country. These include some of the harder consonants, such as the voiced "th," which simply did not exist in many of the African dialects. In this case, a substitution to "d" is made. Again I use as an example Dr. Thomas's setting "Keep Your Lamps!" Instead of *the time is drawing nigh*, with dialect it is, *duha time is drawin' nigh*. Another hard consonant that is softened is "v," which is shifted to "b." For example, instead of *heavenly* you have *heabenly*.

When we deal with the issues of vowels, I strive to eliminate diphthongs through modification. Also, a much more prevalent use of the schwa in words such as *father* is utilized. Specifically, I would use the "uh" sound as schwa for the word *father*. In the word *heavenly*, insertion of the schwa on the second syllable is used. Finally there is the matter of clipping or compressing certain words. For example, the word *plantation* becomes *plantion* and *witness* becomes *widness*.

I have to say this—when dealing with an American group or a group with a mix of ethnic backgrounds, I am careful to explain to the singers why I am using dialect. As a young African American, encountering dialect brought about in me a type of personal embarrassment. So this doesn't happen for other students, I want them to understand the context from which the language emerged and why we are using dialect in this way. This knowledge is also crucial if these materials and songs are to be presented with dignity and respect.

What are your thoughts about a "black sound"? What modifications do you make to create it?

Willoughby: In my experience, there are certain stylistic elements that must be developed in all choruses who are learning to sing spirituals well. These elements include:

- The ability to cultivate an idiomatic understanding of internal (personal) and external (communal) rhythm appropriate to the work.
- A barely discernable but absolutely necessary relaxation of the ongoing pulse in some instances, which can give the spiritual a perceived rhythmic freedom and flexibility for the listener.
- An ability to darken and/or color the vowel—without singing the back of the throat—to give the choral sound

authenticity. This means singing with more [vocal] color (no pun intended) or highlights.

- An ability to sing full out with a different concept of blend that, while in tune, may have more "edges" than the smooth, medium-weight, float, European-cathedral sound.

Then there are the challenges of singing with appropriate vocal weight, text, and phrase accents without "weighing down" or pressing on the voice.

Harry Burleigh's arrangement of the spiritual "My Lord, What a Mornin'" comes to mind as an example of what appears to be a rather straightforward ternary, homophonic, easily sung spiritual. The A sections, in a major key, are warm, legato, and supple, but accurate rhythmically speaking. They are homophonically balanced, with the melody on top and the supporting harmonies underneath (in the alto, tenor, and bass voices). However, the minor-key B section, which talks about "escaping worldly ways" and going to one's "heavenly home," needs a lot of downward weight and rhythmic accent to express the pain and futility of earthly living, yet there can't be vocal pushing. All of these vocal and interpretive challenges coexist in this small spiritual arrangement. The contrast between these elements, which flows from the text as well as the formal structure of the arrangement, should be immediately evident to the listener. (In addition to highlighting the many demands inherent in performing spiritual arrangements, this piece is a good example of a spiritual arrangement that is profound and simple, simultaneously.)

Great attention to the articulation of beginning consonants is also very important in highlighting the appropriate rhythmic energy in faster spirituals.

Armstrong: The issue of vocal timbre and color is an area open for discussion and great debate. When I perform music from any period, I try to gain an understanding of how the people from that time sang the music. If I'm performing music from the Renaissance, I want to know if it was first performed by people who came from Italy, Spain, England, or Germany. Depending upon the region, the music will have a different effect. Also, the language affects the tonal color.

It is a point of fact that for various physiological reasons, the voices of African American singers have a darker quality than those singers of other ethnicities. And this is even truer of the African singers of the folk music. Consequently, for me, striving for that timbre and tone color is part of a respectful and successful interpretation of the slave song (and part of the idea of recreating spirituals with integrity versus authenticity). Coupling the darker sound with the use of dialect (which reflects the speech patterns of that period), you arrive at a tone quality that seems to enhance the singing of the slave songs.[†]

Rather than just impose a dark sound (or a bright sound, if that is needed) I enjoy playing with colors with the singers (particularly when they are children). I will often ask singers to imagine a burgundy sound, an ebony sound, a lime green sound. As we move to the desired sound, all are engaged and we can come to a consensus—can we make that sound? Can we agree that this sound might work in the song? In this way it is a shared process rather just an imposition of my mindset. (I'm always gratified to find that with each ensemble this process is slightly different.)

I want to be sure its clear that in the pursuit of a darker sound, I don't ask singers to manipulate their voices in an unhealthy way, a way that will lead to bad vocalism. (Some conductors will create a so-called darker sound by having singers simply retract their tongue into an uncomfortable vocal position.)

What unique challenges do find when conducting spirituals outside of the United States?

Willoughby: I first became aware of a totally spontaneous quality in American music making (even when the music is of the European classical tradition) when I was privileged to visit the Soviet Union. I spent three weeks there during the height of the Cold War observing the Tchaikovsky competitions in piano, violin, cello, and voice. Musicians traveled from around the world to compete in these simultaneous competitions, held in Moscow, as the guest of the former Soviet Union. The United States and the Soviet Union had the greatest number of competitors in the piano competition (around 70 each), and comparable numbers in the other competition categories.

I heard many musicians from across the globe and the national styles of playing became obvious very quickly. What struck me about the Americans was their total lack of inhibition, relatively speaking, even in the face of nerves created by the high-stakes competition environment. Musicians from the United States exhibited a spontaneity and freshness in their playing—across the board—in every competition that I heard. I am not saying that

---

† We tend to lump all the Negro folk songs together and call them spirituals, but it is the way the slave song functioned in the daily life of the slave that dictates if it's a spiritual or not. Field hollers, for example, don't have religious connotations. Many of the sound concepts and performance practices I'm advocating, though, are appropriate for most Negro folk songs.

every American musician was technically superb. What I am stating is that there was a national characteristic that included spontaneity and rhythmic energy. This, I think, must come from our country's emphasis on the rugged individual, from the very pace and character of our nation, which has long been more spontaneous and "me centered," with the individual and his or her development taking precedence over the needs of the group.

Competitors from other countries exhibited other interesting and sometimes subtle national characteristics. But none, at that time, played or sang with the unabashed internal freedom exhibited by the competitors from the United States. Why do I mention this? Because it has an impact on the way we, as a nation, internalize rhythmic vitality.

When I conduct choruses in the United States, there is a greater chance, because of our culture, that we will find the core of our rhythmic being. And because of our inherent flexibility, we will be able to bring it out in the music. I often have to work harder to get at these elements and bring them forth in the music when working abroad in cultures where elements other than rhythm (e.g. melody, harmony, or form) are the defining elements or central core of the music. This is especially true when it comes to swing or other syncopated rhythms. It can be done, but with a great deal of sweat equity and some luck!

In addition to the more stilted rhythm exhibited by choruses I have conducted abroad, the spiritual text is always a challenge in a different culture. Often, the printed page is taken quite literally, and the conductor must exhibit great creativity through vocal and text modeling and body movement. If your chorus is not self-conscious engaging in this activity in order to shape an interpretation that is true to the spirit of the spiritual, then the possibility for presenting an idiomatic spiritual performance exists.

In Asia I find that singers are particularly drawn to the melodies of spirituals because of their modal qualities. Their immediate connection to this style of music was a happy surprise, and one that made my job easier.

Armstrong: In conducting these songs throughout the world, I have found that the languages of different regions affect the pronunciation of consonants as well as certain vowels. When I worked in Northern Europe (especially Germany, Austria, and certainly in Scandinavia) I found a predominantly brighter timbre in the singing of these choirs. These choirs also sing with much less vibrato; at times, almost no vibrato. So more than just asking them to find a darker timbre, I work to enhance the total color spectrum—not just the vowel color itself but also the release of the sound. I remember working with a fine group of singers in Northern Sweden. Their sound was rather held almost to the point of being truly strained. Doing vocal exercises released the sound and invited a warmer more natural vibrato, which fully enhanced the singing of the spirituals.

In Asian countries, there are issues with certain vowels, but more so with certain consonants that are foreign to their native tongues, for example "r"s and "l"s. (The trilling of the "r" is another problem.) Addressing these issues in a way that doesn't result in a manufactured sound is further complicated by the addition of dialect, and the change of sound that comes with it. As to the sound concept, the elimination of the diphthong also eliminates the much brighter, more spread sound, and often goes hand in hand with trying to get a warmer, fuller, and more released sound.

How do you respond to critics who say, "Singing spirituals is detrimental to good vocal production?"

Willoughby: Singing with authentic understanding of style, vocal color and weight, textual understanding, etc. is a product of good choral teaching and rehearsal technique, followed by the practice and expectation of consistent choral performance. The techniques for singing spirituals successfully need to be applied with the same diligence that has been applied to the mainstream European classical canon of choral literature where, for example, care has been taken to differentiate Baroque vocal performance practice in Bach from Handel from Monteverdi, and certainly from the Romantic Brahms. These are all choral styles that can and should be taught, just as we teach vocal jazz and world music styles, so that choruses (as well as their audiences) are enriched and enlightened by the unique properties of each style of choral singing.

Armstrong: I disagree with that comment. When I conduct any style of music I'm seeking healthy free-release phonation processes. And this is certainly possible when singing spirituals. I think where we get into trouble is thinking there is only one way to sing music. Even in the contemporary African American church we have a tendency to take a very limited view of authentic vocal production. Specifically, vocal production in this context often is influenced by a very contemporary gospel style, which means a lot of use of the heavy mechanism.

I would rather look at the attitude of the piece. I think that often present in these pieces—even when they are dealing with lament—is a key element of people in celebration, celebration of a life yet to come. So what I'm seeking in the performance of this music is a free-release sound, one in which we are not imposing anything that would constrict the vocal production. At the same time, one that will affirm and mirror the celebratory nature of the text.

You obviously get into more trouble with settings that require great rhythmic energy and vocal resonance. Here, rather than trying to get that heavier mechanism (almost a belting sound, some would say), the choice of arrangement and an understanding of what you want to achieve vocally with your choir is paramount.

I know when the St. Olaf Choir was recording the spiritual album of William Dawson's settings, several things happened. I wanted a less controlled sound than that which has been characteristic of the St. Olaf Choir. So for this recording, rather than putting the choir in their block formation, I put them in a more scrambled, mixed formation. (I have done this at times when singing music of African American composers/arrangers, as well as African music and sometimes Latin American music, as well.) I also encouraged a more soloistic approach to the singing, which creates, I think, a different quality of sound. If one was to refer to that Dawson album and listen to "Ezekiel Saw Da Wheel" and "Ain'a That Good News," he or she would hear more individual voices present than might be the norm on any other recording by the St. Olaf Choir.

Really, though, it starts with the conductor. We often think that for music to be exciting it has to be loud and that to achieve that volume we have to abandon good vocal health. I would say that is never the case in my work. These are songs of a noble people and must be sung with respect and beauty. I take my guide from the recordings of the great African American art song singers—Paul Robison, Roland Hayes, Leontyne Price, Marian Anderson, Jessye Norman. I hear a beauty of sound, an understanding of the attitude of the text. This is what guides my interpretation of sound. I attempt to assist the singers in understanding the attitude of the text and the music, and in expressing that understanding in the voice.

Regarding tone, what elements do you change when working with an African American chorus?

Willoughby: I often have to work on creating a unified blend within each section and between sections; the concept of singing longer phrases, using the breath correctly; vowel unification and alignment (which is also part of the "blend"); rhythmic precision in singing the score; mindfully applying or omitting vocal weight to words and phrases; enunciation; and tuning chords. One thing I rarely have to work on is a concept of the individual rhythmic pulse or the communal rhythmic impetus. Almost everyone knows how to clap, tap, and step together!

Armstrong: The two primary issues that I often find myself facing are weight of sound and tonal quality in the color of the sound. Weight of sound is an issue, in part, because of the predominance of gospel music in the African American tradition, especially in the twenty-first century. Often, the model for singers in the contemporary gospel music tradition is the use of a great deal of heavy mechanism or chest voice. Particularly if singers are young or do not have a lot of vocal development, I have to work with them toward a greater use of the light mechanism, and to help them get much more evenness of range and flexibility of voice. After all, many of the arrangements of African American spirituals that are being sung by choirs require a great versatility of vocal technique.

By nature, I think, most African Americans singers (for anatomical and physiological reasons) tend to have a darker hue to our tonal colors. And while that is desirable, many times I want to expand the vocal-timbre palette with which we can interpret these songs, so I work to find some additional shades of vocal colors. (There are some colors that naturally come to the surface as we work with the spirituals, especially as we use aspects of dialect in which we eliminate diphthongs.)

There is also a psychological element inherent in performing spirituals that is specific to African American singers, especially if utilizing dialect. Younger singers in particular (though I've found it also with older singers) see doing these songs as a harkening back to a period in time of which we don't want to be reminded, namely our period as slaves. It behooves me—and puts a great responsibility on me as a music educator—to put these songs in the proper historical and social context for these young singers. To explain to them not only the nobility of these songs but also to find a way to celebrate them, and help the singers understand that our forbearers were great people. And an intelligent people; look how they assimilated a language they were never taught!

What do you do to establish rhythmic energy with your choruses when singing spiritual arrangements?

Willoughby: A variety of tools, such as those outlined below, is used to create rhythmic awareness, internalize the personal and communal rhythm of a piece, and sustain rhythmic energy from the beginning to the end of a piece. These techniques have to be applied ruthlessly until they are internalized.

I create a more palpable awareness of the upbeat—the space between the big beats—through foot stomping (on the big beats) and light clapping (upbeats), or vice versa. I also utilize swaying, walking, or marching, if space allows.

Vocally, I ask the singers to sing schwa vowels on their releases if the releases are active, or conversely, to drop the final active consonant, depending upon the word, and enunciate the consonants that launch their phrases with more energy. I include warm-ups that stress rhythmic breathing in a variety of tempi, on and off the beat, in patterns that will take place in the music. I create easy syncopated patterns (lifted from the music) that help create awareness of the piece's rhythm. One part of the chorus may be assigned a tap/clap activity while the other part(s) speak or sing the text rhythmically; then, that activity will be reversed.

Sometimes I have them lip trill in time and up to tempo because they have to breathe deeply to accomplish that request successfully. Then we quickly transfer that energy into rhythmic energy fueled by deeper breathing. I will continue to return to that technique until the chorus is able to access that energy and use it to keep the rhythmic energy alive throughout the work.

In the fast spirituals I really stress the role of the upbeat, the unarticulated upbeat, as a controlling factor in the rhythmic vitality of the piece. In slow spirituals I also stress the inner, ongoing, common pulse by having the chorus intone a smaller, common unit of time to keep the lines moving in time and forward. I use silent clapping and tapping to remind the singers of the rhythmic pulse. And of course, accurate modeling by the conductor is very important.

Armstrong: It is vital for me that melody and rhythm be the crucial pillars of the spiritual. Those have to be stable and transparent to the listener. Three main ideas influence how I approach the rhythmic articulation of the piece. The first is that my interpretation is tied to a type of oratory. I have tended, in the last few years, to look at the performance of the spirituals as a mirror of the preaching style of the African American clergy person. When I look at the typical pattern in preaching, I see a parallel to many of the spiritual settings, especially those that are more celebratory and rhythmic. There is a sense of beginning then building to an emphasis—all related to how the text is set.

This parallel to black preaching style is rampant, I think, in the arrangements that Moses Hogan has done for us, and even in some of Mr. Hairston's spiritual arrangements. When I look at some of the classic arrangements of William Dawson from this vantage point, one in particular stands out: "In His Care-O." In looking at the text, *an' that day when I was a-walkin' down that lonesome road*, I think the context in which Mr. Dawson intended this music to be sung uses the kind of imagery of the old black gospel quartet. This must be a part of my mind's concept in interpreting this music.

The rhythmic energy I have experienced in black preaching style also comes from call and response. More than part of the compositional style, executing this concept depends on the singers adopting an attitude like these great orators. There are certain spirituals that feel particularly like they are preaching. For example, the Hogan setting of "My God Is So High," where the solo voice serves as leader and the chorus serves as the congregational response—it invites a type of rhythmic energy.

Basic tactus also influences my approach to rhythm. I think the danger so often is that we equate rhythm and tempo. When we see more highly intricate rhythms, we forget the tempo, rushing even already-fast tempos. We need to give intricate rhythms more space to occur. It is like Bach; when we see more black notes, we need to sing slower. This a great issue that has to be dealt with.

I also want to tie the rhythm and tactus to the function of the folk song. What type of spiritual is it and what was the function of that spiritual in the life of slave? Was it sung in the field as they were working? Was it sung in the context of a worship experience? Was it, in fact, an outgrowth of more traditional African ritual; how that might affect the tempo? The driving rhythms? As an example, what was Dawson attempting to portray in his setting of "Ezekiel Saw da Wheel"? Was the wheel at the end of the piece a chariot wheel or the train-engine wheel? Both have a certain noise and rhythm. Which do I bring out in interpretation, and how? The inner rhythms that happen at that point take on a different life. When I look at these rhythms, they often have to be more detached, yet with a sense of line. This is the paradox of the spiritual, and part of what makes it such a challenge to perform.

Do you ever encourage movement or body percussion while performing a spiritual?

Willoughby: Occasionally, when it is appropriate to the structure and mood of the spiritual, I will encourage movement. If it is hard to *not* move, tap, or clap, then it's probably appropriate, at least for some of the up-tempo spirituals. I remember this, actually, from my childhood.

I always encourage a relaxed but appropriate posture which is not stiff, but also not casual. I never snap fingers but if claps or thigh or foot taps seem appropriate for a section of the work, we will experiment with it and perhaps incorporate that motion into the performance.

Armstrong: If some consider me less conservative in my use of dialect, they will certainly find me very conservative in my opinions about movement in the performance of the spiritual. I believe most spirituals are body based; I really do. They come out of folk music and they come from a people who were not performing. So much of the music that comes out of the slave song was part of some type of human activity, whether it was work, a devotional aspect, or a children's game. In my performances, I want to encourage that the body is always singing, and I've moved away from the idea that when we get to the concert hall our singers must stand stiff. I hope that if the music has a sense of a body-based activity or motion, whether it's Bach or Mendelssohn, that that is reflected in how the singers are rendering it. But to impose additional body movements such as clapping, such as the type of body movement you find in gospel music—I tend not to do that with the spirituals. In gospel music, yes, but when I think of the more traditional slave song, I find that if the body is free and released and can reflect the general attitude of the music, that is normally sufficient and, in general, respectful of that genre of music.

Where I will take a minor exception to my own general rule is if I think there is an opportunity to use the slave songs in a different function today. I come back again to Dr. Thomas's setting of "Keep Your Lamps!" I have performed this piece as a processional at the St. Olaf Christmas Festival, and groups such as The American Boychoir have also modeled this in their concert programming. There may be many others who have used this piece as a type of processional, too. Because I have often understood, both from Dr. Thomas and from my own study, that these songs might very possibly have been sung as the slaves were in movement from the fields back to the plantations, I think treating it as a procession is actually very much in keeping with what I said earlier about my interpretations being influenced by the daily cultural function of these pieces. In that sense, these songs served as music in motion. So I think a modern-day application where this type of piece is used in procession works very well, and in some ways mirrors its own cultural origins.

Again, though, tradition has been to not use/impose traditional body percussion. I know that composers of certain types of hybrid arrangements might feel that they need to be encouraged by clapping, and I'm not saying that would be wrong, but, for the most part, I allow this music to stand without that.

Who are ten arrangers whose works you have performed and that would suggest to other colleagues?

Willoughby: Offered in no particular order. I love all of these composer/arrangers and have all of their available work in my personal library. It's hard to pick just ten!

- Undine Smith Moore
- Wendell Whalum
- Moses Hogan
- Nathaniel Dett
- Rosephanye Powell
- Albert McNeil
- Roland Carter
- William Dawson
- André Thomas
- Hall Johnson

Armstrong: At the head of my list is André Thomas, because of the quality and style of his arrangements. (This may seem insincere, as I am offering this assessment in his book, and because we have a close personal and professional relationship, but a review of my programs over the past twenty-seven years would confirm the esteem in which I hold his work.) After Dr. Thomas, the works of Moses Hogan appear most frequently on my programs, particularly in the last ten or twelve years. I always am indebted to the legacy given to these two wonderful contemporary composers by the spiritual arrangements of William Dawson, Jester Hairston, Hall Johnson, John Work, Undine Moore, Albert McNeil, Roland Carter, and L.L. Fleming.

In addition to answering the above questions, Anton Armstrong summarized in our interview his thoughts regarding the performance of spirituals.

The final point I wish to emphasize is this music has to be treated with great dignity. The programming of the spiritual is integral. We often like to program this music at the end, and there is not a problem with it being at the end of the program as long as one understands that there are many other spots on the program that a spiritual could fill. It is the music of a proud and noble people; it is music that celebrates life and the power of goodness over the power of evil. I think for the people of the twenty-first century it represents an affirmation by a people who faced great adversity but never lost their dignity. This music is a vehicle to overcome all of the atrocities and injustices of life. This music does and should serve as inspiration for all generations, for young people understand that one can gain strength, comfort, and inspiration from this music. And for many people, this music leads to healing, to restoration of oneself fully in body, mind, spirit, and voice.

Judith Willoughby

Judith Willoughby is the Wanda L. Bass Professor of Conducting and Choral Music Education at Oklahoma City University and Artistic Director of the Canterbury Academy of the Vocal Arts, the youth choral program of the Canterbury Choral Society. She has conducted choruses of all genres and ages for arts series, honor choirs, and all-state and festival choruses in forty-one states as well as the world's major concert halls throughout North America, Europe, the Caribbean, Australia, and Asia. Professor Willoughby conducted the Women's Honor Choir at the 2003 American Choral Directors Association National Convention—the highest honor accorded a conductor by this organization. She has conducted ACDA Eastern, Central, and North Central divisional convention honor choirs and is a popular featured clinician for conferences, workshops, and master classes.

JUDITH WILLOUGHBY

In 1991, Professor Willoughby founded the Temple University Children's Choir, leading it to international prominence. Highlights of her ten years with this ensemble include four trips to Puerto Rico, an appearance at the ACDA National Convention in San Diego, California, in 1997, numerous appearances with the Philadelphia Orchestra, live radio and television broadcasts on National Public Radio, recordings for the Silver Burdett Ginn Series of elementary music textbooks, and an appearance at the Oregon Bach Festival under the baton of Helmut Rilling.

Prof. Willoughby made her choral/orchestral debut at Carnegie Hall in 2006, conducting the Robert Levin edition of Mozart's *Requiem*. Willoughby has also conducted performances of many of the great choral/orchestral masterworks, including Monteverdi's *Vespers* (1610), concert versions of operas including Bizet's *Carmen*, Haydn's *Creation* and late masses, Mendelssohn's *Elijah*, Britten's *War Requiem*, and Fanshawe's *African Sanctus*.

The editor of a choral series published by Alliance Music, Judith Willoughby received her M.M. from Temple University in piano and conducting and her B.M. from Northwestern University. Her principal teachers in conducting include Elaine Brown, Max Rudolph, and William Smith, and in piano, Natalie Hinderas and Gui Mombaerts. Willoughby has taught at Northwestern University, Temple University, and the Summer Institute programs of Eastman School of Music, Westminster Choir College, and Central Connecticut State University.

A strong interest in the intersection of public policy and the arts has fueled Professor Willoughby's continuing service on numerous panels for the National Endowment for the Arts, as well as state and private arts agencies. She also served on the board of Chorus America for nine years, including two years as secretary, and continues her work on that organization's conducting task force. Willoughby is a member of Chorus America, Music Educators National Conference (MENC), International Federation of Choral Music (IFCM), and College Music Society, and is a life member of ACDA.

Anton Armstrong

Anton Armstrong holds a B.M. in vocal performance from St. Olaf College, an M.M. in choral music from the University of Illinois, and a D.M.A. from Michigan State University. After serving on the faculty at Calvin College, Armstrong returned to St. Olaf in 1990.

As conductor of the St. Olaf Choir, he has toured throughout the United States and to Denmark, Norway, Australia, New Zealand, and Central Europe. On May 5, 2005, he and the St. Olaf Choir sang for President George W. Bush, First Lady Laura Bush, and guests at the White House to commemorate The National Day of Prayer. Together with the St. Olaf Orchestra, the choir was heard live on a national broadcast of Garrison Keillor's *A Prairie Home Companion* radio program. Most recently, the choir was seen and heard on the 2005 PBS Christmas special *A St. Olaf Christmas in Norway*. The choir has recorded 11 CDs during Armstrong's tenure as conductor.

In recent years Armstrong has guest conducted such noted ensembles as the Utah Symphony and Symphony Chorus, the Mormon Tabernacle Choir, and the Saint Paul Chamber Orchestra. He has collaborated in concert with Bobby McFerrin and Garrison Keillor and is active as a guest conductor and lecturer throughout North America, Europe, Scandinavia, Korea, Singapore, Australia, New Zealand, and the Caribbean.

ANTON ARMSTRONG

Dr. Armstrong is widely recognized for his work with youth and children's choral music. He began his tenure as conductor of the Oregon Bach Festival Youth Choral Academy in 1998. In 2001 he served as co-conductor of the World Youth Choir sponsored by the International Federation of Choral Music. That same year, he and Maria Guinand of Venezuela co-conducted the inaugural Multi-Cultural Honor Choir at the American Choral Directors Association National Convention. He served for more than 20 years on the summer faculty of the American Boychoir School in Princeton, N.J., where he had once sung as a Boychoir member. He also was conductor of the St. Cecilia Youth Chorale, a 75-voice treble chorus based in Grand Rapids, Michigan, from 1981 to 1990.

In 2007, Armstrong taught in residence at Baylor University in Texas after receiving the 2006 Robert Foster Cherry Award for Great Teaching. He also edits a multicultural choral series for earthsongs publications and co-edits the revised St. Olaf Choral Series for Augsburg Fortress Publishers.

INDEX OF CONCERT SPIRITUALS BY ARRANGER

Title	Voicing / Soloist	Vocal Ranges				Accomp.	Publisher	© Date	Catalog #
		Soprano	Alto	Tenor	Bass				
ALWES, CHESTER L.									
Hold On!	SATB div	$e\flat^1 - a\flat^2$	$a\flat - f^2$	$c - f^1$	$F - c^1$	a cappella	Roger Dean	2000	10/2350R
Plenty Good Room	SATB div	$e\flat^1 - c^2$	$a\flat - e\flat^2$	$C - c^1$	$E\flat - c^1$	a cappella	Roger Dean	1997	10/2348R
Steal Away	SATB div	$a\flat - a\flat^2$	$g - c^1$	$e\flat - g\flat^1$	$E\flat - c^1$	a cappella	Roger Dean	1997	10/2349R
AMES, JEFFERY									
I've Been in the Storm So Long	SATB div. / Alto	$b - g^2$	$a - c^2$	$e - e^1$	$E - e^1$	a cappella	Walton		HL08501602
Joshua Fit de Battle o'Jericho	TTB			$e\flat - g^1$	$B\flat - c\sharp^1$	piano			
Peter, Go Ring-A Dem Bells	SA	$d^1 - g^2$	$c^1 - d^2$			piano, handbells	Walton	2007	WLG-124
BERG, KEN									
Wayfarin' Stranger	SATB	$d^1 - a^2$	$a - d^2$	$d - f^1$	$D - d^1$	a cappella	Choristers Guild	2004	CGA998
BOATNER, EDWARD									
The Angel Rolled the Stone Away	SATB	$a - g^2$		$A - f^1$		a cappella	Colombo	1954	NY1657
Baby Bethlehem	SATB	$a - g^2$		$G - e^1$		a cappella	Colombo	1964	NY2378
Done Made My Vow	SATB / Ten.	$d^1 - g^2$	$b\flat - c^2$	$g - f^1$	$G - a$	piano	McAfee	1979	M1187
Go Tell It on the Mountain	SATB	$c^1 - a\flat^2$		$A\flat - f^1$		piano	McAfee	1979	M1188
Hold On	SATB	$e^1 - g^2$	$b - c^2$	$e - f\sharp^1$	$G - a$	piano	McAfee	1979	M1189
I Want Jesus to Walk with Me	SATB	$f^1 - a\flat^1$	$b\flat - e\flat^2$	$f - f^1$	$F - c^1$	a cappella	Galaxy	1949	1735

Title	Voicing / Soloist	Vocal Ranges				Accomp.	Publisher	© Date	Catalog #
		Soprano	Alto	Tenor	Bass				
In Bright Mansions	SATB	a - f²			A - f	a cappella	Colombo	1964	NY2377
I've Been 'Buked	SATB	b♭ - g²			G - e¹	piano	McAfee	1979	M1190
Lord, I Can't Stay Away	SATB	a - a²			G - f♯¹	a cappella	Hammon	1952	
Oh, What a Beautiful City	SSATBB	d¹ - g²	b - c²	e - f♯¹	A - b	piano	McAfee	1979	M1191
On Ma Journey	SATB / Alto and Ten.	b♭ - e♭²			A♭ - e♭¹	a cappella	Colombo	1956	NY1778
Rise and Shine	SATB	f¹ - g²	a - c²	e - f¹	F - b♭	piano	McAfee	1979	M1192
Sinner Don't Let This Harvest Pass	SATB	a - g²			G - g¹	a cappella	Hammon	1952	
Soon I Will Be Done	SATB	b♭ - a²			G - f	a cappella	Colombo	1949	NY1655
Trampin'	SATB	b - g²			G - e¹	a cappella	Galaxy	1954	2019
When I Get Home	SATB	f¹ - g²	b♭ - c²	e♭ - g♭¹	A♭ - d¹	a cappella	Ricordi	1954	NY1656-9
Who is That Yonder	SATB	f¹ - f² (a2)	c¹ - c²	B♭ - f¹	F - f	a cappella	Ricordi	1954	NY1660-8
You Hear the Lambs A-Crying	SATB / Ten.	a - g♭²			B - g♭¹	a cappella	Ricordi	1952	217
BRAY, JULIE GARDNER									
David's Golden Harp	Two-part	b♭ - e♭²	b♭ - c²			piano	Heritage	1998	15/1378H
Now Let Me Fly	SATB	d - g²	a♭ - d²	D - d¹	B♭ - c♯¹	piano	Heritage	1996	15/1231H
BROWN, JR., UZEE									
Mary Had a Baby	SATB / Sop.	f - g¹	b♭ - d²	D - e♭¹	G - d¹	a cappella	Roger Dean	1984	HRD121
Oh, the Savior's Comin', Hallelu!	SSAA	e♭¹ - a♭²	f - c²			a cappella	Roger Dean	1997	10/1683R
BURLEIGH, HARRY T.									
Behold That Star	SATB	c - g²			F - f	organ	Ricordi	1928	NY785
Couldn't Hear Nobody Pray	SATB / Sop. and Ten.	a - f²			F - a¹	piano	Ricordi	1922	NY278

Title	Voicing / Soloist	Soprano	Alto	Tenor	Bass	Accomp.	Publisher	© Date	Catalog #
De Creation	TTBB				$E\flat - a\flat^1$	a cappella	Ricordi	1922	NY229
De Gospel Train	TTBB			$f - b\flat'$	$E\flat - d^1$	piano	Ricordi	1921	NY210
Didn't My Lord Deliver Daniel?	SATB	$b\flat - g^2$			$G - f$	a cappella	G. Schirmer	1916	6505
Everytime I Feel de Spirit	SATB / Alto and Bar.	$a - f^2$			$F - f$	a cappella	Ricordi	1925	FC488
Ezekiel Saw de Wheel	SATB	$f - g^2$			$G - f$	a cappella	Ricordi	1927	NY700
Ezekiel Saw de Wheel	SATB	$d\flat^1 - e\flat^2$			$E\flat - f$	a cappella	Ricordi	1928	NY768
Ezekiel Saw de Wheel	SSA	$a - a^2$				a cappella	Ricordi	1927	NY699
Go Tell It on the Mountain	SATB	$a - g^2$			$G - e^1$	organ	Ricordi	1929	NY817
Hear de Lamb A-Cryin'	SATB / Alto and Bar.	$c^1 - a^2$			$E - g^1$	a cappella	Belwin Mills	1927	NY658
Heav'n, Heav'n	SATB	$b\flat - d^2$			$E\flat - f$	piano	Ricordi	1921	NY122
Hold On	SATB	$g - g\sharp^2$			$E - f\sharp^2$	a cappella	Ricordi	1938	NY1113
I Hope My Mother Will Be There	SATB	$c^1 - f^2$			$A\flat - d\flat^1$	a cappella	Ricordi	1924	NY414
I've Been in de Storm So Long	SATB	$a - g^2$			$G - g^1$	a cappella	Ricordi	1944	NY1310
Little Child of Mary	SSA / Sop.	$b\flat - f^2$	$g - g^1$			piano	Ricordi	1940	NY1227-5
Little Mother of Mine	SATB	$c^1 - a^2$			$F - g^1$	piano	Ricordi	1929	NY952
My Lord, What a Mornin'	SATB	$e\flat^1 - a\flat^2$	$b\flat - c^2$	$f - f$	$E\flat - d^1$	a cappella	Belwin Mills	1924	FC412
Nobody Knows the Trouble I've Seen	SATB	$b\flat - a\flat^2$			$E\flat - a\flat^1$	a cappella	Belwin Mills	1924	FCC406
O Lord Have Mercy on Me	TTBB			$d - g^1$	$F - d^1$	a cappella	Ricordi	1935	NY1974-5
Oh Peter go ring-a dem bells	SSA	$c^1 - a\flat^2$	$g - d^2$			piano	Ricordi	1925	NY447

Title	Voicing / Soloist	Soprano	Alto	Tenor	Bass	Accomp.	Publisher	© Date	Catalog #
The Promised Land	SATB / Alto	b♭ - g²			E♭ - f¹	piano	Ricordi	1929	NY831
Scandalize My Name	TTBB			E♭ - g¹	E♭ - g¹	a cappella	Ricordi	1922	NY229
Sometimes I Feel Like a Motherless Child	SSA	a - a²				piano	Ricordi	1949	116543
Steal Away	SATB	b♭ - g²			G - f♯¹	a cappella	Ricordi	1924	NY422
'Tis Me, O Lord	TTBB			F - f¹	F - f¹	a cappella	Ricordi	1924	NY424
Two Negro Spirituals						a cappella	G. Schirmer	1913	5815
Deep River	SATB	e¹ - f♯²	b - d²	e - d¹	A - d¹				
Dig My Grave	SATB	e♭¹ - f²	c¹ - d²	e♭ - f¹	E♭ - c¹				
Wade in de Water	SATB	c¹ - a♭²		F - f¹	F - f¹	a cappella	Ricordi	1925	NY487
Walk Together Children	SSA or TTB	b - g²		B - g¹		a cappella	Ricordi	1938	NY1118
Were You There?	SATB	f - g²	b♭ - f¹	f - g♭¹	E♭ - d¹	a cappella	Belwin Mills	1927	FCC 00423
Were You There?	SSA	g - a♭²				a cappella	Ricordi	1927	NY693
Were You There?	SATB	f¹ - b♭²	b♭ - c²	f - g♭¹	E♭ - d¹	a cappella	Ricordi	1924	NY423
You Goin' to Reap Jus' What You Sow	SATB	a - g²			F - f¹	a cappella	Ricordi	1938	NY1134
BUTLER, MARK									
Glory Hallelujah to the New Born King	SATB div. / Ten.	e¹ - d³	c¹ - e²	e - a¹	G - d¹	a cappella	Hinshaw	2004	HMC1995
Sinner, Please Don't Let This Harvest Pass	SATB div. / Sop. and Ten.	d¹ - e²	a - e²	d - g¹	F - c¹	a cappella	Hinshaw	2006	HMC2056
Wade in the Water	SATB div. / solo	e¹ - c³	b♭ - f²	c - g¹	F - e♭¹	a cappella	Hinshaw	2006	

Title	Voicing / Soloist	Vocal Ranges				Accomp.	Publisher	© Date	Catalog #
		Soprano	Alto	Tenor	Bass				
CAREY, COURTNEY									
Lord, I Want Two Wings	SATB	e♭1 – a♭2	c1 – d♭2	f – a♭1	F – c1	a cappella	Roger Dean	2005	15/1960R
CAREY, PAUL									
Ain' Dat A-Rockin' All Night?	SATB div. / Sop.	c1 – e2	b – d2	e – d1	F – a	a cappella	Roger Dean	2007	15/2309R
CARTER, ROLAND									
Give Me Jesus	SATB	e♭1 – g2	b♭ – c2	g – f1	F – d♭1	a cappella	Mar-Vel	1979	
Go, Tell It on the Mountain	SATB / Sop. or Ten.	d♭1 – a♭2	c1 – d2	e♭ – f1	A♭ – d♭2	a cappella	Mar-Vel	1988	
I Want to Die Easy	SATB	e1 – a2	b – c2	f♯ – e1	E – e1	a cappella	Mar-Vel	1978	
Steal Away	SATB / Alto or Bar.	d1 – g2	g – d2	d – g1	E – e1	a cappella	Mar-Vel	1979	
You Must Have That True Religion	SATB / Sop.	a – a2		F – f1		a cappella	Mar-Vel	1979	
CURTIS, MARVIN									
By An' By	SATB	a – d2		G – f♯		a cappella	manuscript		
Great Day	SATB	f1 – a2	b♭ – c2	f – f1	F – d1	a cappella	Mark Foster	1986	MF 0285
Home In-a Dat Rock	SATB	a – a2	a – d2	G – e1	G – d1	piano	Fostco	1987	MF 290
Roll, Jordan, Roll	SATB	d1 – b2	a – d2	d – g1	F♯ – e1	a cappella	Fostco	1989	MF 2040
DANDRIDGE, DAMON H.									
Git on Boa'd	TTBB / Ten.			b♭ – b♭1	F – b♭	a cappella	manuscript		
I Know I've Been Changed	SATB div. / Sop.	d♭1 – g2	b♭ – d2	f – g1	G – c1	a cappella	Alliance	2000	AMP-0370
I'm Gonna Wait on the Lord	SSAA	c1 – a2	e – c2			a cappella	Alliance	2006	AMP-0666

Title	Voicing / Soloist	Vocal Ranges				Accomp.	Publisher	© Date	Catalog #
		Soprano	Alto	Tenor	Bass				
My God is a Rock	SATB div. / Bass	c¹ – g²	a – c#²	e – g¹	G – e¹	a cappella	Alliance	2002	AMP-0458
Rockin' Jerusalem	SATB div.	e¹ – a²	c¹ – d²	g# – f¹	G# – d¹	a cappella	Alliance	2002	AMP-0481
Witness	SATB div. / Sop. and Ten.	e – a♭²	b♭ – f²	f – a♭¹	F – c¹	a cappella	Alliance	2006	AMP-0650
DAWSON, WILLIAM L.									
Ain'-A That Good News	SATB	d¹ – a²	a – c²	c – g¹	F – d¹	a cappella	Kjos	1937	T103A
Ain'-A That Good News	TTBB			c – a¹	F – e¹	a cappella	Kjos	1937	T104A
Ain'-A That Good News	SSAA	d¹ – a²	f – c²			a cappella	Kjos	1937	T140
Behold That Star	SATB / Sop. and Ten.	d¹ – a²	c¹ – c²	f – f¹	F – c¹	a cappella	Kjos	1946	T111
Ev'ry Time I Feel the Spirit	SATB	e♭¹ – a♭²	b♭ – e♭²	e♭ – e♭¹	G – e♭¹	a cappella	Kjos	1946	T117
Ev'ry Time I Feel the Spirit	SSAA	b – a²	g – e²			a cappella	Kjos	1946	T126
Ev'ry Time I Feel the Spirit	TTBB / Bar.			e♭ – b♭²	E♭ – e♭¹	a cappella	Kjos	1946	T125
Ezekiel Saw De Wheel	SATB	f¹ – b♭²	b♭ – e♭²	f – g²	F – e♭¹	a cappella	Kjos	1942	T110
Feed-A My Sheep	SATB	b♭ – a²	g – c²	c# – f¹	F – c¹	piano	Kjos	1971	T134
Feed-A My Sheep	SSA	b♭ – a²	g – c²			piano	Kjos	1971	T135
Feed-A My Sheep	TTBB			d – a¹	D – d¹	piano	Kjos	1971	T133
Hail Mary	SATB	d¹ – g²	a – c²	B – f¹	G – e¹	a cappella	Kjos	1949	T112
Hail Mary	TTBB			d – g¹	D – d¹	a cappella	Kjos	1949	T113
I Wan' To Be Ready	SATB / Alto and Bar.	b – b♭²	a♭ – e¹	c – b♭¹	E – e♭¹	piano	Kjos	1967	T127A

Title	Voicing / Soloist	Vocal Ranges				Accomp.	Publisher	© Date	Catalog #
		Soprano	Alto	Tenor	Bass				
I Wan'To Be Ready	SSAA / Sop. and Alto	c♯1 – b♭2	g – e♭2			piano	Kjos	1967	T129A
I Wan'To Be Ready	TTBB / Ten. and Bar.			b♭ – b♭1	E – e♭1	piano	Kjos	1967	T128A
In His Care-O	SATB	c♯1 – a2	b♭ – d2	e♭ – g1	B♭ – d1	a cappella	Kjos	1961	T122
In His Care-O	TTBB			B – a1	F – c1	a cappella	Kjos	1961	T123
Jesus Walked This Lonesome Valley	SATB	d1 – g2	g – b1	c – g1	G – e1	piano	Warner Bros.	1927	G821
Jesus Walked This Lonesome Valley	SSA	b – g2	g – g1			piano	Warner Bros.	1927	G823
King Jesus Is A-Listening	TTBB			e♭ – g1	A♭ – d1	a cappella	FitzSimmons	1929	4025
Lit'l' Boy Chile	SATB / Sop., Bar, and Bass	c1 – f2	a – d2	d – g1	F – b	a cappella	Kjos	1947	T120
Mary Had a Baby	SATB	d1 – g2	g – c2	d – g1	E – d1	a cappella	Kjos	1947	T118
Mary Had a Baby	TTBB / Ten.			d – g1	E – d1	a cappella	Kjos	1947	T119
My Lord What a Mourning	SATB	b – g♯2	g♯ – c1	e – f♯1	E – c♯1	a cappella	FitzSimmons	1954	2009
Oh, What a Beautiful City	SATB	d1 – a2	c1 – c2	e – a1	F – c1	a cappella	Kjos	1934	T100
Soon Ah Will Be Done	SATB	b – f♯2	b – d2	f♯ – f♯1	B – d1	a cappella	Kjos	1934	T102A
Soon Ah Will Be Done	TTBB			d – g1	G – d1	a cappella	Kjos	1934	T101A
Steal Away	SATB	e1 – g2	a – d2	c – f1	F – d1	a cappella	Kjos	1942	T108
Steal Away	TTBB			d – a1	D – e1	a cappella	Kjos	1942	T109
Swing Low, Sweet Chariot	SATB	e♭1 – f2	c1 – c2	e♭ – e♭1	A♭ – a♭	a cappella	Kjos	1949	T114
Swing Low, Sweet Chariot	SSA / Sop.	d1 – d2	g – g1			a cappella	Kjos	1946	T116
Swing Low, Sweet Chariot	TTBB			e♭ – a♭1	E♭ – a♭	a cappella	Kjos	1946	T115
There is a Balm in Gilead	SATB / Sop.	e1 – d2	a – a1	e – f♯1	D – c♯1	a cappella	Kjos	1939	T105

Title	Voicing / Soloist	Soprano	Alto	Tenor	Bass	Accomp.	Publisher	© Date	Catalog #
There is a Balm in Gilead	SSA / Sop.	$e\flat^1 - e\flat^2$	$a\flat - a\flat^1$			a cappella	Kjos	1939	T107
There is a Balm in Gilead	TTBB / Ten.			$e\flat - g^1$	$F - b\flat$	a cappella	Kjos	1939	T106
There's a Lit'l'Wheel A-Turnin' In My Heart	SATB	$c^1 - f^2$	$g - d^2$	$c - g^1$	$F - d^1$	a cappella	Kjos	1949	T121
You Got to Reap Just What You Sow	SATB	$e^1 - g^2$	$b - d^2$	$d - g^1$	$G - b\flat$	piano	Kjos	1928	T142
You Got to Reap Just What You Sow	TTBB			$d - a^1$	$E - e^1$	piano	Kjos	1928	T143
You Got to Reap Just What You Sow	SSAA	$b - g^2$	$g - e^2$			piano	Kjos	1928	T144
Zion's Walls	SATB / Sop.	$b\flat - a^2$	$g - d^2$	$B\flat - g^1$	$F - d^1$	a cappella	Kjos	1961	T124
DE PAUR, LEONARD									
All 'Round de Glory Manger	TTBB			$F - b\flat^1$		a cappella	Lawson-Gould	1958	709
A City Called Heaven	SATBB	$c^1 - a\flat^2$	$c^1 - c^2$	$c - g^1$	$F - c^1$	a cappella	Warner Bros.	1959	
Git on Down Dat Road	TTBB			$A\flat - a\flat^1$		a cappella	Library of Congress	1963	
Nobody Knows de Trouble I See	TTBB			$E - g\sharp^1$		a cappella	Lawson-Gould	1954	524
Oh, Po' Little Jesus	TTBB			$f - a^1$	$F - b\flat$	a cappella	Lawson-Gould	1958	710
Swing Low, Sweet Chariot	TTBB			$D - g^1$		a cappella	Lawson-Gould	1954	523
DENNARD, BRAZEAL WAYNE									
Great Day	SATB / solo	$f^1 - f^2$	$c^1 - b\flat^1$	$a - f^1$	$F - f$	a cappella	Shawnee	1990	A-1895
Hush! Somebody's Callin' My Name	Two-part	$f^1 - d^2$	$c^1 - d^2$			opt. piano	Shawnee	1986	EA-144

| Title | Voicing / Soloist | Vocal Ranges | | | | Accomp. | Publisher | © Date | Catalog # |
		Soprano	Alto	Tenor	Bass				
Lord, I Want to Be a Christian	SATB div.	c¹ – g²	a – d²	e – e¹	E – c♯¹	a cappella	Alliance	1994	AMP 0029
Steal Away	TTBB			c – a¹	F – d¹	a cappella	Shawnee	1992	C-279
DETT, R. NATHANIEL									
Dett Collection of Spirituals (originals, settings, anthems, motets)	SATB	a – a²	a♭ – e²	b – g¹	D – d¹	a cappella and piano	Warner Bros.	1936	
Group 1									#13
Group 2									#14
Group 3									#15
Group 4									#16
Done Paid My Vow to the Lord	SSA / Alto and Bar.	g – g²				piano	Presser	1919	322-35007
Don't You Weep No More, Mary	SATB	a – a²	a – a²		D – f¹	a cappella	G. Schirmer	1930	7395
Drink to Me Only With Thine Eyes	SATB	g – g²	g – g²		G – g¹	a cappella	J. Fischer	1933	6700
I'll Never Turn Back No More	SATB	c – a²	a – d²	c – g¹	F – e¹	a cappella	J. Fischer	1918	4435-8
The Lamb	SSA	c♯ – g♯²				a cappella	J. Fischer	1938	7401
Listen to the Lambs	SATB / Sop.	c¹ – a²	a – d²	c – g¹	F – d¹	a cappella	G. Schirmer	1914	
Rise Up Shepherd and Follow	SATB / Sop. and Ten.	g – d♭²			E♭ – d♭¹	piano	J. Fischer	1936	7218
Rise Up Shepherd and Follow	TTBB			G – f¹		piano	J. Fischer	1936	7219
Sit Down, Servant, Sit Down	SATB	c¹ – g²			G – g¹	piano	G. Schirmer	1932	7931
Somebody's Knocking at Your Door	SSA	f♯ – g²				piano	John Church Co.	1921	35186

Title	Voicing / Soloist	Vocal Ranges				Accomp.	Publisher	© Date	Catalog #
		Soprano	Alto	Tenor	Bass				
Somebody's Knocking at Your Door	SATB	g - a²			D - g¹	piano	John Church Co.	1939	35197
There's a Meeting Here Tonight	SSA	g - g²				piano	John Church Co.	1921	35008
Wasn't That a Mighty Day?	SATB / Alto and Bar.	a - a²			F - f¹	a cappella	G. Schirmer	1933	7712
Weeping Mary	SATB / Sop.	g - a²			F - a¹	a cappella	J. Fischer	1918	4434
DILWORTH, ROLLO									
Great Day!	Two-part	e¹ - g²	b - e²			piano	Hal Leonard	2000	8703264
I've Been 'Buked, Children!	SSA	c¹ - a²	b - e²			piano	Santa Barbara	2004	SBMP 547
I've Got Shoes	Two-part	e¹ - f²	c - d²			piano	Hal Leonard	2001	8551500
Lay Your Healing Hands Upon Me	SATB / solo	e¹ - e²	a - c²	a - e¹	A - c¹	piano	Hal Leonard	2002	8711370
My Lord, What a Morning	4-part Treble	e♭¹ - f²	c¹ - d²			piano	Plymouth	1999	21-20263
No Rocks A-Cryin'	SATB div.	a - e²	a - d²	A - f¹	F - c¹	piano	Hal Leonard	2001	9711307
Walk in Jerusalem	SATB	c¹ - a²	c¹ - c²	c - g¹	G - f¹	piano	Hal Leonard	2004	8744360
FARROW, LARRY									
Deep River	SATB / Sop. or Ten.	c¹ - a²	a - c²	d - f¹	F - f¹	a cappella	Gentry	1983	JG-507
Ev'ry Time I Feel the Spirit	SATB	d¹ - g²	b - e²	B - e¹	E - e¹	piano, guitar, bass guitar	Gentry	1982	JG-482

Title	Voicing / Soloist	Vocal Ranges				Accomp.	Publisher	© Date	Catalog #
		Soprano	Alto	Tenor	Bass				
Ev'ry Time I Feel the Spirit	SSAA	b - g²	e - b¹			piano, guitar, bass guitar	Gentry	1982	JG-526
My Lord, What a Mornin'	SSATBB	d#¹ - g#²	b - g#¹	f# - g#¹	E - c#¹	a cappella	Gentry	1983	JG0509
Swing Low, Sweet Chariot	SATB / Alto	b - a♭²	g - b♭¹	e - e¹	F - d¹	a cappella	Gentry	1982	JG-484
When the Saints Go Marching In	SATB	d¹ - f#²	b - d²	e - f#¹	G - f¹	piano, guitar, bass guitar, tambourine	Gentry	1982	JG-481
FOUNTAIN, ROBERT									
Ride On, King Jesus!	SATB div. / Sop. or Ten.	c¹ - c³	b♭ - f²	e - a¹	F - d¹	a cappella	Roger Dean	2000	15/1576R
Roll, Jordan, Roll	SATB div.	f¹ - b♭²	c¹ - e♭²	d - b♭¹	F - e♭¹	a cappella	Roger Dean	1998	15/1398R
GIBBS, STACEY V.									
Certain'ly Lord	SATB	c¹ - a²	b - c²	e - f¹	G - a	a cappella	Alliance	2006	AMP-0664
De Gospel Train	SATB	e♭¹ - b♭²	b♭ - d²	d - g¹	E♭ - d¹	a cappella	Alliance	2005	AMP-0574
I Don' Feel No Ways Tired	SATB	c¹ - b♭²	b♭ - e♭²	g - g¹	F - c¹	a cappella	Alliance	2006	AMP-0580
Lord, If I Got My Ticket	SATB div. / solo	f#¹ - a²	b - c#²	f# - f#¹	F# - c#¹	a cappella	Gentry	2004	JG2320
See Dat Babe	SATB div.	e♭¹ - c³	b♭ - c²	f - a♭¹	F - c¹	a cappella	Gentry	2005	JG2358
Somebody's Knockin' At Yo' Do'	SATB div. / solo	d¹ - a²	g - d¹	d - f¹	E♭ - b	a cappella	Gentry	2004	JG2321
Way Over in Beulah Lan'	SATB div.	c¹ - c³	b♭ - c²	f - f¹	F - d¹	a cappella	Gentry	2007	JG2370

Title	Voicing / Soloist	Vocal Ranges				Accomp.	Publisher	© Date	Catalog #
		Soprano	Alto	Tenor	Bass				
GILPIN, GREG									
Oh, Won't You Sit Down?	SATB	d¹ - f²	c#¹ - c²	d - f¹	B - c¹	piano	Heritage	2007	15/2233H
Oh, Won't You Sit Down?	SAB	d¹ - f²	d¹ - c²		eb - eb¹	piano	Heritage	2007	15/2232H
HAILSTORK, ADOLPHUS C. III									
Crucifixion (He never said a mumblin' word)	SATB div.	b - a²	f# - e²	e - g¹	G - e¹	a cappella	Presser	1994	312-41646
HAIRSTON, JESTER									
Amen	SATB / solo	d¹ - g²	b - bb¹	g - f#¹	G - bb	a cappella	Bourne	1957	CB 1022
Amen	SAB / Sop.	f - eb²	c¹ - f#²	a - a¹	c - e¹	piano	Bourne	1957	103945
Amen	TTBB / Ten.			d - g¹	G - d¹	a cappella	Bourne	1957	103947
Angels Rolled de Stone Away	SATB	f - bb²	c#¹ - bb¹	f - f¹	F - bb	piano	Bourne	1949	105436
Band of Angels	SATB	eb¹ - ab²		Ab - f¹		a cappella	Warner	1940	W3671
Crucifixion	SATB	d#¹ - f#²	f# - d#²	c - g¹	F# - a	a cappella	Bourne	1952	28616
Deep River	SATB / Alto	f# - f²	b - d²	a - f#¹	F# - c#¹	a cappella	Schumann Music Co.	1951	31826
Dis Train	SSATB	c¹ - f²	b - b¹	c - e¹	F - c¹	a cappella	Bourne	1954	32656
Don't Be Weary, Traveler	SSATB	c¹ - g²	g - c²	c - e¹	G - e¹	a cappella	Bourne	1955	CB 1022
Elijah Rock	SSATB	d¹ - g²	g - bb¹	d - f¹	F - d¹	a cappella	Bourne	1955	37376
Elijah Rock	SSA	d¹ - g²	f - b¹			a cappella	Bourne	1956	37378
Free at Last	SATB	d¹ - a²	d¹ - b¹	g - e¹	G - d¹	a cappella	Bourne	1960	306806
Go Down in de Lonesome Valley	SSATB div.	c¹ - ab²	g - e²	c - eb¹	F - eb¹	a cappella	Bourne	1965	CB 1022
Go Tell it on the Mountain	SATB	d¹ - g²	d¹ - d²	f - c¹	G - g	a cappella	Bourne	1967	47356

Title	Voicing / Soloist	Vocal Ranges Soprano	Alto	Tenor	Bass	Accomp.	Publisher	© Date	Catalog #
God's Gonna Buil' Up Zion's Wall	SATB	f¹ - a♭²	c¹ - d²	g - g¹	F - e♭¹	a cappella	Bourne	1960	2938-6
Goin' Down dat Lonesome Road	SATB	f♯¹ - f♯²	d¹ - b¹	d - f	G - d¹	a cappella	Bourne	1965	48006
Great God A'Mighty	SSATB	g¹ - b♭²	c♯¹ - d²	g - g¹	G - d¹	a cappella	Bourne	1959	2914-7
Hand Me Down	SATB	e¹ - g²	b - b¹	f - e¹	G - c¹	a cappella	Bourne	1961	S-1006
Hold On!	SATB div. / solo	f¹ - a♭²	a♭ - c²	f - f¹	F - e¹	a cappella	Bourne	1955	CB 1022
I Can Tell the World	SATB	e¹ - a²	c¹ - c²	f - f¹	c - d¹	a cappella	Bourne	1959	58566
I Want Jesus	SATB	g¹ - g²	g - b¹	g - g¹	G - d¹	a cappella	Bourne	1958	B206151-357
In Dat Great Gittin' Up Mornin'	SATB / Ten.	d¹ - b♭²	g - b♭¹	g - g¹	A♭ - b♭	a cappella	Bourne	1952	65166
It's All Over Me	SATB / Alto	d¹ - g²	c¹ - d²	f - g¹	F - d¹	a cappella	Bourne	1952	69206
Joshua Fit de Battle o'Jericho	SATB	e♭¹ - b²	d¹ - e♭²	e - a¹	F - d¹	a cappella	Bourne	1952	71426
Let the Church Roll On	SSAA	a♭¹ - f²	a♭ - b¹			a cappella	Bourne	1951	75488
Little David, Play on Your Harp	SSAATB	d¹ - a♭²	b - e²	e♭ - e¹	G - e¹	a cappella	Hal Leonard	1976	8601000
Live A-Humble	SSATBB	e¹ - g²	c♯¹ - b♭¹	f - e♯¹	A - c♯¹	a cappella	Bourne	1955	2665-6
Mary, Mary, Where is Your Baby?	SATB	d¹ - g²	b♭ - b♭¹	f - d¹	G - d¹	a cappella	Bourne	1950	82156
Mary's Little Boy Chile	SATB / solo	g¹ - f♯²	c♯¹ - b¹	a - e¹	G♯ - e¹	piano	Schumann Music Co.	1956	S-1024
Mornin'	SATB / Tenor	a - b²		G - g¹		a cappella	Schumann Music Co.	1952	S-1013
Oh, Rocka My Soul	SSATTBB	f¹ - a²	c¹ - b¹	f - a♭¹	F - d¹	a cappella	Bourne	1950	CB 1022
Poor Man Lazrus	TTBB			d - g¹	G - d¹	a cappella	Bourne	1955	2653-7
Poor Man Lazrus	SSA	d¹ - g²	b - d²			a cappella	Bourne	1955	103938
Poor Man Lazrus	SATTBB	d¹ - g²	d¹ - d²	d - g¹	G - d¹	a cappella	Bourne	1955	103936

Title	Voicing / Soloist	Vocal Ranges				Accomp.	Publisher	© Date	Catalog #
		Soprano	Alto	Tenor	Bass				
Rise Up, Shepherd and Follow	SATB	b – d²	a – b¹	d – e¹	A – b	a cappella	Bourne	1974	241706
Scandalized My Name	SSATB	f¹ – b♭²	c¹ – d²	f – e¹	B♭ – d¹	a cappella	Bourne	1959	2917-4
Sometimes I Feel Like a Motherless Child	SATB / Alto	f¹ – b♭²	f – d♭²	f – a♭¹	F – d♭¹		Bourne	1952	120846
Steal Away	SATTBB / solo	d¹ – a♭²	d♯¹ – e²	f♯ – g♯¹	F♯ – e¹	a cappella	Schumann Music Co.	1951	S 1007
Tataleo	SATB	g¹ – e²	c¹ – c²	f – e♯¹	c – c¹	a cappella	Bourne	1971	J-15
Wade in de Water	SATB	b – g²		E – e¹		a cappella	Warner	1950	W3670
What Kind O' Shoes You Gonna Wear?	SATB	d¹ – f²	b♭ – d²	f – f¹	B♭ – c¹	a cappella	Bourne	1959	2867-9
Who'll Be a Witness for My Lord	SATB	f¹ – a²	d¹ – e♭²	f – f¹	B♭ – e♭¹	a cappella	Bourne	1959	146506
You Better Mind	SSATB	e¹ – b²	b¹ – e²	e♭ – e¹	G – d¹	a cappella	Bourne	1965	CB 1022
HALLORAN, JACK									
Witness	SSAATTBB	f♯¹ – g²	a – d²	d – g¹	F♯ – d¹	a cappella	Gentry	1986	JG2010
HARRIS, ROBERT									
Go Down, Moses	SATB / Sop. And Ten.	e – f♯²	a – e²	d – g¹	F♯ – e¹	a cappella	Oxford	1988	94.336
Let Us Break Bread Together	SSAA / Sop.	f – a♭²				a cappella / opt. flute	manuscript	1969	
This Little Light of Mine	Two-part	e¹ – g²	b – e²			piano	Boosey & Hawkes	1997	OCTB6921
HOGAN, MOSES									
Ain't that Good News	SATB	d¹ – f²	c¹ – c²	c – e¹	F – e¹	piano	Hal Leonard	1999	8742075
The Battle of Jericho	SATB	c¹ – b♭²	a♭ – d♭²	c – a♭	F – c¹	a cappella	Marks	1984	

Title	Voicing / Soloist	Vocal Ranges				Accomp.	Publisher	© Date	Catalog #
		Soprano	Alto	Tenor	Bass				
Cert'nly Lord	SATBdDiv. / solo	c¹ – a²	a – c²	e – f¹	F – d¹	a cappella	Hal Leonard	2002	8743356
Climbin' Up the Mountain	SATB div.	e♭¹ – a♭²	a♭ – c¹	e♭ – g♭¹	E – c¹	a cappella	Hal Leonard	2004	8744319
De Blin' Man Stood on de Road An' Cried	SATB div.	f¹ – f²	a♭ – d¹	b – f¹	E♭ – c¹	a cappella	Hal Leonard	2000	8703261
Deep River	SATB div.	b♭ – b♭²	f – a♭²	e♭ – g¹	E♭ – e¹	a cappella	Hal Leonard	2004	8744331
Didn't My Lord Deliver Daniel	SATB / div. small group	f¹ – b♭²	b♭ – d²	d – b♭¹	G – d¹	a cappella	Hal Leonard	1999	8703209
Do, Lord, Remember Me	SATB div.	d¹ – g²	a – c¹	c – d¹	G – g	a cappella	Hal Leonard	2001	8703326
Down by the Riverside	SATB	e♭¹ – d♭²	c¹ – d♭²	e♭ – a♭¹	A♭ – d♭¹	a cappella	Hal Leonard	1999	8703201
Elijah Rock	SATB div.	a – b²	a – e²	a – a¹	E – e¹	a cappella	Hal Leonard	1994	8705532
Ev'ry Time I Feel the Spirit	SATB	c♯¹ – e²	c♯¹ – c♯²	e – e¹	B – c♯¹	piano	Hal Leonard	1999	8742075
Exekiel Saw de Wheel	SATB div.	d¹ – a²	b♭ – e♭²	f – a♭¹	E♭ – c¹	a cappella	Hal Leonard	2001	8703327
Give Me Jesus	SATB div. / solo	e♭¹ – g²	b♭ – b♭¹	e♭ – g¹	D♭ – e♭¹	a cappella	Hal Leonard	1999	8703202
Glory, Glory, Glory to the Newborn King	SATB div.	c¹ – c³	a – d²	c – f¹	F – d¹	a cappella	Hal Leonard	2000	8742097
Go Down Moses	TTBB / Solo			f♯ – b¹	F♯ – d¹	a cappella	Hal Leonard	1999	8703231
God's Gonna Set This World on Fire	SATB	d¹ – b¹	b – g¹	g – e¹	G – g	piano	Hal Leonard	1999	8742075
Good News, The Chariot's Comin'	SATB div.	c¹ – a♭²	c¹ – c²	e♭ – e♭¹	A♭ – c¹	a cappella	Hal Leonard	2001	8703312
Great Day	SATB / solo	e♭¹ – e♭²	b♭ – g¹	f – f¹	G – b♭	a cappella	Hal Leonard	1997	8741181
Hold On!	SATB div. small group	e♭¹ – c³	c♭¹ – d♭²	f – a♭¹	F – d♭¹	a cappella	Hal Leonard	2002	8703351

Title	Voicing / Soloist	Vocal Ranges				Accomp.	Publisher	© Date	Catalog #
		Soprano	Alto	Tenor	Bass				
I Can Tell the World	SATB div.	$d^1 - b^2$	$g - d^1$	$f - g^1$	$F - d^1$	a cappella	Hal Leonard	1998	8703198
I Couldn't Hear Nobody Pray	SATB div / solo	$d^1 - f^2$	$b\flat - c^2$	$d - f^1$	$F - b\flat$	a cappella	Hal Leonard	1999	8703239
I Got a Home in-a Dat Rock	SATB div. / solo	$c^1 - b\flat^2$	$a\flat - a\flat^1$	$c - f^1$	$D\flat - c^1$	a cappella	Hal Leonard	1999	8703228
I Got a Robe	SATB / solo	$d^1 - g^2$	$b - b^1$	$d - d^1$	$G - g$	a cappella	Hal Leonard	1997	8741179
I Know the Lord's Laid His Hands on Me	SATB div. / solo	$c^1 - f^2$	$b\flat - c^2$	$f - f^1$	$F - f$	a cappella	Hal Leonard	1999	8703232
I Stood on the River of Jordan	SATB	$c^1 - c^2$	$f - a^1$	$f - e\flat^1$	$F - g$	a cappella	Hal Leonard	1997	8741178
I Want Jesus to Walk with Me	SATB / solo	$e\flat^1 - a\flat^2$	$d\flat^1 - a\flat$	$e\flat - g^1$	$F - d\flat$	a cappella	Hal Leonard	1997	8740785
I Want to Be Ready	SATB	$c^1 - f^2$	$a\flat - b\flat^1$	$f - f^1$	$F - b\flat$	a cappella	Hal Leonard	2001	8703310
I Want to Thank You, Lord	SATB / Sop. Or Ten.	$b\flat - e\flat^2$	$a\flat - d\flat^2$	$f - e\flat^1$	$E\flat - d\flat^1$	a cappella	Hal Leonard	1995	8740200
I'm Gonna Sing 'Til the Spirit Moves in my Heart	SATB div.	$f - b\flat^2$	$f - c^2$	$f - a\flat^1$	$F - c\flat^1$	a cappella	Hal Leonard	1995	8740284
Jesus Lay Your Head in the Window	SATB div. / Alto or Bass	$e^1 - c^3$	$a - g^1$	$e - e^1$	$E - e$	a cappella / flute	Hal Leonard	1998	8703199
Lily of the Valley	SSAA div.	$c\sharp^1 - a^2$	$g\sharp - a$			a cappella	Hal Leonard	2002	8743330
Little David, Play on Your Harp	SATB	$d^1 - g^2$	$b - c^2$	$d - g^1$	$G - c^1$	a cappella	Hal Leonard	1999	8703229
Lord, I Want to be a Christian	SATB	$d^1 - d^2$	$a - a^1$	$d - d^1$	$G - a$	a cappella	Hal Leonard	1999	8742075
My God is So High	SATB / solo	$d^1 - d^2$	$b\flat - a^1$	$d - f^1$	$G - b\flat$	a cappella	Alliance	1995	AMP-0190
My Soul's Been Anchored in the Lord	SATB div.	$e^1 - a^2$	$a - c^2$	$a - a^1$	$F - d^1$	a cappella	Hal Leonard	1999	8703235
No Hidin' Place	SATB div.	$c^1 - a^2$	$a - f^2$	$f - f^1$	$F - e\flat^1$	a cappella	Hal Leonard	2001	8703328

Title	Voicing / Soloist	Vocal Ranges				Accomp.	Publisher	© Date	Catalog #
		Soprano	Alto	Tenor	Bass				
Oh Mary, Don't You Weep, Don't You Mourn	SATB	$c^1 - d^2$	$a - a^1$	$c - f^1$	$F - f$	a cappella	Hal Leonard	2001	8703329
Old Time Religion	SATB / solo	$a\sharp - g^2$	$f\sharp - g^1$	$c\sharp - d^1$	$G - g$	a cappella	Hal Leonard	1995	8740181
Plenty Good Room	TTBB div.			$e - b\flat^1$	$D - f^1$	a cappella	Hal Leonard	2002	8703330
Ride on, King Jesus	SATB div. / solo	$e\flat^1 - b\flat^2$	$b\flat - e\flat^2$	$e\flat - g^1$	$G - e\flat^1$	keyboard	Hal Leonard	1999	8703210
Ride the Chariot	SATB div.	$b\flat - b\flat^2$	$f - b^1$	$b\flat - f^1$	$E\flat - b\flat$	a cappella	Hal Leonard	2001	8703309
A Spiritual Reflection	SATB div.	$f - g^2$	$b\flat - d^2$	$d - g^1$	$G - c^1$	a cappella	Hal Leonard	2001	8703315
Standin in the Need of Prayer	SATB	$f\sharp - d^2$	$c\sharp - g^1$	$a - d^1$	$G - g$	a cappella	Hal Leonard	1999	8703230
Steal Away	SATB / solo	$f - f^2$	$c^1 - c^2$	$c - f^1$	$F - c^1$	a cappella	Hal Leonard	1999	8703203
Surely He Died on Calvary	SATB div. / solo	$b - e\flat^2$	$g - c^2$	$c - f^1$	$C - c^1$	a cappella	Hal Leonard	2002	8703331
Swing Low, Sweet Chariot	SATB div.	$c^1 - f^2$	$g - a^1$	$c - c^1$	$D\flat - a$	piano, flute	Alliance	1996	AMP-0192
The Battle of Jericho	SATB div.	$c^1 - c^3$	$a\flat - d^2$	$c - f^1$	$F - c^1$	a cappella	Hal Leonard	1996	8703139
There is a Balm in Gilead	SATB div. / solo	$f - f^2$	$c^1 - d^2$	$f - f^1$	$F - b\flat$	a cappella	Hal Leonard	1998	8703200
There's a Man Goin' Round	SSATTB / solo	$e\flat^1 - c^2$	$g - a\flat^1$	$c - e\flat^1$	$E\flat - c^1$	a cappella	Alliance	1996	AMP 0191
This Little Light of Mine	SATB div. / Sop. and Ten.	$e\flat^1 - b\flat^2$	$a\flat - d^2$	$e\flat - f^1$	$E\flat - d^1$	a cappella	Hal Leonard	2002	8743115
Wade in the Water	SATB div. / solo	$g - g^2$	$g - c^2$	$G - f^1$	$G - c^1$	a cappella	Hal Leonard	1997	8741180
Walk Together Children	SATB div.	$d^1 - a^2$	$c^1 - f^2$	$f - a^1$	$F - d^1$	a cappella	Hal Leonard	2001	8703332

Title	Voicing / Soloist	Soprano	Alto	Tenor	Bass	Accomp.	Publisher	© Date	Catalog #
We Shall Walk Through the Valley in Peace	SATB div.	b♭ - g²	g - b¹	e♭ - f¹	E♭ - c¹	a cappella	Hal Leonard	2001	8703314
Who Built the Ark?	SATB div.	d¹ - c³	b♭ - d♭²	f - a♭¹	F - d¹	a cappella	Hal Leonard	2001	8703313
Witness	TTBB div. small group			e - c²	E - d¹	a cappella	Hal Leonard	2002	8743357
You Better Min' How You Talk	SATB	d¹ - d²	a - a¹	c - f¹	F - f	a cappella	Hal Leonard	2001	8703311
JESSYE, EVA									
I Belong to That Band	SATB / Sop. and Bass	b♭ - g²			G - g¹	piano	Skidmore	1965	SK2091
Move! Let Me Shine	SATB	b♭ - a♭²			G - f¹	piano	Skidmore	1965	SK2093
Rock, Mt. Sinai	SATB	c¹ - f²			F - f¹	piano	Skidmore	1965	SK2095
When the Saints Go Marching In	SATB	c¹ - a♭²			B♭ - a♭	piano	Marks	1966	13416-6
Who Is That Yonder?	SATB	c♯¹ - f²			A - f♯¹	piano	Skidmore	1965	SK2096
JOHNSON, HALL									
Cert'nly Lord	SATB / Ten.	c¹ - f²			F - f¹	a cappella	Carl Fischer	1930	CM6641
City Called Heaven	SATB	c♯¹ - f♯²	b - b¹	e - f♯¹	F♯ - c¹	a cappella	Robbins	1958	R3303
Crucifixion	SATB / Ten.	g - g²			D - g¹	a cappella	Carl Fischer	1953	CM 6501
Crucifixion	TTBB			D - d²		a cappella	Carl Fischer	1953	CM6757
Dere's No Hidin' Place Down Dere	SATB	c♯¹ - b♭²			G - g¹	a cappella	Carl Fischer	1930	CM6501
Elijah Rock	SSAATTBB	f¹ - b♭²	a - d²	f - a♭¹	F - f¹	a cappella	G. Schirmer	1956	10354
Fix Me Jesus	SATB / Sop.	d¹ - f²	c¹ - a¹	d - f¹	F - a	a cappella	G. Schirmer	1956	10354
Go Down Moses	SATB / Bar.	d¹ - g²			G - g¹	a cappella	Carl Fischer	1930	CM6739

Title	Voicing / Soloist	Vocal Ranges Soprano	Alto	Tenor	Bass	Accomp.	Publisher	© Date	Catalog #
His Name So Sweet	SATBB	$d^1 - b^2$	$d^1 - g^1$	$b - b^1$	$G - b$	a cappella	Carl Fischer	1935	CM4580
His Name So Sweet	SSA	$a - b^2$				a cappella	Carl Fischer	1935	CM5213
His Name So Sweet	TTBB			$G - b^1$		piano	Carl Fischer	1935	CM2183
Hol' de Light	SATB	$f - f^2$		$F - f^1$		a cappella	Carl Fischer	1959	CM7104
Honor! Honor!	SATBB / Tenor	$e^1 - f\sharp^2$	$b - c^2$	$e - f\sharp^1$	$E - a$	a cappella	G. Schirmer	1935	CM 4579
Honor! Honor!	TTBB			$G\sharp - a^1$		a cappella	Carl Fischer	1935	CM21826
Honor! Honor!	SSA	$b - a^2$				piano	Carl Fischer	1935	CM5212
I Cannot Stay Here by Myself	SATB / Alto	$b - b\flat^2$	$b\flat - b\flat^2$	$E - a^1$		a cappella	Carl Fischer	1940	CM4724
I Couldn't Hear Nobody Pray	SSAATTBB / Sop. and Ten.	$d^1 - a^2$	$c^1 - d^2$	$d - f^1$	$F - d^1$	a cappella	G. Schirmer	1953	10151
I Got Shoes	SATB	$c^1 - e^2$	$c^1 - e^2$		$G - e^1$	a cappella	Robbins	1949	R3413
I'll Never Turn Back No Mo'	SATB	$d^1 - f^2$	$c^1 - b^1$	$g - f^1$	$G - b$	a cappella	Robbins	1949	R3452
I've Been 'Buked	SATB	$c^1 - f^2$	$b\flat - a^1$	$e - e\flat^1$	$F - b$	a cappella	G. Schirmer	1946	9650
Jesus Lay Your Head in de Winder	SATB / Te.	$b\flat - g^2$		$G - e\flat^1$	$G - e\flat^1$	a cappella	Robbins	1930	R3301
Keep a-Inchin' Along	TTBB / Ten.			$E - a^1$	$E - a^1$	a cappella	G. Schirmer	1957	10485
Lord I Want to Be a Christian	SATB / Sop.	$d^1 - g^2$		$G - g^1$	$G - g^1$	a cappella	G. Schirmer	1946	9561
Lord, I Don't Feel Noways Tired	SATB / Ten.	$c^1 - g^2$		$E\flat - g^1$	$E\flat - g^1$	a cappella	Carl Fischer	1930	CM6502
Mary Had a Baby	SATB	$d^1 - e^2$	$d^1 - g^1$	$g - e^1$	$G - c^1$	a cappella	G. Schirmer	1955	10359
Oh Lord, Have Mercy on Me	SATB /Sop.	$a - f^2$		$D - g^1$		a cappella	G. Schirmer	1946	9558
Nobody Knows the Trouble I See	SATB / Ten.	$a\flat - b\flat^2$		$A\flat - a\flat^1$		a cappella	Robbins	1949	R3451
Ride On, Jesus	SATB	$c^1 - a^2$		$F - a^1$		a cappella	G. Schirmer	1957	10483

Title	Voicing / Soloist	Soprano	Alto	Tenor	Bass	Accomp.	Publisher	© Date	Catalog #
Ride On, King Jesus	SATB	a – c³			C – a♭¹	a cappella	Carl Fischer	1951	CM6702
Run Li'l Chillun	SATB / Ten.	a – a²			D – f¹	piano	Robbins	1941	R2164
Scandalize My Name	SATB / Ten.	e¹ – f♯²			A – e♯¹	a cappella	G. Schirmer	1958	10608
Sometimes I Feel Like a Motherless Child	SATB / Alto	a – a²			D – f¹	a cappella	Marks	1956	4007
Steal Away	SSA	b – b²				piano	Carl Fischer	1935	CM5214
Steal Away	SATB	d¹ – b²			G – e¹	a cappella	Carl Fischer	1935	CM4581
Steal Away	TTBB				G – b¹	a cappella	Carl Fischer	1935	CM2184
Trampin'	SATB / Alto	a – a²			F – f¹	a cappella	Marks	1956	4009
Walk Together Children	SATB	d¹ – b²			G – g¹	a cappella	Marks	1956	4006
Way Over in Beluah-Lan'	SATB div. / soli	d¹ – c³	g – d²	f – b¹	G – b	a cappella	Hal Leonard	1956	HL00008006
Way Up in Heaven	SATB	a – g♯²			E – g¹	piano	Robbins	1930	R3300
Were You There?	SATB / Sop. and Ten.	d¹ – g²			G – g¹	a cappella	G. Schirmer	1954	10128
What Kinder Shoes	SATB	d¹ – e²			G – g¹	a cappella	Carl Fischer	1947	CM6209
When I Was Sinking Down	SATB	f – f²	d¹ – c²	f – g♭¹	B♭ – b♭	a cappella	G. Schirmer	1946	9559
Who Built de Ark	TTBB				G – g¹	a cappella	Carl Fischer	1954	CM7444
JOHNSON, JOHN ROSAMOND									
All O' God's Chillun Got Shoes	SATB	e♭¹ – b²	c¹ – b♭¹	g – g♯¹	F – c¹	piano	Handy	1950	HB10
Didn't My Lord Deliver Daniel	SATB / Sop.		d¹ – g²		C – g¹	piano	Handy	1938	
Dry Bones	SATB	c¹ – g²	c¹ – b♭¹	g – f¹	c – b♭	piano	Handy	1938	HB1
Go Chain de Lion Down	SATB	d¹ – f²	a – b♭¹	f – f¹	G – b♭	piano	Handy	1935	HB2

Title	Voicing / Soloist	Vocal Ranges				Accomp.	Publisher	© Date	Catalog #
		Soprano	Alto	Tenor	Bass				
Go Down Moses	SATB	c¹ - a♭²	a♭ - d♭²	c - a♭¹	F - f¹	piano	Handy	1938	HB8
I Ain't Goin' Study War No More	SATB	e♭¹ - d♭²	d♭¹ - a♭¹	b♭ - f¹	A♭ - b♭	piano	Handy	1938	HB3
Joshua Fit de Battle o' Jericho	SATB	e♭¹ - g²	c¹ - c²	g - g¹	B - c¹	piano	Handy	1935	HB4
O Wasn't That a Wide River	SATB	b - a²		F - f¹		piano	Handy	1935	
Same Train	SATB	c¹ - e♭²	b♭¹ - a♭¹	g - e♭¹	E♭ - b♭	piano	Handy	1935	HB5
Steal Away to Jesus	SATB / Alto and Bar.	d¹ - b²	d♯¹ - d¹	a - g¹	G - e¹	piano	Handy	1937	HB6
Who Built de Ark	SATB	e♭¹ - a♭²	c¹ - c²	a♭ - f¹	E♭ - e♭¹	piano	Handy	1938	HB7
JOHNSON, NEIL A.									
Little Innocent Lamb	3-pt. Mxd.	c¹ - e²	b - c²	f - d¹		piano	Heritage	1994	15/1119
JOHNSON, VICTOR C.									
Keep Your Lamps!	SAB	e♭ - g²	b♭ - b♭²	e♭ - d¹		piano	Heritage	2007	15/2253H
Keep Your Lamps!	SSA	b♭ - g²	g - a♭¹			piano	Heritage	2007	15/2237H
Keep Your Lamps!	TTB			c - a¹	G - c¹	piano	Heritage	2007	15/2238H
Mary Had a Baby	TTB			g - a¹	d - b¹	piano	Heritage	1998	15/1377H
Poor Wayfaring Stranger	TTB			d - f¹	B♭ - a	piano	Heritage	1999	15/1449H
Song of Freedom	SATB	c¹ - f²	c¹ - d²	c¹ - f	A - d¹	piano	Heritage	2007	15/2235H
Song of Freedom	3-pt. Mxd.	c¹ - f²	b - d²	f - d¹		piano	Heritage	2007	15/2254H
KING, BETTY JACKSON									
Come Down, Angels	SATB	b - f♯²		E - f♯¹		a cappella	Kjos	1955	ED5393
Ezekiel Saw the Wheel	TTBB			d - b²	G - d¹	a cappella	Lawson-Gould	1982	52185

Title	Voicing / Soloist	Vocal Ranges				Accomp.	Publisher	© Date	Catalog #
		Soprano	Alto	Tenor	Bass				
Great Day	SATB / Sop. or Ten.	$e\flat^1 - e\flat^2$	$b\flat - b\flat^1$	$e\flat - g^1$	$B\flat - c^1$	a cappella	Jacksonian Press	1956	JP 113
Great Gettin' Up Mornin'	SSAA / Sop. and Alto	$c^1 - b\flat^2$	$f - d^2$			a cappella	Jacksonian Press	1992	JP 303
Hear de Lambs A-Cryin'	SATB	$b\flat - g^2$		$G - g^1$		a cappella	Kjos	1961	ED5332
I Couldn't Hear Nobody Pray	SATB / Sop.	$b - f\sharp^2$	$g\sharp^1 - e^2$	$c\sharp^1 - e^1$	$E - e^1$	a cappella	Kjos	1965	ED5394
I Want God's Heaven to be Mine	SATB / Sop. or Ten.	$e^1 - g^2$	$c^1 - d\flat^2$	$f - f^1$	$c - d\flat^1$	a cappella	Marks	1973	MC4601
I'm Going Down to the River Jordan	TTBB / Bar.			$d - g^1$	$F - c^1$	a cappella	Jacksonian Press	1990	JP 203
Let Us Cheer the Weary Traveler	TTBB / Bass			$g - b^1$	$G - d^1$	a cappella	Jacksonian Press	1979	JP 201
Ole Ark's A-Moverin'	TTBB			$a - c^2$	$G - c^1$	a cappella	Jacksonian Press	1992	JP 204
Sinner Please Don't Let This Harvest Pass	SATB div.	$a - a^2$		$A - a^1$		a cappella	Mills	1978	2983
Stan' the Storm	SSA / Sop.	$d^1 - d^2$	$g - g^1$			piano	Jacksonian Press	1956	JP 302
Stand the Storm	SATB / Sop. or Ten.	$d^1 - d^2$	$b - b^1$	$g - f\sharp^1$	$G - g^1$	piano	Hope	1956	HO1814
This Little Light of Mine	SATB	$e\flat^1 - a^2$	$b\flat - e\flat^2$	$e\flat - g^1$	$B\flat - d\flat^1$	a cappella	Hope	1978	HO1812
Two Christmas Spirituals	SATB	$a\flat - f\sharp^2$	$a\flat - b\flat^1$	$E\flat - g\sharp^1$		a cappella	Somerset	1978	AD1998
LARSON, LLOYD									
Ev'ry Time I Feel the Spirit	SATB	$b - g^2$	$a\flat - b\flat^1$	$B - f^1$	$E - b$	a cappella	Exaltation	2004	10/3141L

Title	Voicing / Soloist	Soprano	Alto	Tenor	Bass	Accomp.	Publisher	© Date	Catalog #
MABRY, GEORGE									
Go Tell It On The Mountain	SSATB	d¹ - g²	c¹ - c²	g - f¹	G - g	a cappella	Roger Dean	2000	15/1462R
The Virgin Mary Had-a One Son	SATB div. / Sop.	a - a²	a - e²	c# - f#¹	F# - c#¹	a cappella	Roger Dean	1999	15/1461R
McLIN, LENA									
Cert'nly Lord, Cert'nly Lord	SATB	b♭ - g²	a♭ - b♭¹	e♭ - g¹	B♭ - e♭¹	a cappella	Kjos	1967	ED5458
Done Made My Vow to the Lord	SATB / Bar.	c#¹ - f#²	a - c#²	c# - e¹	f# - c#¹	a cappella	Kjos	1971	ED5872
Don't You Let Nobody Turn You 'Round	SATB / opt. solos	d¹ - g²	b♭ - b♭¹	f# - e¹	G - g	piano	Kjos	1988	GC166
Down by the River	SATB div.	f¹ - g²	c¹ - b¹	f - f¹	G - c¹	a cappella	Kjos	1976	ED5913
Free at Last	SATB / Sop.	a - c³		F - a¹		piano	GWM	1973	GC43
Glory, Glory, Hallelujah	SATB	d¹ - f²	b♭ - a♭¹	d - e¹	G - a♭	piano	Kjos	1966	ED5430
I'm a Soldier, Let me Ride	SATB / Sop. or Bar.	g - g²	g - c#²	d - f#¹	G - e¹	piano opt.	Kjos	1997	8847
The Little Baby	SATB / opt. Solo	d¹ - g²	a - e²	d - e¹	E - g	piano	Kjos	1971	ED5855
Lit'le, Lit'le Lamb	SATB / Sop.	b - b♭²	b♭ - c²	e♭ - e♭¹	F - b♭	a cappella	Kjos	1959	ED5457
My God is So High	SATB	f¹ - g²	c¹ - b♭²	f - e¹	F - c¹	a cappella	Kjos	1972	ED5881
New Born King	SATB	c¹ - a²		F - d¹		a cappella	GWM	1972	EDGC23
Writ'en Down My Name	SATB / Bar.	c¹ - g²	b - e²	e - c¹	G - c¹	a cappella	Kjos	1967	ED5450
McNEIL, ALBERT J.A411									
All My Trials	SATB / solo	c¹ - c²	g - c²	e - c¹	G - c¹	a cappella	Gentry	1987	JG2026

Title	Voicing / Soloist	Vocal Ranges				Accomp.	Publisher	© Date	Catalog #
		Soprano	Alto	Tenor	Bass				
He's Got the Whole World in His Hands	SATB / Sop. or Ten.	b - g²	g - a¹	d - b	D - a¹	a cappella	Gentry	1983	JG-521
Hold Out Your Light	SATB	d¹ - d²	a - g¹	d - d¹	F♯ - b	piano opt.	Gentry	1983	JG-520
O, Mary, Don't You Weep	SATB	c¹ - f²	a♭ - d♭²	e♭ - f¹	A♭ - b♭¹	a cappella	Gentry	1984	JG-536
Open the Window, Noah	SATB / solo	b - d²	a - g¹	d - d¹	G - a	a cappella	Gentry	1986	JG2025
MOORE, UNDINE S.									
Bound for Canaan's Land	SATB	d¹ - a²			A - g¹	a cappella	Warner Bros.	1960	W3653
Come Along in Jesus Name	SATB		g♯ - g♯²		G♯ - e¹	a cappella	Augsburg	1977	11-0558
Daniel, Daniel, Servant of the Lord	SATB	e¹ - a²	a - d²	e - a¹	F♯ - d¹	a cappella	Warner Bros.	1953	W3475
Fare You Well	SATB / Sop. and Ten.	b♭ - e♭²			E♭ - e♭¹	a cappella	M. Witmark and Sons	1951	W3419
I Believe This Is Jesus	SATB	d¹ - a²	a - d²	d - a¹	A - d¹	a cappella	Ausburg Pub. House	1977	11-0559
I Just Come from the Fountain	SATB		a - a²		F♯ - g¹	a cappella	Warner Bros.	1951	W3418
I'm Going Home	SATB / Sop.		g - a²		F - f¹	a cappella	Augsburg	1978	11-0652
The Lamb	SS or Unison	c¹ - f²				piano	Gray	1958	2531
Long Fare You Well	SATB		g - a²		G - g¹	a cappella	Augsburg	1960	11-0563
Lord Have Mercy	SATB		a - a²		G - g¹	a cappella	Augsburg	1978	11-856
Sinner, You Can't Walk My Path	SATB		g - a²		E - g¹	a cappella	M. Witmark and Sons	1958	W3546
Walk Through the Streets of the City	SATB		a - g²		B - g¹	a cappella	Augsburg	1977	11-0564

Title	Voicing / Soloist	Vocal Ranges				Accomp.	Publisher	© Date	Catalog #
		Soprano	Alto	Tenor	Bass				
MORRIS, ROBERT L.									
Children, Go Where I Send Thee	SATB	d¹ - f²	g♯ - b¹	c♯ - f♯¹	D - d¹	a cappella	Alliance	1999	AMP 0347
A City Called Heaven	SATB	d¹ - e²	g - a²	c - e¹	E♯ - e¹	a cappella	Hidden Gems Press	2000	
Fix Me, Jesus	SATB	b - f♯²	a - b¹	c♯ - e¹	F♯ - b	a cappella	Hidden Gems Press	1994	
Glory to the Newborn King	SATB	e¹ - e²	a - a¹	e - e♭¹	F - a	a cappella	Shawnee	1989	MF 0562
I Believe This Is Jesus	SATB div.	e♭¹ - g²	b♭ - e♭¹	f - g♭¹	D♭ - e♭¹	a cappella	Alliance	1997	AMP 0256
I Thank You, Jesus	SATB	d¹ - a²	b - c²	d - e¹	G - d¹	a cappella	Mark Foster	1989	MF 2034
Is A Light Shinin' In The Heavens?	SATB	c♯¹ - g♯²	a - c♯²	c♯ - f♯¹	F♯ - b	a cappella	Alliance	1998	AMP 0273
Now We Take This Body	SATB / Sop. and Bar.	d♯ - e²	b - g♯¹	f♯ - e¹	E - c♯¹	a cappella	Mark Foster	1998	MF 2145
Rockin' Jerusalem	SATB	c¹ - b²	a - e♭²	d - a¹	E - e♭¹	a cappella	Walton	2001	HL08501431
MORROW DAVID									
Got a Mind To Do Right	TTBB			d - a♭¹	D - c¹	a cappella	Lawson-Gould	1989	52502
PARKER, ALICE & SHAW, ROBERT									
By An' By	SATB / Solo	e♭¹ - a♭²	a♭ - c²	e♭ - a♭¹	E♭ - e♭¹	a cappella	Jenson	1991	43509063
Calvary	SATB / Bar.	c¹ - f²	c¹ - e♭²	c - c¹	C - c	a cappella	G. Schirmer	1951	9948
Cert'nly Lord	SATB / solo	c¹ - g²	b♭ - b♭¹	c - e♭¹	B - c¹	a cappella	GIA	1995	G-4239
Come On Up	SSA /sSolo	d¹ - g²	d¹ - d²			a cappella	GIA	1995	G-4231
Dere's No Hidin' Place	SATB / solo	c¹ - f²	a - c²	c - f¹	C - c¹	a cappella	Lawson-Gould	1963	51110

Title	Voicing / Soloist	Vocal Ranges				Accomp.	Publisher	© Date	Catalog #
		Soprano	Alto	Tenor	Bass				
Don't Be Weary, Traveler	SATB / solo	$c^1 - f^2$	$a - c^2$	$d - f^1$	$A - a$	a cappella	GIA	1995	G-4232
Father's Got A Home	SATB	$e^1 - a^2$	$c\#^1 - f\#^2$	$e - a^1$	$A - d^1$	piano	Carl Fischer	1976	CM7993
Free At Las'	TTB / solo			$d - f\#^1$	$d - d^1$	a cappella	GIA	1995	G-4237
Hush!	SATB	$c^1 - f^2$	$a - c^2$	$c - f^1$	$A - b$	a cappella	GIA	1995	G-4233
I Got Shoes	SATBB	$e^{b1} - a^{b2}$	$c^1 - d^{b2}$	$f - f^1$	$E^b - d^{b1}$	a cappella	Lawson-Gould	1953	51116
I Know the Lord	SATB / solo	$b - f\#^2$	$b - c\#^2$	$B - g\#^1$	$B - e^1$	a cappella	GIA	1995	G-4229
I Want Two Wings	SSATB	$e^{b1} - g^2$	$b^b - e^{b2}$	$e^b - g^1$	$E^b - c^1$	a cappella	Jenson	1991	4350062
If I Got My Ticket, Can I Ride?	SSAATTBB / Ten.	$a^{b1} - e^{b2}$	$a^b - e^{b2}$	$a^b - e^{b1}$	$A^b - e^{b1}$	a cappella	G. Schirmer	1952	9933
If I Got My Ticket, Can I Ride?	TBB / Ten.			$g - d^1$	$G - d^1$	a cappella	G. Schirmer	1949	9852
John Saw Duh Numbuh	SSAATTBB	$c^1 - g^2$	$g - c^2$	$c - f^1$	$F - c^1$	a cappella	Lawson-Gould	1963	51109
My Soul's Been Anchored	SATB / Ten.	$e^1 - a^2$	$c^1 - d^2$	$e - f^1$	$E - e^1$	a cappella	Lawson-Gould	1963	51111
Set Down Servant	SATB div. / Alto and Bass	$b - f^2$	$b^b - d^{b2}$	$B - f^1$	$F - c^1$	a cappella	Shawnee	1944	A 0029
Set Down Servant	TTBB div. / Ten. and Bass			$e\# - b^1$	$E - f\#^1$	a cappella	Shawnee	1942	
Stayed On Jesus	SATB / solo	$c^1 - f^2$	$g - d^2$	$c - f^1$	$F - c^1$	a cappella	GIA	1995	G-4230
Take Me to the Water	SAATB / solo	$c^1 - e^{b2}$	$g - c^2$	$c - a^{b1}$	$E^b - c^1$	a cappella	GIA	1995	G-4238
That Lonesome Valley	SATB / Treble voices, Bar.	$b - g^2$	$b - d^2$	$b - e^1$	$D - d^1$	a cappella	Lawson-Gould	1963	51103

Title	Voicing / Soloist	Vocal Ranges				Accomp.	Publisher	© Date	Catalog #
		Soprano	Alto	Tenor	Bass				
Were You There	SATBB / Alto	c#1 - f#2	b - b1	c# - f#1	F# - d1	a cappella	Lawson–Gould	1966	51249
PATTERSON, MARK									
Ain'-a That Good News?	Uni./2-pt.	c1 - g2				piano	Choristers Guild	2004	CGA1029
This Little Light of Mine	Uni./2-pt.	d1 - e♭2				piano	Choristers Guild	2007	CGA1108
PORTERFIELD, SHERRI									
Swing Low, Sweet Chariot	3-pt. mxd.	c1 - g2	b♭ - b1	f - d1		piano	Heritage	1995	15/1179H
POWELL, ROSEPHANYE									
Drinkin' of the Wine	SATB	f1 - f2	c1 - e♭2	c - g1	A♭ - c1	a cappella	Gentry	2002	JG2292
Glory Hallelujah To Duh Newbo'n King	SATB div.	f#1 - g2	d1 - c2	f# - g1	E - c1	a cappella	Gentry	2005	JG2325
Good News!	SSAA	e♭1 - a♭2	a♭ - e♭2			a cappella	Gentry	2003	JG2311
I Wanna Be Ready	SATB / Alto	b♭ - e♭2	b♭ - a♭1	g - e♭1	B♭ - e♭1	piano	Gentry	1996	JG2194
Wade in the Water	SATB div.	d1 - f#2	g - b1	e - g1	B - e1	a cappella	Gentry	2000	JG2241
PRINTZ, BRAD									
Down by the Riverside	3-pt. mxd.	d1 - e2	c1 - c2	f# - e1		piano	Heritage	1993	15/1023
Down by the Riverside	Two-part	c1 - e2	c1 - b♭1			piano	Heritage	1993	15/1012
Dry Bones	SSAA	a - a2	g - d2			small percussion	Heritage	2002	15/1692H
Joshua Fit the Battle of Jericho	3-pt. mxd.	c1 - f2	b♭ - e2	g - e1		piano	Heritage	1998	15/1365H
Joshua Fit the Battle of Jericho	Two-part	c#1 - f2	a - d1			piano	Heritage	1998	15/1348H

Title	Voicing / Soloist	Vocal Ranges				Accomp.	Publisher	© Date	Catalog #
		Soprano	Alto	Tenor	Bass				
Wade in the Water	3-pt. mxd.	c¹ - e♭²	a♭ - c¹	f - e♭¹		piano	Heritage	1996	15/1261H
Wade in the Water	Two-part	c♯¹ - e♭²	b - d²			piano	Heritage	1996	15/1248H
RENTZ, EARLENE									
Every Time I Feel the Spirit	3-pt. mxd.	d¹ - f♯²	b - d²	g - d¹		piano	Heritage	2002	15/1729H
There Is a Balm in Gilead	SATB	d¹ - a²	b - c²	e - g¹	G - c¹	a cappella	Laurel Press	2005	10/3260LA
RINGWALD, ROY									
Deep River	SATB	c¹ - a²	a - c²	c - f¹	F - e¹	a cappella	Shawnee	1948	A-90
He's Got the Whole World in His Hand	SSATB	c¹ - f²	b♭ - a¹	c - e♭¹	F - c¹	piano	Shawnee	1956	
Let Us Break Bread Together	SSA	c¹ - f²	a - d¹			piano or organ	Shawnee	1963	B-259
Steal Away	SSAA	c¹ - g♭²	a♭ - c²			piano	Shawnee	1945	
Three Spirituals	SATB					a cappella	Shawnee	1978	A-1475
1. God's Heaven		e♭¹ - g²	a - b♭¹	d - f¹	E♭ - d¹				
2. O Hear My Prayin'		e♭¹ - g²	f - e♭¹	B♭ - b♭²	E♭ - c¹				
3. The Gospel Train		d¹ - b♭²	b♭ - e♭²	f - g♯¹	E♭ - e♭¹				
Were You There	TTBB			d♭ - b♭¹	D♭ - f♯¹	a cappella	Shawnee	1943	
ROBINSON, RUSSELL									
This Train!	3-pt. mxd.	b♭ - f²	a♭ - a¹	f - d¹		piano	Heritage	2007	15/2289H
This Train!	Two-part	b♭ - f²	b♭ - a¹			piano	Heritage	2007	15/2303H

Title	Voicing / Soloist	Vocal Ranges				Accomp.	Publisher	© Date	Catalog #
		Soprano	Alto	Tenor	Bass				
SHACKLEY, LARRY									
I Been in de Storm So Long	SATB / Sop.	$e^1 - g^2$	$g - b^1$	$e - e^1$	$G - c^1$	piano, soprano sax, rhythm	Monarch	2006	10/3393M
Ride Up in the Chariot	SATB	$c^1 - f^2$	$g - d^1$	$d - f^1$	$G - d^1$	piano	Exaltation	2007	10/3582L
SIMPSON, EUGENE THAMON									
Hold On!	SSATTBB	$c^1 - a^2$	$g - d\flat^2$	$e - f^1$	$F - d\flat^1$	a cappella	Murbo Music Pub.	1974	979
Nobody Knows de Trouble I've Seen	SATB / Bar.	$c^1 - a^2$	$a - c^2$	$c - d^1$	$F - a$	a cappella	Bourne	1976	B231548-358
Sinnuh, Please Don't Let Dis Harves' Pass	SATB / Alto	$d^1 - a^2$	$a - d^2$	$d - g^1$	$G - d^1$	a cappella	Bourne	1976	315146
Sister Mary Had-A But One Child	SSATBB / Ten. or Bar.	$b\flat - a^2$	$a\flat - c^2$	$e - e\flat^1$	$F - b\flat$	a cappella	Bourne	1981	375606
Steal Away	SATB	$d^1 - d^2$	$a - d^2$	$f - g^1$	$A - e^1$	a cappella	Bourne	1975	B231324-358
True Religion	SATB	$c^1 - g^2$	$a - d^2$	$d - e^1$	$F - b$	a cappella	Bourne	1977	B231985-358
SMITH, WILLIAM HENRY									
Children Don't get Weary	SATB / Sop.	$e^1 - g^2$	$b - b^1$	$e - e^1$	$E - b$	a cappella	Kjos	1937	1007
Climbin' Up the Mountain	SATB	$g^1 - e\flat^2$	$e\flat^1 - a^1$	$c^1 - e\flat^1$	$E\flat - a\flat$	a cappella	Kjos	1937	1001
Climbin' Up the Mountain	TTBB			$g - f^1$	$E\flat - a$	a cappella	Kjos	1937	1101
Didn't My Lord Deliver Daniel	SATB	$e\flat^1 - a^2$	$c^1 - c^2$	$a\flat - f^1$	$E\flat - c^1$	a cappella	Kjos	1938	1014
Everytime I Feel the Spirit	SATB	$d^1 - f\sharp^2$	$a - a^1$	$f\sharp - f\sharp^1$	$A - d^1$	a cappella	Kjos	1937	1006
Goin' to Heaven Anyhow	SATB	$e\flat^1 - e\flat^2$	$b\flat - b\flat^1$	$g - e\flat^1$	$E\flat - a\flat$	a cappella	Kjos	1937	1009
Good News	SATB	$a^1 - d^2$	$e^1 - a^1$	$c^1 - g\flat^1$	$A - a$	a cappella	Kjos	1937	1005

Title	Voicing / Soloist	Vocal Ranges				Accomp.	Publisher	© Date	Catalog #
		Soprano	Alto	Tenor	Bass				
Go Tell it on the Mountain	SATB opt. double choir	c¹ - f²	a - a¹	f - f¹	F - f	a cappella	Kjos	1937	1010
I Couldn't Hear Nobody Pray	SATB / Sop. or Ten.	d¹ - f²	c¹ - b¹	f - f¹	F - b♭	a cappella	Kjos	1937	1011
I Stood by the River of Jordan	SATTBB	e♭¹ - a♭²	e♭¹ - c²	a♭ - f¹	A♭ - a♭	a cappella	Kjos	1941	5029
Plenty Good Room	SATB	d¹ - g²	b - c²	f - f♯¹	E - d♯¹	a cappella	Kjos	1937	1003
Ride the Chariot	SATB / Sop.	d¹ - f²	c¹ - d²	f♯ - f♯¹	G - c¹	a cappella	Kjos	1939	1015
Ride the Chariot	TTBB / Ten.			d - f¹	G - a	a cappella	Kjos	1939	1102
Sometimes I Feel Like a Motherless Child	SATB div. / solo	g¹ - a²	a - d²	f - f¹	A - d¹	piano / organ	Kjos	1939	1013
Sometimes I Feel Like a Motherless Child	TTBB / Sop.			b - f¹	G - b	a cappella	Kjos	1937	1113
SOUTHALL, MITCHELL									
The Blind Man Stood on the Road and Cried	SATB	g¹ - g²	b♭ - a¹	d - f¹	F - c¹	a cappella	Jusko	1960	J-205
The Blind Man Stood on the Road and Cried	SSAA	d¹ - g²	f♯ - g¹			a cappella	Jusko	1960	J-206
The Blind Man Stood on the Road and Cried	TTBB			g - g¹	F - e¹	a cappella	Jusko	1960	J-207
I Want Jesus to Walk With Me	SATB / Sop. or Ten.	c¹ - e♭²	a♭ - a♭¹	f - f¹	F - c¹	a cappella	Jusko	1960	J-208
I Want Jesus to Walk With Me	SSA / Sop.	a♭ - d♭²	f - g¹			a cappella	Jusko	1960	J-170
I Want Jesus to Walk With Me	TTBB / Ten.			f - g¹	F - d♭¹	a cappella	Jusko	1960	J-210
Joshua Fit de Battle of Jericho	TTBB			e - a¹	D - d¹	a cappella	Jusko	1959	J-211

Title	Voicing / Soloist	Vocal Ranges				Accomp.	Publisher	© Date	Catalog #
		Soprano	Alto	Tenor	Bass				
Nobody Knows the Trouble I've Seen	SATB	f - f²	c¹ - b♭¹	e♭ - g¹	F - c¹	a cappella	Jusko	1960	J-209
Nobody Knows the Trouble I've Seen	SSA	c¹ - f²	f - a¹			a cappella	Jusko	1960	J-171
Sometimes I Feel Like a Motherless Child	SATB	g - g²		E - g¹		a cappella	Carl Fischer	1959	9167
Steal Away	SATTBB	b♭ - e²	a - a¹	f - g¹	G - c¹	a cappella	Jusko	1959	J-212
There's No Hiding Place Down There	SATB	f¹ - a♭²	a♭ - c²	e♭ - f¹	F - e♭¹	a cappella	Jusko	1959	J-213
Wade in de Waters	SATB / Sop.	f - f²		F - d♭¹		opt. piano	Handy	1957	
SPEVACEK, LINDA									
Deep River	SATB	b♭ - g²	b♭ - c²	f - e♭¹	A♭ - g	piano	Heritage	1993	15/1068
Deep River	3-pt. mxd.	b♭ - g²	a♭ - c¹	f - e♭¹		piano	Heritage	1994	15/1087
Now Let Me Fly	SATB	d¹ - g²	d¹ - d²	e♭ - e¹	A - c¹	piano	Heritage	2003	15/1775H
Now Let Me Fly	SAB	d¹ - b♭²	b♭ - d²		A - e¹	piano	Heritage	2003	15/1783H
Now Let Me Fly	SSA	d¹ - b♭²	a - d²			piano	Heritage	2003	15/1845H
Now Let Me Fly	TB / TTB			e♭ - b♭¹	A - e¹	piano	Heritage	2003	15/1846H
Rock-a My Soul	SATB	c¹ - f²	c¹ - e²	f - e¹	F - c¹	piano	Heritage	2004	15/1891H
Rock-a My Soul	3-pt. mxd.	c¹ - f²	c¹ - e²	f - e♭¹		piano	Heritage	2001	15/1652H
Rock-a My Soul	Two-part	c¹ - f²	c¹ - e²			piano	Heritage	2001	15/1656H
Spiritual Jubilee	SATB	a - e²	a - e²	f - e¹	A - c¹	piano	Heritage	2002	15/1749H
Spiritual Jubilee	TTBB			g - a♭¹	A - e¹	piano	Heritage	2007	15/2280H
Spiritual Jubilee	3-pt. mxd.	a - e²	a - e²	f - e¹		piano	Heritage	2002	15/1724H
Spiritual Jubilee	Two-part	a - e²	a - e²			piano	Heritage	2002	15/1718H
Wayfarin' Stranger	3-pt. mxd.	c¹ - d²	c¹ - d²	f - d¹		piano	Heritage	2007	15/2297H

Title	Voicing / Soloist	Vocal Ranges Soprano	Alto	Tenor	Bass	Accomp.	Publisher	© Date	Catalog #
STILL, WILLIAM GRANT									
The Blind Man	SATB div.	b♭ - e♭²	g - a♭¹	c - e♭¹	A♭ - a♭	piano	Gemini	1974	GP-406
Ev'ry Time I Feel the Spirit	SATB	d¹ - f²	b - d²	c - f¹	G - b♭	piano	Gemini	1977	GP-405
Here's One	SATB / Sop.	d¹ - f♯²	a - b♭¹	e - f♯¹	A - c¹	a cappella	Presser	1941	322-40037
I Feel Like My Time Ain't Long	SATB	c¹ - f²			c - d¹	a cappella	Presser	1956	322-40304
Is There Anybody Here	SATB	c¹ - e²			c - e¹	piano	Presser	1956	312-40305
Lawd, Ah Wants to Be a Christian	SATB	g¹ - g²	d¹ - d²	f - a¹	G - c¹	piano	Handy	1938	HB9
Three Rhythmic Spirituals	SATB						Bourne	1961	
1. Lord, I Looked Down the Road		d¹ - f♯²	a - f♯²	d - f♯¹	d - d¹	piano			2951-9
2. Hard Trials									
3. Holy Spirit, Don't You Leave Me									
Where Shall I Be?	SATB div.	c¹ - f²	g - f¹	d - f¹	F - c¹	piano	Gemini	1977	GP-408
THOMAS, ANDRÉ J.									
Band of Angels	SATB div.	d¹ - g²	b♭ - e²	d - f¹	G - e¹	piano	Heritage	2000	15/1580H
Beautiful City	SATB	b♭ - b♭²	a♭ - d♭²	B♭ - g¹	G - b♭	piano	Heritage	2006	15/2124H
Death is Gonna Lay His Cold Icy Hands on Me	SSATB / Bar.	c¹ - g²	c¹ - d²	c - e¹	G - d¹	piano	Mark Foster	1993	MF 2098
Deep River	SATB	c¹ - a²	a - c²	c - f¹	F - a	a cappella	Heritage	2002	15/1750H
Go Down 'n the Valley and Pray!	SATB	c¹ - a²	a♭ - c²	f - a♭¹	F - c¹	a cappella	Heritage	2007	15/2348H
Good News!	SSA	e¹ - g²	c¹ - e²			piano	Heritage	2004	15/1886H
Good News!	TTB			e - g¹	c - c¹	piano	Heritage	2004	15/1890H

Title	Voicing / Soloist	Vocal Ranges				Accomp.	Publisher	© Date	Catalog #
		Soprano	Alto	Tenor	Bass				
Go Where I Send Thee	SATB div. / Bar.	c¹ - a♭²	a - c²	e - g♭¹	F - d♭	piano	Mark Foster	1989	MF 2044
Great Day!	SATB	f¹ - a♭²	c¹ - f²	f - f¹	c - d¹	piano	FitzSimmons	1989	F2270
Heaven	SATB	c¹ - a²	c¹ - f²	c - a♭¹	G - d¹	piano	Mark Foster	1989	MF 2051
Heaven	TTBB			c - a♭¹	F - c¹	piano	Mark Foster	1988	MF 1016
Here's a Pretty Little Baby	SATB / Sop. or Ten.	e¹ - g²	c¹ - g♯¹	f♯ - e¹	A - a	synthesizer, tenor steel drum, flute, percussion, string bass	earthsongs	1997	
I'm A-Rollin'	SATB	b♭ - g²	b♭ - c²	e♭ - e♭¹	B♭ - c¹	piano	Hinshaw	1986	HMC-842
I Open My Mouth	SATB	d♯¹ - e²	b - b¹	f♯ - g¹	A - d¹	a cappella	Hinshaw	1990	HMC-1168
John Saw Duh Numbuh	SATB	c¹ - b²	c¹ - d²	c - g♭¹	c - d¹	piano	Heritage	2001	15/1665H
John Saw Duh Numbuh	SSAA	c¹ - a²	c¹ - a♭¹	b - d²	b - b♭¹	piano	Heritage	2001	15/1666H
Keep Your Lamps	SATB	e♭¹ - e♭²	b♭ - a♭¹	g - f¹	B♭ - a♭	conga drums	Hinshaw	1982	HMC-577
Keep Your Lamps	SSA	b - g²	g - c²			piano	Hinshaw	2005	HMC-2048
Peter, Go Ring Dem Bells	SATB	c¹ - a♭²	b♭ - c²	c - f¹	c - c¹	piano	Heritage	2001	15/1592H
Ride the Chariot	SATB	e¹ - e²	b - c♯²	f♯ - e¹	B - c♯¹	opt. conga drum	Hinshaw	1987	HMC-931
Rise Up, Shepherd, and Follow	SATB	b♭ - f²	b♭ - b♭¹	c - f¹	G - c¹	a cappella	Heritage	2001	15/1591H
Rockin' Jerusalem	SATB	c¹ - a♭²	g - c²	c - f¹	G - c¹	a cappella	Mark Foster	1986	MF 2002
Swing Down, Chariot	SATB	f¹ - f²	b♭ - d²	f - f¹	F - b♭	a cappella	Heritage	2003	15/1798H
Swing Down, Chariot	TTBB			f - b♭¹	F - d¹	a cappella	Heritage	2003	15/1778H

Title	Voicing / Soloist	Vocal Ranges				Accomp.	Publisher	© Date	Catalog #
		Soprano	Alto	Tenor	Bass				
When The Trumpet Sounds	SATB	$c^1 - e\flat^2$	$a\flat - c^2$	$c - f^1$	$G - c^1$	piano	Mark Foster	1985	MF 261
VOLLINGER, BILL									
Ezekiel!	Two-part	$c^1 - c^2$	$c^1 - c^2$			piano and small perc	Heritage	2004	15/1927H
WAGNER, DOUGLAS E.									
WEBB, JEFFREY L.									
Give Me Jesus	SATB	$c^1 - a^2$	$g - b^1$	$c - f\sharp^1$	$G - d^1$	piano	Exaltation	1986	E103
Oh, What a Beautiful City	SATB div. / Sop.	$c^1 - f^2$	$c^1 - d^2$	$e - f^1$	$F - d^1$	piano	Roger Dean	2007	15/2311R
WHALUM, WENDELL									
Been in the Storm	TTBB / Bar.			$d - b\flat^1$	$G - d^1$	a cappella	Lawson-Gould	1982	52246
Drinkin' of the Wine	SATB	$b - a^2$	$g - c\sharp^2$	$d - g^1$	$E - d^1$	a cappella	Lawson-Gould	1989	52495
Give Me Jesus	SATB / Sop.	$c^1 - g^2$	$a\flat - d^2$	$e\flat - f^1$	$D\flat - d^1$	a cappella	Lawson-Gould	1978	52039
The Lily of the Valley	SATB	$e\flat^1 - a\flat^2$	$a\flat - d\flat^2$	$c - a\flat^1$	$A\flat - d\flat^1$	a cappella	Lawson-Gould	1981	52141
Mary was the Queen of Galilee	SATB / Sop.	$d^1 - g^2$	$a - b\flat^1$	$d - a^1$	$G - c^1$	a cappella	Lawson-Gould	1974	51808
My Lord, What a Morning	TTBB			$G - a^1$		a cappella	Lawson-Gould	1979	51917
Somebody's Calling My Name	TTBB			$g - a\flat^1$	$A\flat - c^1$	a cappella	Lawson-Gould	1975	51932

Title	Voicing / Soloist	Vocal Ranges Soprano	Alto	Tenor	Bass	Accomp.	Publisher	© Date	Catalog #
Sweet Home	SATB / Sop.	d♭1 – f2	a♭ – c2	c – e♭1	A♭ – c1	a cappella	Lawson-Gould	1975	51869
You'd Better Run	TTBB / Bar.			A♭ – a♭1		a cappella	Lawson-Gould	1976	51749
Who'll Be a Witness?	SATB / Ten.	d1 – b♭2	b♭ – d♭2	f – g1	F – d♭1	a cappella	Lawson-Gould	1986	52279
WORK III, JOHN									
The Angels Done Bowed Down	SATB / SATB	c1 – f2		F – d♭1		a cappella	Presser	1943	21515
Done Made My Vow	SATB / Sop. or Ten.	c#1 – g#2	f# – c#2	f# – f#1	F# – c#1	a cappella	Galaxy	1956	2110
For the Beauty of the Earth	SATB	c1 – g2		G – f1		organ	J. Fischer	1936	6815
Glory to That New-born King	TTBB / Ten. 2 and Bar.			f – g1	G – b♭	a cappella	Presser	1929	20885
Go Tell it on the Mountain	SATB / Sop. and Ten.	e♭1 – c2	a♭ – c2	e – f1	E♭ – a♭	a cappella	Galaxy	1945	1532
Go Tell it on the Mountain	TTBB / Ten.			e♭ – f1	E♭ – c1	a cappella	Galaxy	1946	1583
Go Tell it on the Mountain	SSA / Sop.	e1 – f2	a – c2			piano	Galaxy	1953	1753
Go Tell it on the Mountain	SA / Sop.	e – f#2	a – a1			piano	Galaxy	1953	1960
Going Home to Live with God	SATB / Sop.	b♭ – a♭2		F – a♭1		a cappella	J. Fischer	1934	6794
I, John, Saw the Holy Number	SATB	f#1 – f#2	c#1 – d2	f# – g#1	F# – d1	a cappella	Galaxy	1962	2236
Jesus, Lay Your Head in the Window	SATB / Sop. and Ten.	g#1 – a2	c1 – a1	a – g1	A – d	a cappella	Galaxy	1960	GMC2166
Jesus is a Rock in a Weary Lan'	SATB / Sop.	d1 – g2	b – b1	f – g1	F – d1	a cappella	Presser	1937	

Title	Voicing / Soloist	Vocal Ranges				Accomp.	Publisher	© Date	Catalog #
		Soprano	Alto	Tenor	Bass				
John, Saw the Holy Number	SATB / Sop.	c¹ - a²		F - g¹		a cappella	Galaxy	1962	GMC2236
Listen to the Angels Shouting	SAA	e¹ - a²	a - b¹	a - b¹		a cappella	Galaxy	1947	1649
Little Black Train	SAATB / Alto and Ten.	e¹ - f#²	a - a¹	e - d¹	E - a	a cappella	Galaxy	1956	2088
My Lord, What a Mornin'	SATB / Sop. and Bar.	e♭¹ - e♭²	b♭ - b♭¹	g♭ - g♭¹	G♭ - g♭	a cappella	Presser	1964	312-40622
Po' Ol' Laz'rus	TTBB / Ten. and Bass			E♭ - e♭¹		a cappella	J. Fischer	1931	6513
Rock, Mount Sinai	SATB	c¹ - e²	a - a¹	d - f¹	F - c¹	a cappella	Galaxy	1962	2237
Rockin' Jerusalem	SATB	a¹ - e²	e¹ - c²	e - d¹	A - a	a cappella	Presser	1940	312-21427
Sinner Please Don't Let This Harvest Pass	SATB / Sop.	d¹ - a²	g - c²	f - a¹	F - d¹	a cappella	Presser	1952	322-40020
There's a Meeting Here Tonight	TTBB			f - f¹	F - b♭	a cappella	E.C. Schirmer	1950	2150
This Little Light of Mine	SATB / Sop.	e¹ - e²	g# - b¹	d# - e¹	F# - a	a cappella	Galaxy	1973	1384
Wasn't That a Mighty Day	TTBB			d - g¹	E♭ - d¹	a cappella	J. Fischer	1931	6515
Wasn't That a Mighty Day	SSA	c¹ - f²				piano	J. Fischer	1934	FE6845
Way Over in Eygpt Land	SATB	a♭ - a♭²		F - f¹		a cappella	Galaxy	1947	1574

INDEX OF CONCERT SPIRITUALS BY TITLE
(Organized by voicing, from fullest to smallest, then by arranger)

Title	Arranger	Voicing / Solosit	Accomp.	Publisher	© Date	Catalog #
Ain' Dat A-Rockin' All Night?	Carey, Paul	SATB div. / Sop.	a cappella	Roger Dean	2007	15/2309R
Ain'-A That Good News	Dawson, William L.	SATB	a cappella	Kjos	1937	T103A
Ain't that Good News	Hogan, Moses	SATB	piano	Hal Leonard	1999	8742075
Ain'-A That Good News	Dawson, William L.	SSAA	a cappella	Kjos	1937	T140
Ain'-A That Good News	Dawson, William L.	TTBB	a cappella	Kjos	1937	T104A
Ain'-a That Good News?	Patterson, Mark	Uni./2-pt.	piano	Choristers Guild	2004	CGA1029
All My Trials	McNeil, Albert J.	SATB / solo	a cappella	Gentry	1987	JG2026
All O' God's Chillun Got Shoes	Johnson, John Rosamond	SATB	piano	Handy	1950	HB10
All 'Round de Glory Manger	de Paur, Leonard	TTBB	a cappella	Lawson-Gould	1958	709
Amen	Hairston, Jester	SATB / solo	a cappella	Bourne	1957	CB 1022
Amen	Hairston, Jester	SAB / Sop.	piano	Bourne	1957	103945
Amen	Hairston, Jester	TTBB / Ten.	a cappella	Bourne	1957	103947
The Angels Done Bowed Down	Work III, John	SATB / SATB	a cappella	Presser	1943	21515
Angels Rolled de Stone Away	Hairston, Jester	SATB	piano	Bourne	1949	105436
The Angel Rolled the Stone Away	Boatner, Edward	SATB	a cappella	Colombo	1954	NY1657
Baby Bethlehem	Boatner, Edward	SATB	a cappella	Colombo	1964	NY2378
Band of Angels	Thomas, André J.	SATB div.	piano	Heritage	2000	15/1580H
Band of Angels	Hairston, Jester	SATB	a cappella	Warner	1940	W3671
The Battle of Jericho	Hogan, Moses	SATB div.	a cappella	Hal Leonard	1996	8703139

Title	Arranger	Voicing / Solosit	Accomp.	Publisher	© Date	Catalog #
The Battle of Jericho	Hogan, Moses	SATB	a cappella	Marks	1984	
Been in the Storm	Whalum, Wendell	TTBB / Bar.	a cappella	Lawson-Gould	1982	52246
Behold That Star	Dawson, William L.	SATB / Sop. and Ten.	a cappella	Kjos	1946	T111
Behold That Star	Burleigh, Harry T.	SATB	organ	Ricordi	1928	NY785
The Blind Man	Still, William Grant	SATB div.	piano	Gemini	1974	GP-406
The Blind Man Stood on the Road and Cried	Southall, Mitchell	SATB	a cappella	Jusko	1960	J-205
The Blind Man Stood on the Road and Cried	Southall, Mitchell	SSAA	a cappella	Jusko	1960	J-206
The Blind Man Stood on the Road and Cried	Southall, Mitchell	TTBB	a cappella	Jusko	1960	J-207
Bound for Canaan's Land	Moore, Undine S.	SATB	a cappella	Warner Bros.	1960	W3653
By An' By	Parker, Alice & Shaw, Robert	SATB / Solo	a cappella	Jenson	1991	43509063
By An' By	Curtis, Marvin	SATB	a cappella	manuscript		
Calvary	Parker, Alice & Shaw, Robert	SATB / Bar.	a cappella	G. Schirmer	1951	9948
Cert'nly Lord	Hogan, Moses	SATB div. / solo	a cappella	Hal Leonard	2002	8743356
Cert'nly Lord	Johnson, Hall	SATB / Ten.	a cappella	Carl Fischer	1930	CM6641
Cert'nly Lord	Parker, Alice & Shaw, Robert	SATB / solo	a cappella	GIA	1995	G-4239
Certain'y Lord	Gibbs, Stacey V.	SATB	a cappella	Alliance	2006	AMP-0664
Cert'nly Lord, Cert'nly Lord	McLin, Lena	SATB	a cappella	Kjos	1967	ED5458
Children Don't get Weary	Smith, William Henry	SATB / Sop.	a cappella	Kjos	1937	1007
Children, Go Where I Send Thee	Morris, Robert L.	SATB	a cappella	Alliance	1999	AMP 0347
A City Called Heaven	de Paur, Leonard	SATBB	a cappella	Warner Bros.	1959	
City Called Heaven	Johnson, Hall	SATB	a cappella	Robbins	1958	R3303

Title	Arranger	Voicing / Solosit	Accomp.	Publisher	© Date	Catalog #
A City Called Heaven	Morris, Robert L.	SATB	a cappella	Hidden Gems Press	2000	
Climbin' Up the Mountain	Hogan, Moses	SATB div.	a cappella	Hal Leonard	2004	8744319
Climbin' Up the Mountain	Smith, William Henry	SATB	a cappella	Kjos	1937	1001
Climbin' Up the Mountain	Smith, William Henry	TTBB	a cappella	Kjos	1937	1101
Come Along in Jesus Name	Moore, Undine S.	SATB	a cappella	Augsburg	1977	11-0558
Come Down, Angels	King, Betty Jackson	SATB	a cappella	Kjos	1955	ED5393
Come On Up	Parker, Alice & Shaw, Robert	SSA /sSolo	a cappella	GIA	1995	G-4231
Couldn't Hear Nobody Pray	Burleigh, Harry T.	SATB / Sop. and Ten.	piano	Ricordi	1922	NY278
Crucifixion (He never said a mumblin' word)	Hailstork, Adolphus C.	SATB div.	a cappella	Presser	1994	312-41646
Crucifixion	Hairston, Jester	SATB	a cappella	Bourne	1952	28616
Crucifixion	Johnson, Hall	SATB / Ten.	a cappella	Carl Fischer	1953	CM 6501
Crucifixion	Johnson, Hall	TTBB	a cappella	Carl Fischer	1953	CM6757
Daniel, Daniel, Servant of the Lord	Moore, Undine S.	SATB	a cappella	Warner Bros.	1953	W3475
David's Golden Harp	Bray, Julie Gardner	Two-part	piano	Heritage	1998	15/1378H
De Blin' Man Stood on de Road An' Cried	Hogan, Moses	SATB div.	a cappella	Hal Leonard	2000	8703261
De Creation	Burleigh, Harry T.	TTBB	a cappella	Ricordi	1922	NY229
De Gospel Train	Gibbs, Stacey V.	SATB	a cappella	Alliance	2005	AMP-0574
De Gospel Train	Burleigh, Harry T.	TTBB	piano	Ricordi	1921	NY210
Death is Gonna Lay His Cold Icy Hands on Me	Thomas, André J.	SSATB / Bar.	piano	Mark Foster	1993	MF 2098
Deep River	Hogan, Moses	SATB div.	a cappella	Hal Leonard	2004	8744331
Deep River	Farrow, Larry	SATB / Sop. or Ten.	a cappella	Gentry	1983	JG-507

Title	Arranger	Voicing / Solosit	Accomp.	Publisher	© Date	Catalog #
Deep River	Hairston, Jester	SATB / Alto	a cappella	Schumann Music Co.	1951	31826
Deep River (from *Two Negro Spirituals*)	Burleigh, Harry T.	SATB	a cappella	G. Schirmer	1913	5815
Deep River	Ringwald, Roy	SATB	a cappella	Shawnee	1948	A-90
Deep River	Spevacek, Linda	SATB	piano	Heritage	1993	15/1068
Deep River	Thomas, André J.	SATB	a cappella	Heritage	2002	15/1750H
Deep River	Spevacek, Linda	3-pt. mxd.	piano	Heritage	1994	15/1087
Dere's No Hidin' Place	Parker, Alice & Shaw, Robert	SATB / solo	a cappella	Lawson-Gould	1963	51110
Dere's No Hidin' Place Down Dere	Johnson, Hall	SATB	a cappella	Carl Fischer	1930	CM6501
Didn't My Lord Deliver Daniel	Hogan, Moses	SATB / div. small group	a cappella	Hal Leonard	1999	8703209
Didn't My Lord Deliver Daniel	Johnson, John Rosamond	SATB / Sop.	piano	Handy	1938	
Didn't My Lord Deliver Daniel?	Burleigh, Harry T.	SATB	a cappella	G. Schirmer	1916	6505
Didn't My Lord Deliver Daniel	Smith, William Henry	SATB	a cappella	Kjos	1938	1014
Dig My Grave (from *Two Negro Spirituals*)	Burleigh, Harry T.	SATB	a cappella	G. Schirmer	1913	5815
Dis Train	Hairston, Jester	SSATB	a cappella	Bourne	1954	32656
Do, Lord, Remember Me	Hogan, Moses	SATB div.	a cappella	Hal Leonard	2001	8703326
Done Made My Vow	Boatner, Edward	SATB / Ten.	piano	McAfee	1979	M1187
Done Made My Vow	Work III, John	SATB / Sop. or Ten.	a cappella	Galaxy	1956	2110
Done Made My Vow to the Lord	McLin, Lena	SATB / Bar.	a cappella	Kjos	1971	ED5872
Done Paid My Vow to the Lord	Dett, R. Nathaniel	SSA / Alto and Bar.	piano	Presser	1919	322-35007
Don't Be Weary, Traveler	Hairston, Jester	SSATB	a cappella	Bourne	1955	CB 1022

Title	Arranger	Voicing / Solosit	Accomp.	Publisher	© Date	Catalog #
Don't Be Weary, Traveler	Parker, Alice & Shaw, Robert	SATB / solo	a cappella	GIA	1995	G-4232
Don't You Let Nobody Turn You 'Round	McLin, Lena	SATB / opt. solos	piano	Kjos	1988	GC166
Don't You Weep No More, Mary	Dett, R. Nathaniel	SATB	a cappella	G. Schirmer	1930	7395
Down by the River	McLin, Lena	SATB div.	a cappella	Kjos	1976	ED5913
Down by the Riverside	Hogan, Moses	SATB	a cappella	Hal Leonard	1999	8703201
Down by the Riverside	Printz, Brad	3-pt. mxd.	piano	Heritage	1993	15/1023
Down by the Riverside	Printz, Brad	Two-part	piano	Heritage	1993	15/1012
Drink to Me Only With Thine Eyes	Dett, R. Nathaniel	SATB	a cappella	J. Fischer	1933	6700
Drinkin' of the Wine	Powell, Rosephanye	SATB	a cappella	Gentry	2002	JG2292
Drinkin' of the Wine	Whalum, Wendell	SATB	a cappella	Lawson-Gould	1989	52495
Dry Bones	Johnson, John Rosamond	SATB	piano	Handy	1938	HB1
Dry Bones	Printz, Brad	SSAA	small percussion	Heritage	2002	15/1692H
Elijah Rock	Johnson, Hall	SSAATTBB	a cappella	G. Schirmer	1956	10354
Elijah Rock	Hairston, Jester	SSATB	a cappella	Bourne	1955	37376
Elijah Rock	Hogan, Moses	SATB div.	a cappella	Hal Leonard	1994	8705532
Elijah Rock	Hairston, Jester	SSA	a cappella	Bourne	1956	37378
Everytime I Feel de Spirit	Burleigh, Harry T.	SATB / Alto and Bar.	a cappella	Ricordi	1925	FC488
Everytime I Feel the Spirit	Smith, William Henry	SATB	a cappella	Kjos	1937	1006
Ev'ry Time I Feel the Spirit	Dawson, William L.	SATB	a cappella	Kjos	1946	T117
Ev'ry Time I Feel the Spirit	Farrow, Larry	SATB	piano, guitar, bass guitar	Gentry	1982	JG-482
Ev'ry Time I Feel the Spirit	Hogan, Moses	SATB	piano	Hal Leonard	1999	8742075

Title	Arranger	Voicing / Solosit	Accomp.	Publisher	© Date	Catalog #
Ev'ry Time I Feel the Spirit	Larson, Lloyd	SATB	a cappella	Exaltation	2004	10/3141L
Ev'ry Time I Feel the Spirit	Still, William Grant	SATB	piano	Gemini	1977	GP-405
Ev'ry Time I Feel the Spirit	Dawson, William L.	SSAA	a cappella	Kjos	1946	T126
Ev'ry Time I Feel the Spirit	Farrow, Larry	SSAA	piano, guitar, bass guitar	Gentry	1982	JG-526
Ev'ry Time I Feel the Spirit	Dawson, William L.	TTBB / Bar.	a cappella	Kjos	1946	T125
Every Time I Feel the Spirit	Rentz, Earlene	3–pt. mxd.	piano	Heritage	2002	15/1729H
Exekiel Saw de Wheel	Hogan, Moses	SATB div.	a cappella	Hal Leonard	2001	8703327
Ezekiel Saw de Wheel	Burleigh, Harry T.	SATB	a cappella	Ricordi	1927	NY700
Ezekiel Saw de Wheel	Burleigh, Harry T.	SATB	a cappella	Ricordi	1928	NY768
Ezekiel Saw De Wheel	Dawson, William L.	SATB	a cappella	Kjos	1942	T110
Ezekiel Saw de Wheel	Burleigh, Harry T.	SSA	a cappella	Ricordi	1927	NY699
Ezekiel Saw the Wheel	King, Betty Jackson	TTBB	a cappella	Lawson–Gould	1982	52185
Ezekiel!	Vollinger, Bill	Two–part	piano and small perc	Heritage	2004	15/1927H
Fare You Well	Moore, Undine S.	SATB / Sop. and Ten.	a cappella	M. Witmark and Sons	1951	W3419
Father's Got A Home	Parker, Alice & Shaw, Robert	SATB	piano	Carl Fischer	1976	CM7993
Feed-A My Sheep	Dawson, William L.	SATB	piano	Kjos	1971	T134
Feed-A My Sheep	Dawson, William L.	SSA	piano	Kjos	1971	T135
Feed-A My Sheep	Dawson, William L.	TTBB	piano	Kjos	1971	T133
Fix Me Jesus	Johnson, Hall	SATB / Sop.	a cappella	G. Schirmer	1956	10354
Fix Me, Jesus	Morris, Robert L.	SATB	a cappella	Hidden Gems Press	1994	

Title	Arranger	Voicing / Solosit	Accomp.	Publisher	©Date	Catalog #
For the Beauty of the Earth	Work III, John	SATB	organ	J. Fischer	1936	6815
Free at Last	McLin, Lena	SATB / Sop.	piano	GWM	1973	GC43
Free at Last	Hairston, Jester	SATB	a cappella	Bourne	1960	306806
Free At Las'	Parker, Alice & Shaw, Robert	TTB / solo	a cappella	GIA	1995	G-4237
Git on Boad	Dandridge, Damon H.	TTBB / Ten.	a cappella	manuscript		
Git on Down Dat Road	de Paur, Leonard	TTBB	a cappella	Library of Congress	1963	
Give Me Jesus	Hogan, Moses	SATB div. / solo	a cappella	Hal Leonard	1999	8703202
Give Me Jesus	Whalum, Wendell	SATB / Sop.	a cappella	Lawson-Gould	1978	52039
Give Me Jesus	Carter, Roland	SATB	a cappella	Mar-Vel	1979	
Give Me Jesus	Wagner, Douglas E.	SATB	piano	Exaltation	1986	E103
Glory Hallelujah to the New Born King	Butler, Mark	SATB div. / Ten.	a cappella	Hinshaw	2004	HMC1995
Glory, Glory, Glory to the Newborn King	Hogan, Moses	SATB div.	a cappella	Hal Leonard	2000	8742097
Glory Hallelujah To Duh Newbo'n King	Powell, Rosephanye	SATB div.	a cappella	Gentry	2005	JG2325
Glory to the Newborn King	Morris, Robert L.	SATB	a cappella	Shawnee	1989	MF 0562
Glory to That New-born King	Work III, John	TTBB / Ten. 2 and Bar.	a cappella	Presser	1929	20885
Glory, Glory, Hallelujah	McLin, Lena	SATB	piano	Kjos	1966	ED5430
Go Chain de Lion Down	Johnson, John Rosamond	SATB	piano	Handy	1935	HB2
Go Down in de Lonesome Valley	Hairston, Jester	SSATB div.	a cappella	Bourne	1965	CB 1022
Go Down, Moses	Harris, Robert	SATB / Sop. And Ten.	a cappella	Oxford	1988	94.336
Go Down Moses	Johnson, John Rosamond	SATB	piano	Handy	1938	HB8

Title	Arranger	Voicing / Solosit	Accomp.	Publisher	© Date	Catalog #
Go Down Moses	Johnson, Hall	SATB / Bar.	a cappella	Carl Fischer	1930	CM6739
Go Down Moses	Hogan, Moses	TTBB / Solo	a cappella	Hal Leonard	1999	8703231
Go Down 'n the Valley and Pray!	Thomas, André J.	SATB	a cappella	Heritage	2007	15/2348H
Go Tell it on the Mountain	Smith, William Henry	SATB opt. double choir	a cappella	Kjos	1937	1010
Go Tell It on the Mountain	Mabry, George	SSATB	a cappella	Roger Dean	2000	15/1462R
Go, Tell It on the Mountain	Carter, Roland	SATB / Sop. or Ten.	a cappella	Mar-Vel	1988	
Go Tell it on the Mountain	Work III, John	SATB / Sop. and Ten.	a cappella	Galaxy	1945	1532
Go Tell It on the Mountain	Boatner, Edward	SATB	piano	McAfee	1979	M1188
Go Tell It on the Mountain	Burleigh, Harry T.	SATB	organ	Ricordi	1929	NY817
Go Tell it on the Mountain	Hairston, Jester	SATB	a cappella	Bourne	1967	47356
Go Tell it on the Mountain	Work III, John	SSA / Sop.	piano	Galaxy	1953	1753
Go Tell it on the Mountain	Work III, John	SA / Sop.	piano	Galaxy	1953	1960
Go Tell it on the Mountain	Work III, John	TTBB / Ten.	a cappella	Galaxy	1946	1583
Go Where I Send Thee	Thomas, André J.	SATB div. / Bar.	piano	Mark Foster	1989	MF 2044
God's Gonna Buil' Up Zion's Wall	Hairston, Jester	SATB	a cappella	Bourne	1960	2938-6
God's Gonna Set This World on Fire	Hogan, Moses	SATB	piano	Hal Leonard	1999	8742075
God's Heaven (from *Three Spirituals*)	Ringwald, Roy	SATB	a cappella	Shawnee	1978	A-1475
Goin' Down dat Lonesome Road	Hairston, Jester	SATB	a cappella	Bourne	1965	48006
Goin' to Heaven Anyhow	Smith, William Henry	SATB	a cappella	Kjos	1937	1009
Going Home to Live with God	Work III, John	SATB / Sop.	a cappella	J. Fischer	1934	6794
Good News, The Chariot's Comin'	Hogan, Moses	SATB div.	a cappella	Hal Leonard	2001	8703312

Title	Arranger	Voicing / Solosit	Accomp.	Publisher	© Date	Catalog #
Good News	Smith, William Henry	SATB	a cappella	Kjos	1937	1005
Good News!	Powell, Rosephanye	SSAA	a cappella	Gentry	2003	JG2311
Good News!	Thomas, André J.	SSA	piano	Heritage	2004	15/1886H
Good News!	Thomas, André J.	TTB	piano	Heritage	2004	15/1890H
The Gospel Train (from *Three Spirituals*)	Ringwald, Roy	SATB	a cappella	Shawnee	1978	A-1475
Got a Mind To Do Right	Morrow David	TTBB	a cappella	Lawson-Gould	1989	52502
Great Day	Curtis, Marvin	SATB	a cappella	Mark Foster	1986	MF 0285
Great Day	Dennard, Brazeal Wayne	SATB / solo	a cappella	Shawnee	1990	A-1895
Great Day	Hogan, Moses	SATB / solo	a cappella	Hal Leonard	1997	8741181
Great Day	King, Betty Jackson	SATB / Sop. or Ten.	a cappella	Jacksonian Press	1956	JP 113
Great Day!	Thomas, André J.	SATB	piano	H.T. Fitzsimons	1989	F2270
Great Day!	Dilworth, Rollo	Two-part	piano	Hal Leonard	2000	8703264
Great Gettin' Up Mornin'	King, Betty Jackson	SSAA / Sop. and Alto	a cappella	Jacksonian Press	1992	JP 303
Great God A' Mighty	Hairston, Jester	SSATB	a cappella	Bourne	1959	2914-7
Hail Mary	Dawson, William L.	SATB	a cappella	Kjos	1949	T112
Hail Mary	Dawson, William L.	TTBB	a cappella	Kjos	1949	T113
Hand Me Down	Hairston, Jester	SATB	a cappella	Bourne	1961	S-1006
Hard Trials (from *Three Rhythmic Spirituals*)	Still, William Grant	SATB	piano	Bourne	1961	2951-9
Hear de Lamb A-Cryin'	Burleigh, Harry T.	SATB / Alto and Bar.	a cappella	Belwin Mills	1927	NY658
Hear de Lambs A-Cryin'	King, Betty Jackson	SATB	a cappella	Kjos	1961	ED5332

Title	Arranger	Voicing / Solosit	Accomp.	Publisher	©Date	Catalog #
Hear My Prayer	Hogan, Moses	SATB	a cappella	Hal Leonard	2001	8703308
Heaven	Thomas, André J.	SATB	piano	Mark Foster	1989	MF 2051
Heaven	Thomas, André J.	TTBB	piano	Mark Foster	1988	MF 1016
Heav'n, Heav'n	Burleigh, Harry T.	SATB	piano	Ricordi	1921	NY122
Here's a Pretty Little Baby	Thomas, André J.	SATB / Sop. or Ten.	synthesizer, ten-or steel drum, flute, percussion, string bass	earthsongs	1997	
Here's One	Still, William Grant	SATB / Sop.	a cappella	Presser	1941	322-40037
He's Got the Whole World in His Hand	Ringwald, Roy	SSATB	piano	Shawnee	1956	
He's Got the Whole World in His Hands	McNeil, Albert J.	SATB / Sop. or Ten.	a cappella	Gentry	1983	JG-521
His Name So Sweet	Johnson, Hall	SATBB	a cappella	Carl Fischer	1935	CM4580
His Name So Sweet	Johnson, Hall	SSA	a cappella	Carl Fischer	1935	CM5213
His Name So Sweet	Johnson, Hall	TTBB	piano	Carl Fischer	1935	CM2183
Hol' de Light	Johnson, Hall	SATB	a cappella	Carl Fischer	1959	CM7104
Hold On!	Simpson, Eugene Thamon	SSATTBB	a cappella	Murbo Music Pub.	1974	979
Hold On!	Alwes, Chester L.	SATB div	a cappella	Roger Dean	2000	10/2350R
Hold On!	Hairston, Jester	SATB div./ solo	a cappella	Bourne	1955	CB 1022
Hold On!	Hogan, Moses	SATB div. small group	a cappella	Hal Leonard	2002	8703351
Hold On	Boatner, Edward	SATB	piano	McAfee	1979	M1189
Hold On	Burleigh, Harry T.	SATB	a cappella	Ricordi	1938	NY1113
Hold Out Your Light	McNeil, Albert J.	SATB	piano opt.	Gentry	1983	JG-520

Title	Arranger	Voicing / Soloist	Accomp.	Publisher	©Date	Catalog #
Holy Spirit, Don't You Leave Me (from *Three Rhythmic Spirituals*)	Still, William Grant	SATB	piano	Bourne	1961	2951-9
Home In-a Dat Rock	Curtis, Marvin	SATB	piano	Fostco	1987	MF 290
Honor! Honor!	Johnson, Hall	SATBB / Tenor	a cappella	G. Schirmer	1935	CM 4579
Honor! Honor!	Johnson, Hall	SSA	piano	Carl Fischer	1935	CM5212
Honor! Honor!	Johnson, Hall	TTBB	a cappella	Carl Fischer	1935	CM21826
Hush!	Parker, Alice & Shaw, Robert	SATB	a cappella	GIA	1995	G-4233
Hush! Somebody's Callin' My Name	Dennard, Brazeal Wayne	Two-part	opt. piano	Shawnee	1986	EA-144
I Ain't Goin' Study War No More	Johnson, John Rosamond	SATB	piano	Handy	1938	HB3
I Been in de Storm So Long	Shackley, Larry	SATB / Sop.	piano, soprano sax, rhythm	Monarch	2006	10/3393M
I Believe This Is Jesus	Morris, Robert L.	SATB div.	a cappella	Alliance	1997	AMP 0256
I Believe This Is Jesus	Moore, Undine S.	SATB	a cappella	Ausburg Pub. House	1977	11-0559
I Belong to That Band	Jessye, Eva	SATB / Sop. and Bass	piano	Skidmore	1965	SK2091
I Can Tell the World	Hogan, Moses	SATB div.	a cappella	Hal Leonard	1998	8703198
I Can Tell the World	Hairston, Jester	SATB	a cappella	Bourne	1959	58566
I Cannot Stay Here by Myself	Johnson, Hall	SATB / Alto	a cappella	Carl Fischer	1940	CM4724
I Couldn't Hear Nobody Pray	Johnson, Hall	SSAATTBB / Sop. and Ten.	a cappella	G. Schirmer	1953	10151
I Couldn't Hear Nobody Pray	Hogan, Moses	SATB div / solo	a cappella	Hal Leonard	1999	8703239
I Couldn't Hear Nobody Pray	King, Betty Jackson	SATB / Sop.	a cappella	Kjos	1965	ED5394

Title	Arranger	Voicing / Solosit	Accomp.	Publisher	© Date	Catalog #
I Couldn't Hear Nobody Pray	Smith, William Henry	SATB / Sop. or Ten.	a cappella	Kjos	1937	1011
I Don' Feel No Ways Tired	Gibbs, Stacey V.	SATB	a cappella	Alliance	2006	AMP–0580
I Feel Like My Time Ain't Long	Still, William Grant	SATB	a cappella	Presser	1956	322–40304
I Got a Home in-a Dat Rock	Hogan, Moses	SATB div. / solo	a cappella	Hal Leonard	1999	8703228
I Got a Robe	Hogan, Moses	SATB / solo	a cappella	Hal Leonard	1997	8741179
I Got Shoes	Parker, Alice & Shaw, Robert	SATBB	a cappella	Lawson–Gould	1953	51116
I Got Shoes	Johnson, Hall	SATB	a cappella	Robbins	1949	R3413
I Hope My Mother Will Be There	Burleigh, Harry T.	SATB	a cappella	Ricordi	1924	NY414
I Just Come from the Fountain	Moore, Undine S.	SATB	a cappella	Warner Bros.	1951	W3418
I Know I've Been Changed	Dandridge, Damon H.	SATB div. / Sop.	a cappella	Alliance	2000	AMP–0370
I Know the Lord	Parker, Alice & Shaw, Robert	SATB / solo	a cappella	GIA	1995	G–4229
I Know the Lord's Laid His Hands on Me	Hogan, Moses	SATB div. / solo	a cappella	Hal Leonard	1999	8703232
I Open My Mouth	Thomas, André J.	SATB	a cappella	Hinshaw	1990	HMC–1168
I Stood by the River of Jordan	Smith, William Henry	SATTBB	a cappella	Kjos	1941	5029
I Stood on the River of Jordan	Hogan, Moses	SATB	a cappella	Hal Leonard	1997	8741178
I Thank You, Jesus	Morris, Robert L.	SATB	a cappella	Mark Foster	1989	MF 2034
I Wan'To Be Ready	Dawson, William L.	SATB / Alto and Bar.	piano	Kjos	1967	T127A
I Wanna Be Ready	Powell, Rosephanye	SATB / Alto	piano	Gentry	1996	JG2194
I Wan'To Be Ready	Dawson, William L.	SSAA / Sop. and Alto	piano	Kjos	1967	T129A
I Wan'To Be Ready	Dawson, William L.	TTBB / Ten. and Bar.	piano	Kjos	1967	T128A
I Want God's Heaven to be Mine	King, Betty Jackson	SATB / Sop. or Ten.	a cappella	Marks	1973	MC4601

Title	Arranger	Voicing / Solosit	Accomp.	Publisher	© Date	Catalog #
I Want Jesus	Hairston, Jester	SATB	a cappella	Bourne	1958	B206151-357
I Want Jesus to Walk with Me	Boatner, Edward	SATB	a cappella	Galaxy	1949	1735
I Want Jesus to Walk with Me	Hogan, Moses	SATB / solo	a cappella	Hal Leonard	1997	8740785
I Want Jesus to Walk With Me	Southall, Mitchell	SATB / Sop. or Ten.	a cappella	Jusko	1960	J-208
I Want Jesus to Walk With Me	Southall, Mitchell	SSA / Sop.	a cappella	Jusko	1960	J-170
I Want Jesus to Walk With Me	Southall, Mitchell	TTBB / Ten.	a cappella	Jusko	1960	J-210
I Want to Be Ready	Hogan, Moses	SATB	a cappella	Hal Leonard	2001	8703310
I Want to Die Easy	Carter, Roland	SATB	a cappella	Mar-Vel	1978	
I Want to Thank You, Lord	Hogan, Moses	SATB / Sop. or Ten.	a cappella	Hal Leonard	1995	8740200
I Want Two Wings	Parker, Alice & Shaw, Robert	SSATB	a cappella	Jenson	1991	43509062
If I Got My Ticket, Can I Ride?	Parker, Alice & Shaw, Robert	SSAATTBB / Ten.	a cappella	G. Schirmer	1952	9933
If I Got My Ticket, Can I Ride?	Parker, Alice & Shaw, Robert	TBB / Ten.	a cappella	G. Schirmer	1949	9852
I'll Never Turn Back No Mo'	Johnson, Hall	SATB	a cappella	Robbins	1949	R3452
I'll Never Turn Back No More	Dett, R. Nathaniel	SATB	a cappella	J. Fischer	1918	J.F.&B. 4435-8
I'm a Soldier, Let me Ride	McLin, Lena	SATB / Sop. or Bar.	piano opt.	Kjos	1997	8847
I'm A-Rollin'	Thomas, André J.	SATB	piano	Hinshaw	1986	HMC-842
I'm Going Down to the River Jordan	King, Betty Jackson	TTBB / Bar.	a cappella	Jacksonian Press	1990	JP 203
I'm Going Home	Moore, Undine S.	SATB / Sop.	a cappella	Augsburg	1978	11-0652
I'm Gonna Sing 'Til the Spirit Moves in my Heart	Hogan, Moses	SATB div.	a cappella	Hal Leonard	1995	8740284

Title	Arranger	Voicing / Solosit	Accomp.	Publisher	© Date	Catalog #
I'm Gonna Wait on the Lord	Dandridge, Damon H.	SSAA	a cappella	Alliance	2006	AMP-0666
In Bright Mansions	Boatner, Edward	SATB	a cappella	Colombo	1964	NY2377
In Dat Great Gittin' Up Mornin'	Hairston, Jester	SATB/ Ten.	a cappella	Bourne	1952	65166
In His Care-O	Dawson, William L.	SATB	a cappella	Kjos	1961	T122
In His Care-O	Dawson, William L.	TTBB	a cappella	Kjos	1961	T123
Is A Light Shinin' In The Heavens?	Morris, Robert L.	SATB	a cappella	Alliance	1998	AMP 0273
Is There Anybody Here	Still, William Grant	SATB	piano	Presser	1956	312–40305
It's All Over Me	Hairston, Jester	SATB / Alto	a cappella	Bourne	1952	69206
I've Been 'Buked	Boatner, Edward	SATB	piano	McAfee	1979	M1190
I've Been 'Buked	Johnson, Hall	SATB	a cappella	G. Schirmer	1946	9650
I've Been 'Buked, Children!	Dilworth, Rollo	SSA	piano	Santa Barbara	2004	SBMP 547
I've Been in the Storm So Long	Ames, Jeffery	SATB div. / Alto	a cappella	Walton		HL08501602
I've Been in de Storm So Long	Burleigh, Harry T.	SATB	a cappella	Ricordi	1944	NY1310
I've Got Shoes	Dilworth, Rollo	Two-part	piano	Hal Leonard	2001	8551500
Jesus is a Rock in a Weary Lan'	Work III, John	SATB / Sop.	a cappella	Presser	1937	
Jesus Lay Your Head in the Window	Hogan, Moses	SATB div. / Alto or Bass	a cappella / flute	Hal Leonard	1998	8703199
Jesus Lay Your Head in de Winder	Johnson, Hall	SATB / Ten.	a cappella	Robbins	1930	R3301
Jesus Walked This Lonesome Valley	Dawson, William L.	SATB	piano	Warner Bros.	1927	G821
Jesus Walked This Lonesome Valley	Dawson, William L.	SSA	piano	Warner Bros.	1927	G823
Jesus, Lay Your Head in the Window	Work III, John	SATB / Sop. and Ten.	a cappella	Galaxy	1960	GMC2166
John Saw Duh Numbuh	Parker, Alice & Shaw, Robert	SSAATTBB	a cappella	Lawson–Gould	1963	51109

Title	Arranger	Voicing / Solosit	Accomp.	Publisher	© Date	Catalog #
John, Saw the Holy Number	Work III, John	SATB / Sop.	a cappella	Galaxy	1962	GMC2236
I, John, Saw the Holy Number	Work III, John	SATB	a cappella	Galaxy	1962	2236
John Saw Duh Numbuh	Thomas, André J.	SATB	piano	Heritage	2001	15/1665H-2
John Saw Duh Numbuh	Thomas, André J.	SSAA	piano	Heritage	2001	15/1666H-2
Joshua Fit de Battle o'Jericho	Hairston, Jester	SATB	a cappella	Bourne	1952	71426
Joshua Fit de Battle o'Jericho	Johnson, John Rosamond	SATB	piano	Handy	1935	HB4
Joshua Fit de Battle o'Jericho	Southall, Mitchell	TTBB	a cappella	Jusko	1959	J-211
Joshua Fit de Battle o'Jericho	Ames, Jeffery	TTB	piano			
Joshua Fit the Battle o'Jericho	Printz, Brad	3-pt. mxd.	piano	Heritage	1998	15/1365H
Joshua Fit the Battle o'Jericho	Printz, Brad	Two-part	piano	Heritage	1998	15/1348H
Keep a-Inchin' Along	Johnson, Hall	TTBB / Ten.	a cappella	G. Schirmer	1957	10485
Keep Your Lamps	Thomas, André J.	SATB	conga drums	Hinshaw	1982	HMC-577
Keep Your Lamps!	Johnson, Victor C.	SAB	piano	Heritage	2007	15/2253H
Keep Your Lamps!	Johnson, Victor C.	SSA	piano	Heritage	2007	15/2237H
Keep Your Lamps	Thomas, André J.	SSA	piano	Hinshaw	2005	HMC-2048
Keep Your Lamps!	Johnson, Victor C.	TTB	piano	Heritage	2007	15/2238H
King Jesus Is A-Listening	Dawson, William L.	TTBB	a cappella	FitzSimmons	1929	No. 4025
The Lamb	Moore, Undine S.	SS or Unison	piano	Gray	1958	2531
The Lamb	Dett, R. Nathaniel	SSA	a cappella	J. Fischer	1938	7401
Lawd, Ah Wants to Be a Christian	Still, William Grant	SATB	piano	Handy	1938	HB9
Lay Your Healing Hands Upon Me	Dilworth, Rollo	SATB / solo	piano	Hal Leonard	2002	8711370
Let the Church Roll On	Hairston, Jester	SSAA	a cappella	Bourne	1951	75488

Title	Arranger	Voicing / Soloist	Accomp.	Publisher	© Date	Catalog #
Let Us Break Bread Together	Harris, Robert	SSAA / Sop.	a cappella / opt. flute	Manuscript	1969	
Let Us Break Bread Together	Ringwald, Roy	SSA	piano or organ	Shawnee	1963	B-259
Let Us Cheer the Weary Traveler	King, Betty Jackson	TTBB / Bass	a cappella	Jacksonian Press	1979	JP 201
The Lily of the Valley	Whalum, Wendell	SATB	a cappella	Lawson-Gould	1981	52141
Lily of the Valley	Hogan, Moses	SSAA div.	a cappella	Hal Leonard	2002	8743330
Listen to the Angels Shouting	Work III, John	SAA	a cappella	Galaxy	1947	1649
Listen to the Lambs	Dett, R. Nathaniel	SATB / Sop.	a cappella	G. Schirmer	1914	
Lit'l' Boy Chile	Dawson, William L.	SATB / Sop., Bar., and Bass	a cappella	Kjos	1947	T120
Lit'le, Lit'le Lamb	McLin, Lena	SATB / Sop.	a cappella	Kjos	1959	ED5457
The Little Baby	McLin, Lena	SATB / opt. Solo	piano	Kjos	1971	ED5855
Little Black Train	Work III, John	SAATB / Alto and Ten.	a cappella	Galaxy	1956	2088
Little Child of Mary	Burleigh, Harry T.	SSA / Sop.	piano	Ricordi	1940	NY1227-5
Little David, Play on Your Harp	Hairston, Jester	SSAATB	a cappella	Hal Leonard	1976	8601000
Little David, Play on Your Harp	Hogan, Moses	SATB	a cappella	Hal Leonard	1999	8703229
Little Innocent Lamb	Johnson, Neil A.	3-pt. Mxd.	piano	Heritage	1994	15/1119
Little Mother of Mine	Burleigh, Harry T.	SATB	piano	Ricordi	1929	NY952
Live A-Humble	Hairston, Jester	SSATBB	a cappella	Bourne	1955	2665-6
Long Fare You Well	Moore, Undine S.	SATB	a cappella	Augsburg	1960	11-0563
Lord Have Mercy	Moore, Undine S.	SATB	a cappella	Augsburg	1978	11-856
Lord, I Can't Stay Away	Boatner, Edward	SATB	a cappella	Hammon	1952	

Title	Arranger	Voicing / Solosit	Accomp.	Publisher	© Date	Catalog #
Lord, I Don't Feel Noways Tired	Johnson, Hall	SATB / Ten.	a cappella	Carl Fischer	1930	CM6502
Lord, I Looked Down the Road (from *Three Rhythmic Spirituals*)	Still, William Grant	SATB	piano	Bourne	1961	2951-9
Lord, I Want to Be a Christian	Dennard, Brazeal Wayne	SATB div.	a cappella	Alliance	1994	AMP 0029
Lord I Want to Be a Christian	Johnson, Hall	SATB / Sop.	a cappella	G. Schirmer	1946	9561
Lord, I Want to be a Christian	Hogan, Moses	SATB	a cappella	Hal Leonard	1999	8742075
Lord, I Want Two Wings	Carey, Courtney	SATB	a cappella	Roger Dean	2005	15/1960R+
Lord, If I Got My Ticket	Gibbs, Stacey V.	SATB div. / solo	a cappella	Gentry	2004	JG2320
Mary Had a Baby	Brown, Jr., Uzee	SATB / Sop.	a cappella	Roger Dean	1984	HRD121
Mary Had a Baby	Johnson, Hall	SATB	a cappella	G. Schirmer	1955	10359
Mary Had a Baby	Dawson, William L.	SATB	a cappella	Kjos	1947	T118
Mary Had a Baby	Dawson, William L.	TTBB / Ten.	a cappella	Kjos	1947	T119
Mary Had a Baby	Johnson, Victor C.	TTB	piano	Heritage	1998	15/1377H
Mary, Mary, Where is Your Baby?	Hairston, Jester	SATB	a cappella	Bourne	1950	82156
Mary was the Queen of Galilee	Whalum, Wendell	SATB / Sop.	a cappella	Lawson-Gould	1974	51808
Mary's Little Boy Chile	Hairston, Jester	SATB / solo	piano	Schumann Music Co.	1956	S-1024
Mornin'	Hairston, Jester	SATB / Tenor	a cappella	Schumann Music Co.	1952	S-1013
Move! Let Me Shine	Jessye, Eva	SATB	piano	Skidmore	1965	SK2093
My God is a Rock	Dandridge, Damon H.	SATB div. / Bass	a cappella	Alliance	2002	AMP-0458
My God is So High	Hogan, Moses	SATB / solo	a cappella	Alliance	1995	AMP-0190
My God is So High	McLin, Lena	SATB	a cappella	Kjos	1972	ED5881
My Lord, What a Mornin'	Farrow, Larry	SSATBB	a cappella	Gentry	1983	JG0509

Title	Arranger	Voicing / Solosit	Accomp.	Publisher	© Date	Catalog #
My Lord, What a Mornin'	Work III, John	SATB / Sop. and Bar.	a cappella	Presser	1964	312-40622
My Lord What a Mourning	Dawson, William L.	SATB	a cappella	FitzSimmons	1954	2009
My Lord, What a Mornin'	Burleigh, Harry T.	SATB	a cappella	Belwin Mills	1924	FC412
My Lord, What a Morning	Dilworth, Rollo	4-part Treble	piano	Plymouth	1999	21-20263
My Lord, What a Morning	Whalum, Wendell	TTBB	a cappella	Lawson-Gould	1979	51917
My Soul's Been Anchored in the Lord	Hogan, Moses	SATB div.	a cappella	Hal Leonard	1999	8703235
My Soul's Been Anchored	Parker, Alice & Shaw, Robert	SATB / Ten.	a cappella	Lawson-Gould	1963	51111
New Born King	McLin, Lena	SATB	a cappella	GWM	1972	EDGC23
No Hidin' Place	Hogan, Moses	SATB div.	a cappella	Hal Leonard	2001	8703328
No Rocks A-Cryin'	Dilworth, Rollo	SATB div.	piano	Hal Leonard	2001	9711307
Nobody Knows the Trouble I See	Johnson, Hall	SATB / Ten.	a cappella	Robbins	1949	R3451
Nobody Knows de Trouble I've Seen	Simpson, Eugene Thamon	SATB / Bar.	a cappella	Bourne	1976	B231548-358
Nobody Knows the Trouble I've Seen	Burleigh, Harry T.	SATB	a cappella	Belwin Mills	1924	FCC406
Nobody Knows the Trouble I've Seen	Southall, Mitchell	SATB	a cappella	Jusko	1960	J-209
Nobody Knows the Trouble I've Seen	Southall, Mitchell	SSA	a cappella	Jusko	1960	J-171
Nobody Knows de Trouble I See	de Paur, Leonard	TTBB	a cappella	Lawson-Gould	1954	524
Now Let Me Fly	Bray, Julie Gardner	SATB	piano	Heritage	1996	15/1231H
Now Let Me Fly	Spevacek, Linda	SATB	piano	Heritage	2003	15/1775H
Now Let Me Fly	Spevacek, Linda	SAB	piano	Heritage	2003	15/1783H
Now Let Me Fly	Spevacek, Linda	SSA	piano	Heritage	2003	15/1845H
Now Let Me Fly	Spevacek, Linda	TB / TTB	piano	Heritage	2003	15/1846H

Title	Arranger	Voicing / Solosit	Accomp.	Publisher	© Date	Catalog #
Now We Take This Body	Morris, Robert L.	SATB / Sop. and Bar.	a cappella	Mark Foster	1998	MF 2145
O Hear My Prayin' (from *Three Spirituals*)	Ringwald, Roy	SATB	a cappella	Shawnee	1978	A-1475
Oh Lord, Have Mercy on Me	Johnson, Hall	SATB /Sop.	a cappella	G. Schirmer	1946	9558
O Lord Have Mercy on Me	Burleigh, Harry T.	TTBB	a cappella	Ricordi	1935	NY1974-5
Oh Mary, Don't You Weep, Don't You Mourn	Hogan, Moses	SATB	a cappella	Hal Leonard	2001	8703329
O, Mary, Don't You Weep	McNeil, Albert J.	SATB	a cappella	Gentry	1984	JG-536
O Wasn't That a Wide River	Johnson, John Rosamond	SATB	piano	Handy	1935	
Oh, Po' Little Jesus	de Paur, Leonard	TTBB	a cappella	Lawson–Gould	1958	710
Oh, the Savior's Comin', Hallelu!	Brown, Jr., Uzee	SSAA	a cappella	Roger Dean	1997	10/1683R
Oh, What a Beautiful City	Webb, Jeffrey L.	SATB div. / Sop.	piano	Roger Dean	2007	15/2311R
Oh, What a Beautiful City	Boatner, Edward	SSATBB	piano	McAfee	1979	M1191
Oh, What a Beautiful City	Dawson, William L.	SATB	a cappella	Kjos	1934	T100
Beautiful City	Thomas, André J.	SATB	piano	Heritage	2006	15/2124H
Oh, Won't You Sit Down?	Gilpin, Greg	SAB	piano	Heritage	2007	15/2232H
Oh, Won't You Sit Down?	Gilpin, Greg	SATB	piano	Heritage	2007	15/2233H
Old Time Religion	Hogan, Moses	SATB / solo	a cappella	Hal Leonard	1995	8740181
Ole Ark's A-Moverin'	King, Betty Jackson	TTBB	a cappella	Jacksonian Press	1992	JP 204
On Ma Journey	Boatner, Edward	SATB / Alto and Ten.	a cappella	Colombo	1956	NY1778
Open the Window, Noah	McNeil, Albert J.	SATB / solo	a cappella	Gentry	1986	JG2025
Peter, Go Ring–A Dem Bells	Ames, Jeffery	SA	piano, handbells	Walton	2007	WLG–124

Title	Arranger	Voicing / Solosit	Accomp.	Publisher	© Date	Catalog #
Peter, Go Ring Dem Bells	Thomas, André J.	SATB	piano	Heritage	2001	15/1592H-3
Oh Peter go ring-a dem bells	Burleigh, Harry T.	SSA	piano	Ricordi	1925	NY447
Plenty Good Room	Alwes, Chester L.	SATB div	a cappella	Roger Dean	1997	10/2348R
Plenty Good Room	Smith, William Henry	SATB	a cappella	Kjos	1937	1003
Plenty Good Room	Hogan, Moses	TTBB div.	a cappella	Hal Leonard	2002	8703330
Poor Man Lazrus	Hairston, Jester	SATTBB	a cappella	Bourne	1955	103936
Poor Man Lazrus	Hairston, Jester	SSA	a cappella	Bourne	1955	103938
Po'Ol' Laz'rus	Work III, John	TTBB / Ten. and Bass	a cappella	J. Fischer	1931	6513
Poor Man Lazrus	Hairston, Jester	TTBB	a cappella	Bourne	1955	2653-7
Poor Wayfaring Stranger	Johnson, Victor C.	TTB	piano	Heritage	1999	15/1449H
The Promised Land	Burleigh, Harry T.	SATB / Alto	piano	Ricordi	1929	NY831
Ride On, Jesus	Johnson, Hall	SATB	a cappella	G. Schirmer	1957	10483
Ride on, King Jesus	Hogan, Moses	SATB div. / solo	keyboard	Hal Leonard	1999	8703210
Ride On, King Jesus!	Fountain, Robert	SATB div. / Sop. or Ten.	a cappella	Roger Dean	2000	15/1576R
Ride On, King Jesus	Johnson, Hall	SATB	a cappella	Carl Fischer	1951	CM6702
Ride the Chariot	Hogan, Moses	SATB div.	a cappella	Hal Leonard	2001	8703309
Ride the Chariot	Smith, William Henry	SATB / Sop.	a cappella	Kjos	1939	1015
Ride the Chariot	Thomas, André J.	SATB	opt. conga drum	Hinshaw	1987	HMC-931
Ride the Chariot	Smith, William Henry	TTBB / Ten.	a cappella	Kjos	1939	1102
Ride Up in the Chariot	Shackley, Larry	SATB	piano	Exaltation	2007	10/3582L

Title	Arranger	Voicing / Solosit	Accomp.	Publisher	© Date	Catalog #
Rise and Shine	Boatner, Edward	SATB	piano	McAfee	1979	M1192
Rise Up Shepherd and Follow	Dett, R. Nathaniel	SATB / Sop. and Ten.	piano	J. Fischer	1936	7218
Rise Up, Shepherd and Follow	Hairston, Jester	SATB	a cappella	Bourne	1974	241706
Rise Up, Shepherd, and Follow	Thomas, André J.	SATB	a cappella	Heritage	2001	15/1591H
Rise Up Shepherd and Follow	Dett, R. Nathaniel	TTBB	piano	J. Fischer	1936	7219
Rock, Mt. Sinai	Jessye, Eva	SATB	piano	Skidmore	1965	SK2095
Rock, Mount Sinai	Work III, John	SATB	a cappella	Galaxy	1962	2237
Oh, Rocka My Soul	Hairston, Jester	SSATTBB	a cappella	Bourne	1950	CB 1022
Rock-a My Soul	Spevacek, Linda	SATB	piano	Heritage	2004	15/1891H
Rock-a My Soul	Spevacek, Linda	3-pt. mxd.	piano	Heritage	2001	15/1652H
Rock-a My Soul	Spevacek, Linda	Two-part	piano	Heritage	2001	15/1656H
Rockin' Jerusalem	Dandridge, Damon H.	SATB div.	a cappella	Alliance	2002	AMP-0481
Rockin' Jerusalem	Morris, Robert L.	SATB	a cappella	Walton	2001	HL08501431
Rockin' Jerusalem	Thomas, André J.	SATB	a cappella	Mark Foster	1986	MF 2002
Rockin' Jerusalem	Work III, John	SATB	a cappella	Presser	1940	312–21427
Roll, Jordan, Roll	Fountain, Robert	SATB div.	a cappella	Roger Dean	1998	15/1398R
Roll, Jordan, Roll	Curtis, Marvin	SATB	a cappella	Fostco	1989	MF 2040
Run Li'l Chillun	Johnson, Hall	SATB / Ten.	piano	Robbins	1941	R2164
Same Train	Johnson, John Rosamond	SATB	piano	Handy	1935	HB5
Scandalized My Name	Hairston, Jester	SSATB	a cappella	Bourne	1959	2917–4
Scandalize My Name	Johnson, Hall	SATB / Ten.	a cappella	G. Schirmer	1958	10608
Scandalize My Name	Burleigh, Harry T.	TTBB	a cappella	Ricordi	1922	NY229

Title	Arranger	Voicing / Soloist	Accomp.	Publisher	© Date	Catalog #
See Dat Babe	Gibbs, Stacey V.	SATB div.	a cappella	Gentry	2005	JG2358
Set Down Servant	Parker, Alice & Shaw, Robert	SATB div. / Alto and Bass	a cappella	Shawnee	1944	A 0029
Set Down Servant	Parker, Alice & Shaw, Robert	TTBB div. / Ten. and Bass	a cappella	Shawnee	1942	
Sinner, Please Don't Let This Harvest Pass	Butler, Mark	SATB div. / Sop. and Ten.	a cappella	Hinshaw	2006	HMC2056
Sinner Please Don't Let This Harvest Pass	King, Betty Jackson	SATB div.	a cappella	Mills	1978	2983
Sinner Don't Let This Harvest Pass	Boatner, Edward	SATB	a cappella	Hammon	1952	
Sinnuh, Please Don't Let Dis Harves' Pass	Simpson, Eugene Thamon	SATB / Alto	a cappella	Bourne	1976	315146
Sinner Please Don't Let This Harvest Pass	Work III, John	SATB / Sop.	a cappella	Presser	1952	322–40020
Sinner, You Can't Walk My Path	Moore, Undine S.	SATB	a cappella	M. Witmark and Sons	1958	W3546
Sister Mary Had-A But One Child	Simpson, Eugene Thamon	SSATBB / Ten. or Bar.	a cappella	Bourne	1981	375606
The Virgin Mary Had-a One Son	Mabry, George	SATB div. / Sop.	a cappella	Roger Dean	1999	15/1461R
Sit Down, Servant, Sit Down	Dett, R. Nathaniel	SATB	piano	G. Schirmer	1932	7931
Somebody's Calling My Name	Whalum, Wendell	TTBB	a cappella	Lawson-Gould	1975	51932
Somebody's Knockin' At Yo' Do'	Gibbs, Stacey V.	SATB div. / solo	a cappella	Gentry	2004	JG2321
Somebody's Knocking at Your Door	Dett, R. Nathaniel	SATB	piano	John Church Co.	1939	35197
Somebody's Knocking at Your Door	Dett, R. Nathaniel	SSA	piano	John Church Co.	1921	35186
Sometimes I Feel Like a Motherless Child	Smith, William Henry	SATB div. / solo	piano / organ	Kjos	1939	1013
Sometimes I Feel Like a Motherless Child	Hairston, Jester	SATB / Alto	a cappella	Bourne	1952	120846
Sometimes I Feel Like a Motherless Child	Johnson, Hall	SATB / Alto	a cappella	Marks	1956	4007

Title	Arranger	Voicing / Soloist	Accomp.	Publisher	© Date	Catalog #
Sometimes I Feel Like a Motherless Child	Southall, Mitchell	SATB	a cappella	Carl Fischer	1959	9167
Sometimes I Feel Like a Motherless Child	Burleigh, Harry T.	SSA	piano	Ricordi	1949	116543
Sometimes I Feel Like a Motherless Child	Smith, William Henry	TTBB / Sop.	a cappella	Kjos	1937	1113
Song of Freedom	Johnson, Victor C.	3-pt. Mxd.	piano	Heritage	2007	15/2254H
Song of Freedom	Johnson, Victor C.	SATB	piano	Heritage	2007	15/2235H
Soon I Will Be Done	Boatner, Edward	SATB	a cappella	Colombo	1949	NY1655
Soon Ah Will Be Done	Dawson, William L.	SATB	a cappella	Kjos	1934	T102A
Soon Ah Will Be Done	Dawson, William L.	TTBB	a cappella	Kjos	1934	T101A
Spiritual Jubilee	Spevacek, Linda	SATB	piano	Heritage	2002	15/1749H
Spiritual Jubilee	Spevacek, Linda	TTBB	piano	Heritage	2007	15/2280H
Spiritual Jubilee	Spevacek, Linda	3-pt. mxd.	piano	Heritage	2002	15/1724H
Spiritual Jubilee	Spevacek, Linda	Two-part	piano	Heritage	2002	15/1718H
A Spiritual Reflection	Hogan, Moses	SATB div.	a cappella	Hal Leonard	2001	8703315
Stand the Storm	King, Betty Jackson	SATB / Sop. or Ten.	piano	Hope	1956	HO1814
Stan' the Storm	King, Betty Jackson	SSA / Sop.	piano	Jacksonian Press	1956	JP 302
Standin in the Need of Prayer	Hogan, Moses	SATB	a cappella	Hal Leonard	1999	8703230
Stayed On Jesus	Parker, Alice & Shaw, Robert	SATB / solo	a cappella	GIA	1995	G-4230
Steal Away	Hairston, Jester	SATTBB / solo	a cappella	Schumann Music Co.	1951	S 1007
Steal Away	Alwes, Chester L.	SATB div	a cappella	Roger Dean	1997	10/2349R
Steal Away	Southall, Mitchell	SATTBB	a cappella	Jusko	1959	J-212
Steal Away	Carter, Roland	SATB / Alto or Bar.	a cappella	Mar-Vel	1979	
Steal Away	Hogan, Moses	SATB / solo	a cappella	Hal Leonard	1999	8703203

Title	Arranger	Voicing / Solosit	Accomp.	Publisher	©Date	Catalog #
Steal Away	Burleigh, Harry T.	SATB	a cappella	Ricordi	1924	NY422
Steal Away	Dawson, William L.	SATB	a cappella	Kjos	1942	T108
Steal Away	Johnson, Hall	SATB	a cappella	Carl Fischer	1935	CM4581
Steal Away to Jesus	Johnson, John Rosamond	SATB / Alto and Bar.	piano	Handy	1937	HB6
Steal Away	Simpson, Eugene Thamon	SATB	a cappella	Bourne	1975	B231324-358
Steal Away	Ringwald, Roy	SSAA	piano	Shawnee	1945	
Steal Away	Johnson, Hall	SSA	piano	Carl Fischer	1935	CM5214
Steal Away	Dawson, William L.	TTBB	a cappella	Kjos	1942	T109
Steal Away	Dennard, Brazeal Wayne	TTBB	a cappella	Shawnee	1992	C-279
Steal Away	Johnson, Hall	TTBB	a cappella	Carl Fischer	1935	CM2184
Surely He Died on Calvary	Hogan, Moses	SATB div. / solo	a cappella	Hal Leonard	2002	8703331
Sweet Home	Whalum, Wendell	SATB / Sop.	a cappella	Lawson-Gould	1975	51869
Swing Down, Chariot	Thomas, André J.	SATB	a cappella	Heritage	2003	15/1798H
Swing Down, Chariot	Thomas, André J.	TTBB	a cappella	Heritage	2003	15/1778H
Swing Low, Sweet Chariot	Hogan, Moses	SATB div.	piano, flute	Alliance	1996	AMP-0192
Swing Low, Sweet Chariot	Farrow, Larry	SATB / Alto	a cappella	Gentry	1982	JG-484
Swing Low, Sweet Chariot	Dawson, William L.	SATB	a cappella	Kjos	1949	T114
Swing Low, Sweet Chariot	Dawson, William L.	SSA / Sop.	a cappella	Kjos	1946	T116
Swing Low, Sweet Chariot	Dawson, William L.	TTBB	a cappella	Kjos	1946	T115
Swing Low, Sweet Chariot	de Paur, Leonard	TTBB	a cappella	Lawson-Gould	1954	523
Swing Low, Sweet Chariot	Porterfield, Sherri	3-pt. mxd.	piano	Heritage	1995	15/1179H
Take Me to the Water	Parker, Alice & Shaw, Robert	SAATB / solo	a cappella	GIA	1995	G-4238

Title	Arranger	Voicing / Solosit	Accomp.	Publisher	©Date	Catalog #
Tataleo	Hairston, Jester	SATB	a cappella	Bourne	1971	J-15
That Lonesome Valley	Parker, Alice & Shaw, Robert	SATB / Treble voices, Bar.	a cappella	Lawson-Gould	1963	51103
There is a Balm in Gilead	Hogan, Moses	SATB div. / solo	a cappella	Hal Leonard	1998	8703200
There is a Balm in Gilead	Dawson, William L.	SATB / Sop.	a cappella	Kjos	1939	T105
There Is a Balm in Gilead	Rentz, Earlene	SATB	a cappella	Laurel	2005	10/3260L
There is a Balm in Gilead	Dawson, William L.	SSA / Sop.	a cappella	Kjos	1939	T107
There is a Balm in Gilead	Dawson, William L.	TTBB / Ten.	a cappella	Kjos	1939	T106
There's a Lit'l'Wheel A-Turnin' In My Heart	Dawson, William L.	SATB	a cappella	Kjos	1949	T121
There's a Man Goin' Round	Hogan, Moses	SSATTB / solo	a cappella	Alliance	1996	AMP 0191
There's a Meeting Here Tonight	Dett, R. Nathaniel	SSA	piano	John Church Co.	1921	35008
There's a Meeting Here Tonight	Work III, John	TTBB	a cappella	E.C. Schirmer	1950	2150
There's No Hiding Place Down There	Southall, Mitchell	SATB	a cappella	Jusko	1959	J-213
This Little Light of Mine	Hogan, Moses	SATB div. / Sop. and Ten.	a cappella	Hal Leonard	2002	8743115
This Little Light of Mine	Work III, John	SATB / Sop.	a cappella	Galaxy	1973	1384
This Little Light of Mine	King, Betty Jackson	SATB	a cappella	Hope	1978	HO1812
This Little Light of Mine	Harris, Robert	Two-part	piano	Boosey & Hawkes	1997	OCTB6921
This Little Light of Mine	Patterson, Mark	Uni./2-pt.	piano	Choristers Guild	2007	CGA1108
This Train!	Robinson, Russell	3-pt. mxd.	piano	Heritage	2007	15/2289H
This Train!	Robinson, Russell	Two-part	piano	Heritage	2007	15/2303H
'Tis Me, O Lord	Burleigh, Harry T.	TTBB	a cappella	Ricordi	1924	NY424
Trampin'	Boatner, Edward	SATB	a cappella	Galaxy	1954	2019

Title	Arranger	Voicing / Solosit	Accomp.	Publisher	© Date	Catalog #
Trampin'	Johnson, Hall	SATB / Alto	a cappella	Marks	1956	4009
True Religion	Simpson, Eugene Thamon	SATB	a cappella	Bourne	1977	B231985-358
Two Christmas Spirituals	King, Betty Jackson	SATB	a cappella	Somerset	1978	AD1998
Wade in the Water	Butler, Mark	SATB div. / solo	a cappella	Hinshaw	2006	
Wade in the Water	Hogan, Moses	SATB div. / solo	a cappella	Hal Leonard	1997	8741180
Wade in the Water	Powell, Rosephanye	SATB div.	a cappella	Gentry	2000	JG2241
Wade in de Waters	Southall, Mitchell	SATB / Sop.	opt. piano	Handy	1957	
Wade in de Water	Burleigh, Harry T.	SATB	a cappella	Ricordi	1925	NY487
Wade in de Water	Hairston, Jester	SATB	a cappella	Warner	1950	W3670
Wade in the Water	Printz, Brad	3-pt. mxd.	piano	Heritage	1996	15/1261H
Wade in the Water	Printz, Brad	Two-part	piano	Heritage	1996	15/1248H
Walk in Jerusalem	Dilworth, Rollo	SATB	piano	Hal Leonard	2004	8744360
Walk Through the Streets of the City	Moore, Undine S.	SATB	a cappella	Augsburg	1977	11-0564
Walk Together Children	Hogan, Moses	SATB div.	a cappella	Hal Leonard	2001	8703332
Walk Together Children	Johnson, Hall	SATB	a cappella	Marks	1956	4006
Walk Together Children	Burleigh, Harry T.	SSA or TTB	a cappella	Ricordi	1938	NY1118
Wasn't That a Mighty Day?	Dett, R. Nathaniel	SATB / Alto and Bar.	a cappella	G. Schirmer	1933	7712
Wasn't That a Mighty Day	Work III, John	SSA	piano	J. Fischer	1934	FE6845
Wasn't That a Mighty Day	Work III, John	TTBB	a cappella	J. Fischer	1931	6515
Way Over in Beluah-Lan'	Johnson, Hall	SATB div. / soli	a cappella	Hal Leonard	1956	HL00008006
Way Over in Beulah Lan'	Gibbs, Stacey V.	SATB div.	a cappella	Gentry	2007	JG2370
Way Over in Eygpt Land	Work III, John	SATB	a cappella	Galaxy	1947	1574

Title	Arranger	Voicing / Solosit	Accomp.	Publisher	© Date	Catalog #
Way Up in Heaven	Johnson, Hall	SATB	piano	Robbins	1930	R3300
Wayfarin' Stranger	Berg, Ken	SATB	a cappella	Choristers Guild	2004	CGA998
Wayfarin' Stranger	Spevacek, Linda	3-pt. mxd.	piano	Heritage	2007	15/2297H
We Shall Walk Through the Valley in Peace	Hogan, Moses	SATB div.	a cappella	Hal Leonard	2001	8703314
Weeping Mary	Dett, R. Nathaniel	SATB / Sop.	a cappella	J. Fischer	1918	4434
Were You There	Parker, Alice & Shaw, Robert	SATBB / Alto	a cappella	Lawson-Gould	1966	51249
Were You There?	Johnson, Hall	SATB / Sop. and Ten.	a cappella	G. Schirmer	1954	10128
Were You There?	Burleigh, Harry T.	SATB	a cappella	Ricordi	1924	NY423
Were You There?	Burleigh, Harry T.	SATB	a cappella	Belwin Mills	1927	FCC 00423
Were You There?	Burleigh, Harry T.	SSA	a cappella	Ricordi	1927	NY693
Were You There	Ringwald, Roy	TTBB	a cappella	Shawnee	1943	
What Kind O' Shoes You Gonna Wear?	Hairston, Jester	SATB	a cappella	Bourne	1959	2867-9
What Kinder Shoes	Johnson, Hall	SATB	a cappella	Carl Fischer	1947	CM6209
When I Get Home	Boatner, Edward	SATB	a cappella	Ricordi	1954	NY1656-9
When I Was Sinking Down	Johnson, Hall	SATB	a cappella	G. Schirmer	1946	9559
When the Saints Go Marching In	Farrow, Larry	SATB	piano, guitar, bass guitar, tambourine	Gentry	1982	JG-481
When the Saints Go Marching In	Jessye, Eva	SATB	piano	Marks	1966	13416-6
When The Trumpet Sounds	Thomas, André J.	SATB	piano	Mark Foster	1985	MF 261
Where Shall I Be?	Still, William Grant	SATB div.	piano	Gemini Press	1977	GP-408
Who Built the Ark?	Hogan, Moses	SATB div.	a cappella	Hal Leonard	2001	8703313
Who Built de Ark	Johnson, John Rosamond	SATB	piano	Handy	1938	HB7

Title	Arranger	Voicing / Solosit	Accomp.	Publisher	© Date	Catalog #
Who Built de Ark	Johnson, Hall	TTBB	a cappella	Carl Fischer	1954	CM7444
Who is That Yonder	Boatner, Edward	SATB	a cappella	Ricordi	1954	NY1660-8
Who Is That Yonder?	Jessye, Eva	SATB	piano	Skidmore	1965	SK2096
Who'll Be a Witness?	Whalum, Wendell	SATB / Ten.	a cappella	Lawson-Gould	1986	52279
Who'll Be a Witness for My Lord	Hairston, Jester	SATB	a cappella	Bourne	1959	146506
Witness	Halloran, Jack	SSAATTBB	a cappella	Gentry	1986	JG2010
Witness	Dandridge, Damon H.	SATB div. / Sop. and Ten.	a cappella	Alliance	2006	AMP-0650
Witness	Hogan, Moses	TTBB div. small group	a cappella	Hal Leonard	2002	8743357
Writ'en Down My Name	McLin, Lena	SATB / Bar.	a cappella	Kjos	1967	ED5450
You Better Min' How You Talk	Hogan, Moses	SATB	a cappella	Hal Leonard	2001	8703311
You Better Mind	Hairston, Jester	SSATB	a cappella	Bourne	1965	CB 1022
You Goin' to Reap Jus' What You Sow	Burleigh, Harry T.	SATB	a cappella	Ricordi	1938	NY1134
You Got to Reap Just What You Sow	Dawson, William L.	SATB	piano	Kjos	1928	T142
You Got to Reap Just What You Sow	Dawson, William L.	SSAA	piano	Kjos	1928	T144
You Got to Reap Just What You Sow	Dawson, William L.	TTBB	piano	Kjos	1928	T143
You Hear the Lambs A–Crying	Boatner, Edward	SATB / Ten.	a cappella	Ricordi	1952	217
You Must Have That True Religion	Carter, Roland	SATB / Sop.	a cappella	Mar-Vel	1979	
You'd Better Run	Whalum, Wendell	TTBB / Bar.	a cappella	Lawson-Gould	1976	51749
Zion's Walls	Dawson, William L.	SATB / Sop.	a cappella	Kjos	1961	T124

NOTES

Chapter 1: Singing in a Strange Land

1. Eileen Southern, *The Music of Black Americans*, 3rd ed. (New York: W.W. Norton & Co., 1997), 6.

2. James Walvin, *The Slave Trade* (Gloucestershire, UK: Sutton Publishing Limited, 1999).

3. *The Interesting Narrative of the Life of Olaudah Equiano* (London: T. Wilkins, 1789), 58.

4. Hildred Roach, *Black American Music: Past and Present*, 2nd ed. (Malabar, FL: Krieger Publishing Company, 1992), 4.

5. James W. Johnson and J. Rosamond Johnson, *The Books of American Negro Spirituals* (1925; reprint, Cambridge: Da Capo Press, 2005) 17.

6. Southern, *The Music of Black Americans*, 10.

7. Bruno Nettl, *Folk and Traditional Music of the Western Continents* (Englewood Cliffs, N.J.: Prentice Hall, Inc., 1965).

8. Robert Newman, *Go Down Moses: Celebrating the African-American Spiritual* (New York: Clarkson Potter, 1998).

9. Johnson and Johnson, *The Books of American Negro Spirituals*, 20.

10. Henry Edward Krehbiel, *Afro-American Folksongs* (Baltimore: Clearfield Company, 1914), 3; John Lovell, *Black Song: The Forge and the Flame; The Story of How the Afro-American Spiritual was Hammered Out* (New York: Macmillan, 1972), 13.

11. Southern, *The Music of Black Americans*, 155.

12. Arthur C. Jones, *Wade in the Water: The Wisdom of the Spirituals* (Maryknoll: Orbis Books, 1993), 6; Roach, *Black American Music*, 23.

13. Jones, *Wade in the Water*, 6.

14. Krehbiel, *Afro-American Folksongs*, 33.

15. Johnson and Johnson, *The Books of American Negro Spirituals*, 33; Southern, *The Music of Black Americans*, 170.

16. Southern, *The Music of Black Americans*, 164.

17. Lovell, *Black Song*, 23.

18. Krehbiel, *Afro-American Folksongs*, vi–vii.

19. Lovell, *Black Song*, 198.

20. Newman, *Go Down Moses*, 19.

Chapter 2: From the Oral Tradition to the Printed Page

1. Southern, *The Music of Black Americans*, 151.

2. William Francis Allen, Charles Pickard Ware, and Lucy McKim Garrison, eds. *Slave Songs of the United States* (New York: Simpson, 1867), ii.

3. Ibid., vi.

4. J.B.T Marsh, *The Story of the Jubilee Singers: With Their Songs* (Boston: Houghton, Osgood, 1880), 121.

5. Thomas P. Fenner, arr, *Cabin and plantation songs as sung by the Hampton Students* (New York: G. P. Putnam's Sons, 1891), vi.

6. Edward Avery McIlhenny and Henry Whermann, *Befo' De War Spirituals* (Boston: Christopher Publishing House, 1933).

Chapter 3: Beyond the Printed Page to Shaping an Art

1. Anne Key Simpson, *Hard Trials: The Life and Music of Harry T. Burleigh* (Metuchen, New Jersey: Scarecrow Press, 1990) 16, 32.

2. Johnson and Johnson, *The Books of American Negro Spirituals*, 48.

3. Charlotte W. Murray, "The Story of Harry T. Burleigh," *The Hymn 17*, no. 4 (October 1966): 105.

4. Southern, *The Music of Black Americans*, 270; Irving S. Gilmore Music Library, "J. Rosamond Johnson Papers," Irving S. Gilmore Music Library, http://webtext.library.yale.edu/mxl2html/music/jrj-d.htm. These sources provided important biographical information.

5. Johnson and Johnson, *The Books of American Negro Spirituals*, 50.

6. R. Nathaniel Dett, "Helping to Lay Foundation for Negro Music of Future," *Black Perspective in Music 1/1*, (Spring 1973): 64–69. Previously published in *Musical America* (July 8, 1918).

7. Ibid.

8. R. Nathaniel Dett, "From Bell Stand to Throne Room," *Black Perspective in Music 1/1*, (Spring 1973): 73–81. Previously published in *The Etude LII*, (February 1934): 79–80.

9. Anne Key Simpson, *Follow Me: The Life and Music of R. Nathaniel Dett* (Metuchen, New Jersey: Scarecrow Press, 1993) 21–22.

10. Vivian Flagg McBrier, *R. Nathaniel Dett: His Life and Works, 1882–1943* (Washington: Associated Publishers, 1977) 52.

11. George Pullen Jackson, *White and Negro Spirituals: Their Life Span and Kinship* (New York: Augustin, 1944) 141–142.

12. Eileen Southern, *Readings in Black American Music* (New York: W.W. Norton & Co., 1983) 272.

13. Ibid., 274.

14. Southern, *The Music of Black Americans*, 414.

15. Roach, *Black American Music*, 123.

16. William Grant Still, interview by R. Donald Brown, *The Oral History Program*, California State University, Fullerton, 1984. Important biographical information was obtained from this interview.

17. Edward Boatner, *The Story of the Spirituals: 30 Spirituals and Their Origins* (Miami: Belwin Mills, 1973).

18. Southern, *The Music of Black Americans*, 416.

19. Biographical information was obtained from Mr. Malone's dissertation "William Levi Dawson: American Music Educator," Southern, *The Music of Black Americans*, 418, and Roach, *Black American Music*, 129.

20. Mark Malone, "William Levi Dawson: American Music Educator," (PhD diss., Florida State University, 1981) 119.

21. Southern, *The Music of Black Americans*, 277.

22. The Library of Congress, "Fisk University Mississippi Delta Collection," The Library of Congress, http://www.loc.gov/folklife/guides/fisk.html. Much of this impressive collection is available at this site.

23. Roach, *Black American Music*, 131.

24. Colored Reflections, "Jester Hairston," Colored Reflections, http://www.coloredreflections.com/decades/Decade.cfm?Dec=5&Typ=2&Sty=1&SID=95.

25. Biographical information was obtained from Southern, *The Music of Black Americans*, 524, and Evelyn Davidson White, *Choral Music by African American Composers: A Selected, Annotated Bibliography* (Lanham, Maryland: Scarecrow Press, 1996) 208. The Library of Virginia, "Working Out Her Destiny: Notable Virginia Women," The Library of Virginia, http://www.lva.lib.va.us/whoweare/exhibits/destiny/notable/smith.htm. This site contains Ms. Moore's description of herself.

26. White, *Choral Music by African American Composers*, 210.

27. Shawnee Press, "Roy Ringwald," Shawnee Press Inc., http://www.shawneepress.com/composers.asp. Mr. Ringwald's biographical information was obtained from this site.

28. Roach, *Black American Music*, 142–144; Southern, *The Music of Black Americans*, 460–461; The Center for Black Music Research, "Leonard de Paur," The Center for Black Music Research, http://www.cbmr.org/depaur/depaur.htm. These sources provided important biographical information; "Music Giant Leonard de Paur is Dead at 83," *New York Amsterdam News* (November 25, 1998). This article is a good representation of the media's opinions of Mr. de Paur.

29. Roach, *Black American Music*, 146.

30. Alice Parker, interview by Anne Daugherty and André J. Thomas, *The Spiritual Tradition in the United States: A Glance Back, A Look Forward*, Public Radio International, February, 1994.

31. White, *Choral Music by African American Composers*, 206; Roach, *Black American Music*, 166.

32. Brazeal Wayne Dennard, *The Spiritual Tradition in the United States*.

33. White, *Choral Music by African American Composers*, 210; Roach, *Black American Music*, 150.

34. Eugene Simpson, e-mail message to author, March 21, 2007.

35. Robert Morris, personal correspondence with author, March 19, 2007.

36. Larry Farrow, *The Spiritual Tradition in the United States*.

37. Marvin Curtis, personal correspondence with author, March 23, 2007.

38. Moses Hogan, *The Spiritual Tradition in the United States*.

39. David Morrow, personal correspondence with author, October 24, 2006.

40. Stacey Gibbs, e-mail message to author, August 2006.

41. The Evangelical Covenant Church, "Dilworth Directs Boston Chorus in King Tribute," The Evangelical Covenant Church, http://www.covchurch.org/dilworth-directs-boston-chorus-in-king-tribute.

42. Mark Butler, personal correspondence with author, August 16, 2006.

43. Damon Dandridge, personal correspondence with author, August 4, 2006.

44. Victor Johnson, e-mail message to author, March 23, 2007.

Chapter 4: From the Printed Page to the Concert Stage

1. Johnson and Johnson, *The Books of American Negro Spirituals*, 43.

2. Ibid., 46.

3. Southern, *The Music of Black Americans*, 201.

4. Alice Parker, *The Spiritual Tradition in the United States*.

5. Samuel A. Floyd, Jr., *The Power of Black Music: Interpreting Its History From Africa to the United States* (New York: Oxford Univ. Press, 1995) 61.

6. James Monroe Trotter, *Music and Some Highly Musical People* (Boston: Lee and Shepard, 1878) 258–259.

BIBLIOGRAPHY

Allen, William Francis, Charles Pickard Ware, and Lucy McKim Garrison, eds. *Slave Songs of the United States.* New York: Simpson, 1867.

Armstrong, Orland Kay. *Old Massa's People: The Old Slaves Tell Their Story.* Indianapolis: Bobbs-Merrill, 1931.

Barton, William E. *Old Plantation Hymns.* New York: AMS Press, 1972. First published 1899 by Lamson, Wolffe.

Still, William Grant. "William Grant Still Interviewed by R. Donald Brown." By Donald R. Brown. *Oral History Program*, California State University, (1984).

Buchanan, Heather J and Matthew W. Mehaffey eds. *Teaching Music Through Performance in Choir.* Vol. 1. Chicago: GIA, 2005.

Courlander, Harold. *Negro Folk Music U.S.A.* New York: Columbia Univ. Press, 1963.

Curtis, Marvin V. and Lee V. Clour. "The African-American Spiritual: Traditions and Performance Practices." *Choral Journal 32*, no. 4 (November 1991): 15-22.

Daugherty, Anne and André J. Thomas. *The Spiritual Tradition in the United States: A Glance Back, A Look Forward* (includes interviews with Larry Farrow, Moses Hogan, Adolphus Hailstork, Alice Parker, and Brazeal Dennard). Public Radio International, February, 1994.

DeLerma, Dominique-René. *Bibliography of Black Music,* Volume 3, *Geographical Studies.* Westport: Greenwood Press, 1982.

Dett, Robert Nathaniel. *The Collected Piano Works of R. Nathaniel Dett.* Evanston, Illinois: Summy-Birchard, 1973.

———. "From Bell Stand to Throne Room." *Black Perspective in Music, 1/1* (Spring 1973): 73–81. Reprinted from *Etude, LII,* (February 1934): 79-80.

———. "Helping to Lay Foundation for Negro Music of Future." *Black Perspective in Music 1/1*, (Spring 1973): 64–69. Reprinted from *Musical America* (July 8, 1918).

Dett, R. Nathaniel, ed. *The Dett Collection of Negro Spirituals.* Chicago: Hall & McCreary, 1936.

———. *Religious Folk-Songs of the Negro as Sung at Hampton Institute.* Hampton, Virginia: Hampton Institute Press, 1927.

Du Bois, W.E.B. *The Souls of Black Folk: Essays and Sketches.* New York: Bantam Books, 1989. First published 1903 by A. C. McClurg & Co.

Epstein, Dena J. Polacheck. *Sinful Tunes and Spirituals: Black Folk Music to the Civil War.* Urbana: Univ. of Illinois Press, 1977.

Equiano, Olaudah. *The Interesting Narrative of the Life of Olaudah Equiano, or, Gustavus Vassa the African/Written by Himself.* London: T. Wilkins, 1789.

Evans, Arthur Lee. "The Development of the Negro Spiritual as Choral Art Music by Afro-American Composers with an Annotated Guide to the Performance of Selected Spirituals." PhD diss., University of Miami, 1972.

Fenner, Thomas P. arr. *Cabin and plantation songs as sung by the Hampton Students*. New York: G. P. Putnam's Sons, 1891.

Floyd, Jr., Samuel A. *The Power of Black Music: Interpreting Its History from Africa to the United States*. New York: Oxford Univ. Press, 1995.

Franklin, John Hope. *From Slavery to Freedom; a History of Negro Americans*. 3rd ed. New York: Knopf, 1967.

Haas, Robert Bartlett. *William Grant Still and the Fusion of Cultures in American Music*. Los Angeles: Black Sparrow Press, 1972.

Hickman, Cynthia. *Spirituals: A Folk Anthology*. New York: Dunbar, 2002.

Hogan, Moses. *Feel the Spirit*. Vol. 1. Milwaukee: Hal Leonard, 2003.

———. *Feel the Spirit*. Vol. 2. Milwaukee: Hal Leonard, 2005.

Hogan, Moses, ed. *The Oxford Book of Spirituals*. Oxford: Oxford Univ. Press, 2002.

Jackson, George Pullen. *White and Negro Spirituals: Their Life Span and Kinship*. New York: Augustin, 1944.

Johnson, James Weldon, and J. Rosamond Johnson. *The Books of American Negro Spirituals*. Cambridge: Da Capo Press, 1969. First published 1925 and 1926 by Viking Press.

Jones, Arthur C. *Wade in the Water: The Wisdom of the Spirituals*. Maryknoll: Orbis Books, 1993.

Jones, Bessie and Bess Lomax Hawes. *Step it Down: Games, Plays, Songs and Stories from the Afro-American Heritage*. Athens: Univ. of Georgia Press, 1987. First published 1972 by Harper and Row.

Krehbiel, Henry Edward. *Afro-American Folksongs*. Baltimore: Clearfield Company, 1914.

Locke, Alain. *The Negro and His Music*. New York: Arno Press, 1969. First published 1936 by Associates in Negro Education.

Lomax, John A., and Alan Lomax. *American Ballads and Folk Songs*. New York: Dover, 1994. First published 1934 by Macmillan.

Lovell, John. *Black Song: The Forge and the Flame; The Story of How the Afro-American Spiritual was Hammered Out*. New York: Macmillan, 1972.

Mallard, Robert Q. *Plantation Life Before Emancipation*. Richmond: Whittet & Shepperson, 1892.

Malone, Mark Hugh. "William Levi Dawson: American Music Educator." PhD diss., Florida State University, 1981.

Marsh, J.B.T. *The Story of the Jubilee Singers: With Their Songs*. Boston: Houghton, Osgood, 1880.

McBrier, Vivian Flagg. *R. Nathaniel Dett: His Life and Works, 1882–1943*. Washington: Associated Publishers, 1977.

McIlhenny, Edward Avery, and Henry Whermann. *Befo' De War Spirituals*. Boston: Christopher Publishing House, 1933.

Murray, Charlotte W. "The Story of Harry T. Burleigh." *The Hymn 17*, no. 4. (October 1966): 101–111.

Nettl, Bruno. *Folk and Traditional Music of the Western Continents*. Englewood Cliffs: Prentice-Hall, 1965.

Newman, Richard. *Go Down, Moses: A Celebration of the African-American Spiritual.* New York: Clarkson Potter, 1998.

Northup, Solomon. *Twelve Years a Slave: The Narrative of Solomon Northup, A Citizen of New York, Kidnapped in Washington City in 1841, and Rescued in 1853, from a Cotton Plantation near the Red River, in Louisiana.* Auburn, Derby and Miller; Buffalo, Derby, Orton and Mulligan; [etc., etc.], 1853.

Ragon, Bernice Johnson. *If You Don't Go, Don't Hinder Me: The African American Sacred Song Tradition.* Lincoln: Univ. of Nebraska Press, 2001.

Roach, Hildred. *Black American Music: Past and Present.* 2nd ed. Malabar, FL: Krieger Publishing Company, 1992.

Simpson, Anne Key. *Follow Me: The Life and Music of R. Nathaniel Dett.* Metuchen, New Jersey: Scarecrow Press, 1993.

———. *Hard Trials: The Life and Music of Harry T. Burleigh.* Metuchen, New Jersey: Scarecrow Press, 1990.

Smith, Catherine Parsons. *William Grant Still: A Study in Contradictions.* Berkley: Univ. of California Press, 2000.

Southern, Eileen. *Biographical Dictionary of Afro-American and African Musicians.* Westport: Greenwood Press, 1982.

———. *The Music of Black Americans: A History.* 3rd ed. New York: W.W. Norton & Co., 1997.

———. *Readings in Black American Music,* 2nd ed. New York: W.W. Norton & Co., 1983.

Thomas, André J. "Singing Black Gospel Music and Spirituals." *Reformed Worship,* no. 14. (December 1989): 36–37.

Thurman, Howard. *Deep River and The Negro Spiritual Speaks of Life and Death,* Richmond Virginia: Friends United Press, 1975. Reprints, 1990, 1993, 1996, 1999.

———. *Jesus and the Disinherited.* Boston: Beacon Press, 1996.

Toelken, Barre. *Morning Dew and Roses: Nuance, Metaphor, and Meaning in Folksongs.* Urbana: Univ. of Illinois Press, 1995.

Trice, Patricia Johnson. *Choral Arrangements of the African-American Spirituals: Historical Overview and Annotated Listings.* Westport: Greenwood Press, 1998.

Vanden Wyngaard, Margueite A. "African-American Choral Music for Secondary Schools." M.A.T. Thesis, University of Minnesota – Morris, 1993.

Walvin, James. *The Slave Trade.* Gloucestershire: Sutton Publishing Limited, 1999.

Ward, Andrew. *Dark Midnight When I Rise: the Story of the Jubilee Singers, Who Introduced the World to the Music of Black America.* New York: Farrar, Straus, and Giroux, 2000.

Wiencek, Henry. *The Hairstons: An American Family in Black and White.* New York: St.Martin's Press, 1999.

White, Evelyn Davidson. *Choral Music by African American Composers: A Selected, Annotated Bibliography.* Lanham, Maryland: Scarecrow Press, 1996.

Work III, John W. *American Negro Songs: 230 Folk Songs and Spirituals, Religious and Secular.* Mineola: Dover, 1998. First published 1940 by Howell, Soskin.

SELECTED AUDIO AND VIDEO RECORDINGS

Recordings by/of the arrangers discussed in Chapter 3

(organized alphabetically by arranger)

Dawson, William L., conductor. Tuskegee Institute Choir. *Spirituals.* MCA Records. B000MDE3QC. CD, 1992.

The Dawson Days: The Story of William Levi Dawson and the Tuskegee Institute Choir from 1931–1955. Leonard B. Horton. Florida A&M University. Documentary Video (master's thesis), 2003.

The Spirituals of William L. Dawson. The St. Olaf Choir, Anton Armstrong, conductor. St. Olaf Records. B00021YYNQ. CD, 1997.

The Nathaniel Dett Chorale. *An Indigo Christmas Live!* Marquis Music. B000A2XBF4. DVD, 2005.

Listen to the Lambs: The Music of R. Nathaniel Dett. The Nathaniel Dett Chorale, Brainerd Blyden-Taylor, artistic director. Marquis Music. B00007EB7C. CD, 2003.

The Fisk Jubilee Singers, Paul T. Kwami, conductor. *In Bright Mansions.* Curb Records. B00007MB2L. CD, 2003.

The Fisk Jubilee Singers, Paul T. Kwami, conductor. *Rise Shine: Fisk Jubilee Singers Live In Concert.* CD.

The McCullough Chorale in Concert Singing the Music of Adolphus Hailstork. The McCullough Chorale, Donald McCullough, conductor. Albany Records. TROY156. CD, 1995.

Hairston, Jester. *The Afro-American Slave Song: Its African Roots and American Development.* Hinshaw Music. CD, 1978.

Hairston, Jester. *The Black Spiritual in America, Volume 3.* The American Choral Directors Association. CD.

Hogan, Moses, conductor. The Moses Hogan Chorale. *Abide With Me: A Collection of Spirituals and Hymns.* MGH Records. B000IV2662. CD, 1998.

Hogan, Moses, conductor. The Moses Hogan Chorale – Community Ensemble. *The Battle of Jericho.* MGH Records. CD, 1995.

Hogan, Moses, conductor. The Moses Hogan Chorale. *The Best of The Moses Hogan Chorale.* MGH Records. CD, 1998.

Hogan, Moses, conductor. The Moses Hogan Chorale. *The Choral and Vocal Arrangements of Moses Hogan, Volume One.* MGH Records. CD, 1995.

Hogan, Moses, conductor. The New World Ensemble Chamber Choir. *Ev'ry Time I Feel the Spirit.* Channel Classics. CCS2991. CD, 1991.

Hogan, Moses, conductor. The Moses Hogan Singers. *Lift Every Voice for Freedom*. MGH Records. CD, 2001.

Hogan, Moses, conductor. The Moses Hogan Chorale and The Moses Hogan Singers. *The Moses Hogan Choral Series 2002*. MGH Records. CD, 2001.

Hogan, Moses, conductor. The Moses Hogan Chorale. *Our Choral Heritage Series, Volume 1: I Can Tell the World*. MGH Records. CD, 1997.

Hogan, Moses, conductor. The Moses Hogan Chorale. *Songs of Reflection*. MGH Records. CD, 1997.

Hogan, Moses and Albert McNeil, conductors. The Mormon Tabernacle Choir. *An American Heritage of Spirituals*. BWE Classic. B00000586G. CD, 1996.

Jessye, Eva, conductor. The Eva Jessye Chorale. *Gershwin: Porgy and Bess (with members of the original cast)*. Decca. B000002OJM. CD, 1992.

Jessye, Eva, music director. *King Vidor's Hallelujah* (1929). Warner Home Video. B000BNTME6. DVD, 2006.

Johnson, Hall, conductor. *The Green Pastures*. Warner Home Video. B000BNTMDC. DVD, 2006.

McNeil, Albert, conductor. Albert McNeil Jubilee Singers. *The Best of Jubilee, Volume I*. B000MB8GFS. CD, 2001.

McNeil, Albert, conductor. Albert McNeil Jubilee Singers. *The Best of Jubilee, Volume II*. Aya World Productions. CD, 2005.

McNeil, Albert, conductor. Albert McNeil Jubilee Singers. *They've Got the Whole World in Their Hands, Volume II*. CD.

Shaw, Robert, conductor. Robert Shaw Festival Singers. *Amazing Grace: American Hymns and Spirituals*. Telarc. B000003CZ1. CD, 1993.

Shaw, Robert, conductor. The Robert Shaw Chorale. *Deep River and Other Spirituals*. RCA Victor. LM 2247. LP, 1958.

Shaw, Robert, conductor. The Robert Shaw Chorale. *I'm Goin' to Sing: Sixteen Spirituals*. RCA Victor. LM 2580. LP, 1961.

Shaw, Robert, conductor. The Robert Shaw Chorale. *The Robert Shaw Chorale on Tour*. RCA Victor. LSC 2676. LP, 1963.

Thomas, André J., guest conductor. Rundfunkchor Berlin. *True Light—The Berlin Christmas Concert*. Coviello Classics. COV 50508. CD, 2004.

Thomas, André J. and Anton Armstrong, conductors. Florida State University Choirs and St. Olaf Choir. *Songs From My Heart—Choral Music of André Thomas*. CT0029. CD, 2004.

Recommended recordings of spirituals by various arrangers and conductors

(organized alphabetically by title)

21 Spirituals for the 21ˢᵗ Century. The Raise Chorale, Raymond Wise, conductor. Raise Records. B000A38TWI. CD, 2005.

Black Christmas: Spirituals in the African-American Tradition. Thomas Young, Vanessa Ayers and Robert Mosely, chorus directed by Ronald Isaac. Essay Recordings. B000CDUHIA. CD, 1990.

Folk Visions & Voices: Traditional Music & Song in Northern Georgia, Vol. 1. Smithsonian Folkways Recordings. FW34161. CD, 1984.

Jubilate Spirituals & Gospel. Jubilate, Nelson Hall, conductor. CDJ001. CD, 1996.

Negro Folk Music of Alabama, Vol. 5: Spirituals. Smithsonian Folkways Recordings. FW04473. CD, original recording 1950.

Singing For Freedom: A Concert For the Child in Each of Us. Sweet Honey in the Rock, Bernice Johnson Reagon, director. Music for Little People. B0009UZGOG. DVD, 2005.

A Tradition of Spirituals. The Claflin College Concert Choir, James A McDaniel, director. 12106. CD, 1994.

United We Sing. The Turtle Creek Chorale, Hamilton Park Men's Chorus, and New Arts Six, Timothy Seelig, artistic director. Turtle Creek Chorale Recording. B000A2H998. CD, 1994.

Wade In The Water, Vol. 1: African American Spirituals: The Concert Tradition. Smithsonian Folkways Recording. B000001DJE. CD, 1994.

Where the Sun Will Never Go Down: Spirituals and Traditional Gospel Music. Chanticleer. Teldec. B000000SJN. CD, 1994.

Witness: What a Mighty God – Spirituals and Gospels for Chorus. VocalEssence Ensemble Singers and Chorus, Phillip Brunelle, conductor. Clarion. B0001FVEPE. CD, 2004.

ABOUT THE AUTHOR

André J. Thomas, the Owen F. Sellers Professor of Music, is Director of Choral Activities and Professor of Choral Music Education at Florida State University. A previous faculty member at the University of Texas, Austin, Dr. Thomas received his degrees from Friends University (B.A.), Northwestern University (M.M.), and the University of Illinois (D.M.A).

In demand as a choral adjudicator, clinician, and director of honor/all-state choirs throughout the United States, Europe, Asia, New Zealand, and Australia, Dr. Thomas has conducted choirs at the state, division, and national conventions of the Music Educators National Conference (MENC) and American Choral Directors Association (ACDA). He has conducted the summer residency of the World Youth Choir in the Republic of China and the Philippines, winter residency of the World Youth Choir in Europe. Other international credits include a premier performance by an American choir (Florida State University Singers) in Vietnam. He has been the guest conductor of such distinguished orchestras and choirs as the Birmingham Symphony Orchestra in England, and guest conductor for the Berlin Radio Choir in Germany and the Netherlands Radio Choir. He has also guest conducted the Tallahassee Symphony.

As a clinician he has appeared at two of the World Symposiums of Choral Music, the National Music Educators Conference, the Swedish Choral Directors Association, the Australian Choral Directors Association, Presbyterian Association of Musicians, The Fellowship of Methodist Musicians, BonClarken Music Conference, Fellowship of American Baptist Musicians, Conference on Liturgy and Worship at St. Olaf College, Chautauqua Institute, Zimriya World Assembly of Choirs in Israel, Choir Fest Vancouver, Alpe Adria Cantat in Italy, and a host of other events. He has been a choral adjudicator for the Llangollen International Eisteddfod in North Wales and the International Choral Festival in Helsingborg, Sweden. He has also been one of the Instructors at the Eric Ericson Choral Conducting Master Classes in Holland. His 2007 engagements include serving as conductor/clinician for the Estonian Choral Association, the China National Choir Association, and the Asia Cantat in Taiwan.

Dr. Thomas has also distinguished himself as a composer/arranger. Hinshaw Music Company, Mark Foster Music Company, FitzSimmon Music Co., Lawson-Gould Music, earthsongs, and Heritage Music Press (a division of The Lorenz Corporation) publish his compositions and arrangements. Dr. Thomas has produced two instructional videos: *What They See Is What You Get*, on choral conducting, with Rodney Eichenberger; and *Body, Mind, Spirit, Voice,* on adolescent voices, with Anton Armstrong.

Thomas serves or has served on numerous boards including the National Board of Choristers Guild, National Board of ACDA and The Singing City. He has been active as an officer in both Music Educators National Conference (MENC) and American Choral Directors Association (ACDA), where he served as Past President of both Florida and the Southern Division.